Praise for iZombie

"[A] wealth of densely quirky elements . . . which send the book soaring past merely "high-concept" into ... just plain high. Gwen, a character whose savvy, sardonic, world-weary attitude shines through all the genre trappings..."
—NPR

"Quirky and hypercolorful, at once neo-noir and post-Gothic."
—FLAVORWIRE

"iZombie is flat out my favorite new title this year...The main cast is really fun and have solid voices, and the recurring set pieces give the series a welcoming feel, more like a favorite TV show than a typical monthly."
—CBR/COMICS SHOULD BE GOOD

"Roberson hands down is one of the best writers of strong and smart female characters that can embrace their femininity without ever transcending into objectification."
—AIN'T IT COOL NEWS

"The smart zombie gimmick felt like a nice tweak on brain-eater lore... I love the character design, and I love Laura A.'s sense of color."
—TIME/TECHLAND

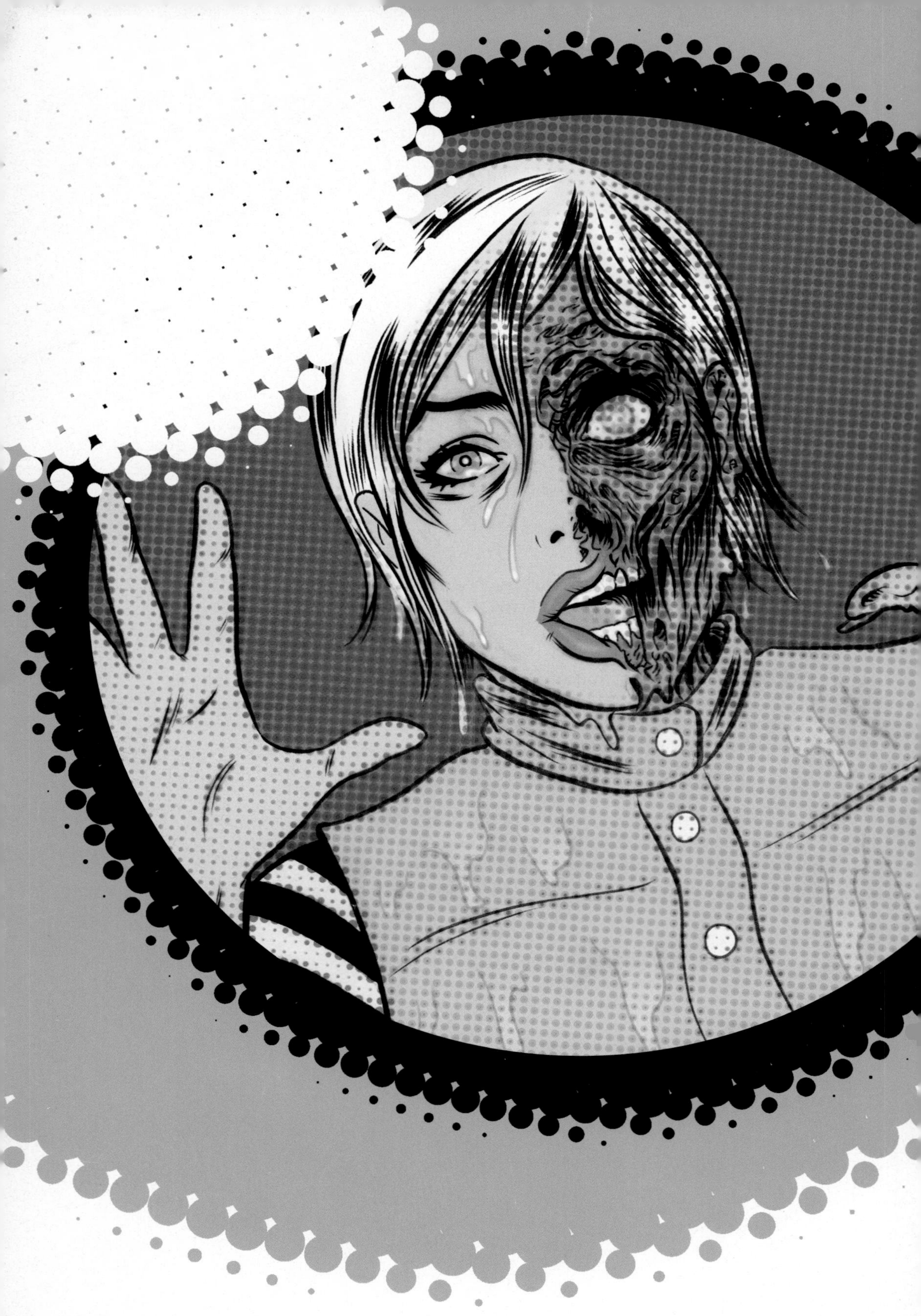

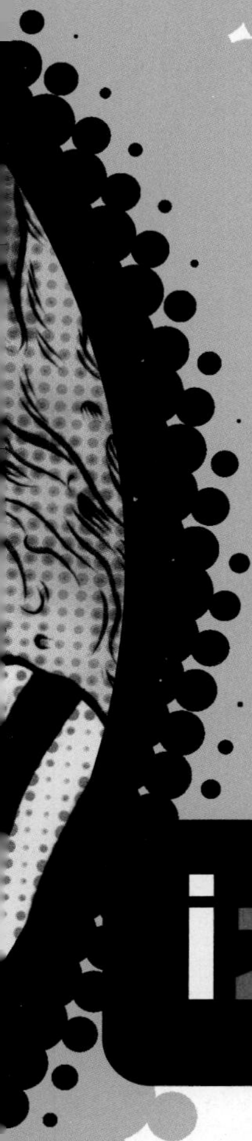

iZombie

Dead to the World

Chris Roberson Writer

Michael Allred Artist

Laura Allred Colorist

Todd Klein Letterer

Michael Allred Cover

iZombie created by Roberson and Allred

Karen Berger SVP-Executive Editor

Shelly Bond Editor-original series

Angela Rufino Associate Editor-original series

Bob Harras Group Editor-Collected Editions

Robbin Brosterman Design Director-Books

Louis Prandi Art Director

DC COMICS

Diane Nelson President

Dan DiDio and Jim Lee Co-Publishers

Geoff Johns Chief Creative Officer

Patrick Caldon EVP-Finance and Administration

John Rood EVP-Sales, Marketing and Business Development

Amy Genkins SVP-Business and Legal Affairs

Steve Rotterdam SVP-Sales and Marketing

John Cunningham VP-Marketing

Terri Cunningham VP-Managing Editor

Alison Gill VP-Manufacturing

David Hyde VP-Publicity

Sue Pohja VP-Book Trade Sales

Alysse Soll VP-Advertising and Custom Publishing

Bob Wayne VP-Sales

Mark Chiarello Art Director

iZOMBIE: DEAD TO THE WORLD
Published by DC Comics. Cover and compilation Copyright © 2011
Monkey Brain, Inc. and Michael Allred. All Rights Reserved.

Originally published in single magazine form in iZOMBIE 1-5 and
THE HOUSE OF MYSTERY HALLOWEEN ANNUAL #1. Copyright ©
2010 Monkey Brain, Inc. and Michael Allred. All Rights Reserved.
All characters, their distinctive likenesses and related elements
featured in this publication are trademarks of DC Comics. The
stories, characters and incidents featured in this publication are
entirely fictional. DC Comics does not read or accept unsolicited
submissions of ideas, stories or artwork.

DC Comics, 1700 Broadway, New York, NY 10019
A Warner Bros. Entertainment Company
Printed in the USA. First Printing.
ISBN: 978-1-4012-2965-8

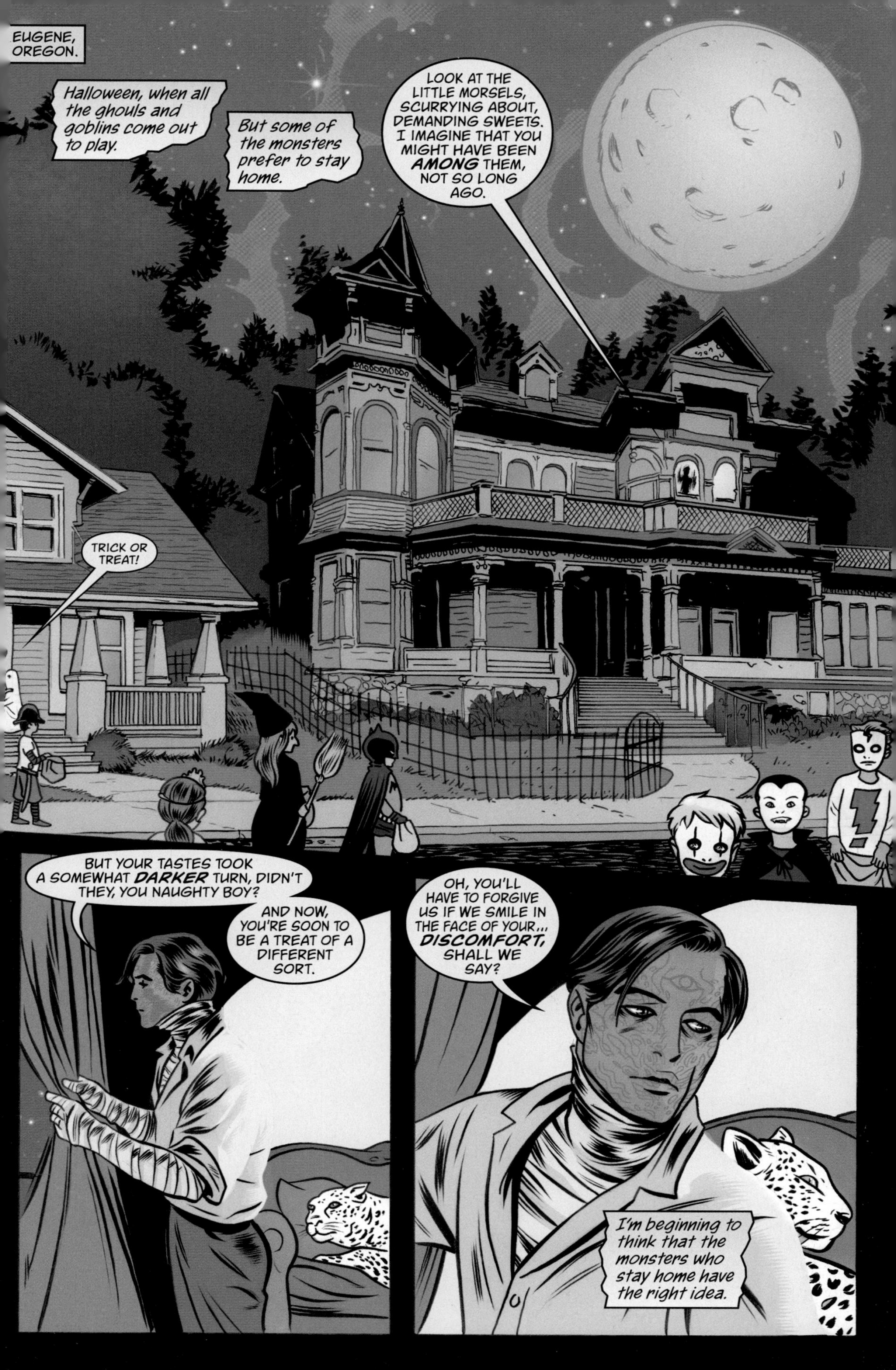
EUGENE, OREGON.
Halloween, when all the ghouls and goblins come out to play.
But some of the monsters prefer to stay home.
LOOK AT THE LITTLE MORSELS, SCURRYING ABOUT, DEMANDING SWEETS. I IMAGINE THAT YOU MIGHT HAVE BEEN AMONG THEM, NOT SO LONG AGO.
TRICK OR TREAT!
BUT YOUR TASTES TOOK A SOMEWHAT DARKER TURN, DIDN'T THEY, YOU NAUGHTY BOY?
AND NOW, YOU'RE SOON TO BE A TREAT OF A DIFFERENT SORT.
OH, YOU'LL HAVE TO FORGIVE US IF WE SMILE IN THE FACE OF YOUR... DISCOMFORT, SHALL WE SAY?
I'm beginning to think that the monsters who stay home have the right idea.

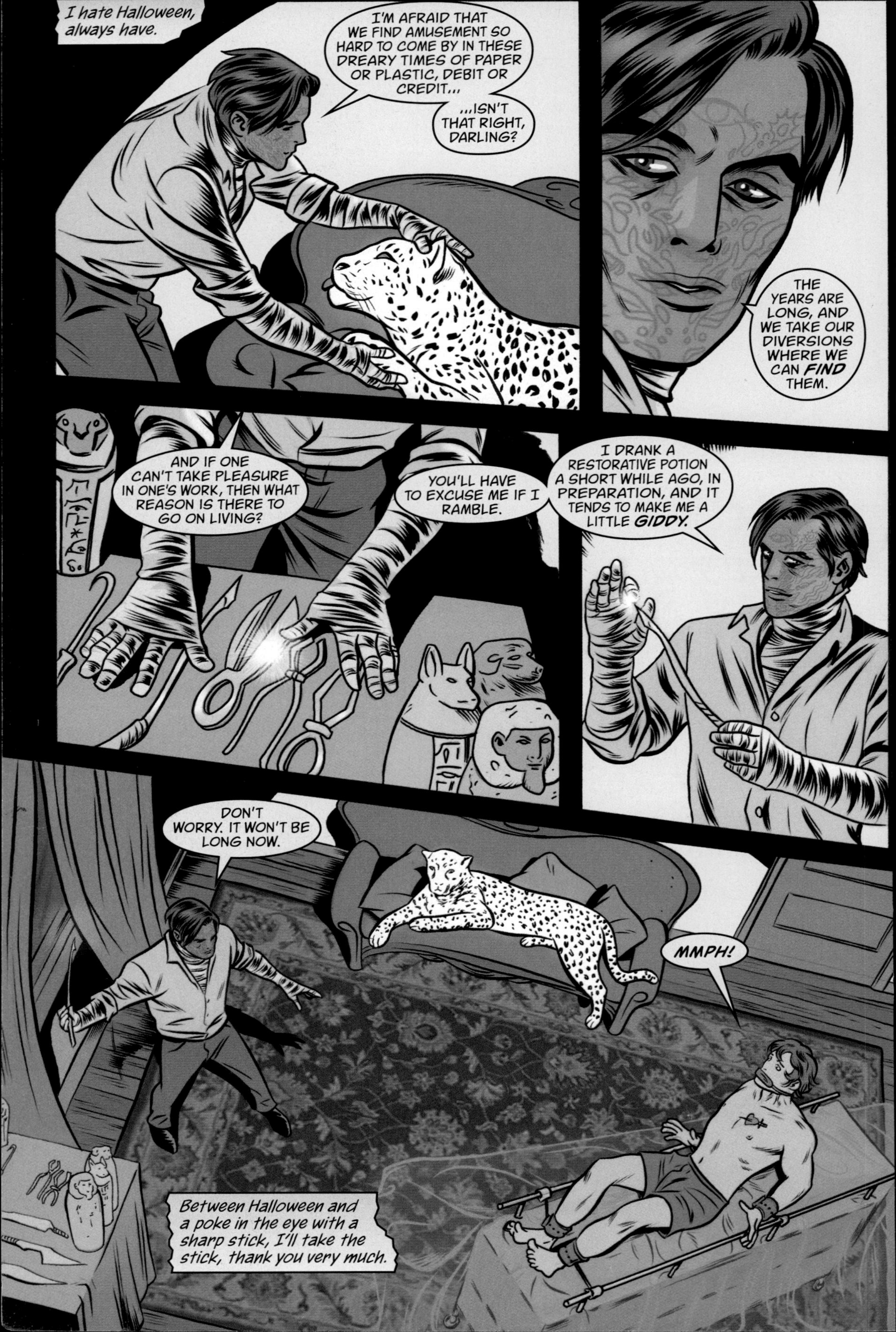

I hate Halloween, always have.
I'M AFRAID THAT WE FIND AMUSEMENT SO HARD TO COME BY IN THESE DREARY TIMES OF PAPER OR PLASTIC, DEBIT OR CREDIT...
...ISN'T THAT RIGHT, DARLING?
THE YEARS ARE LONG, AND WE TAKE OUR DIVERSIONS WHERE WE CAN FIND THEM.
AND IF ONE CAN'T TAKE PLEASURE IN ONE'S WORK, THEN WHAT REASON IS THERE TO GO ON LIVING?
YOU'LL HAVE TO EXCUSE ME IF I RAMBLE.
I DRANK A RESTORATIVE POTION A SHORT WHILE AGO, IN PREPARATION, AND IT TENDS TO MAKE ME A LITTLE GIDDY.
DON'T WORRY. IT WON'T BE LONG NOW.
MMPH!
Between Halloween and a poke in the eye with a sharp stick, I'll take the stick, thank you very much.

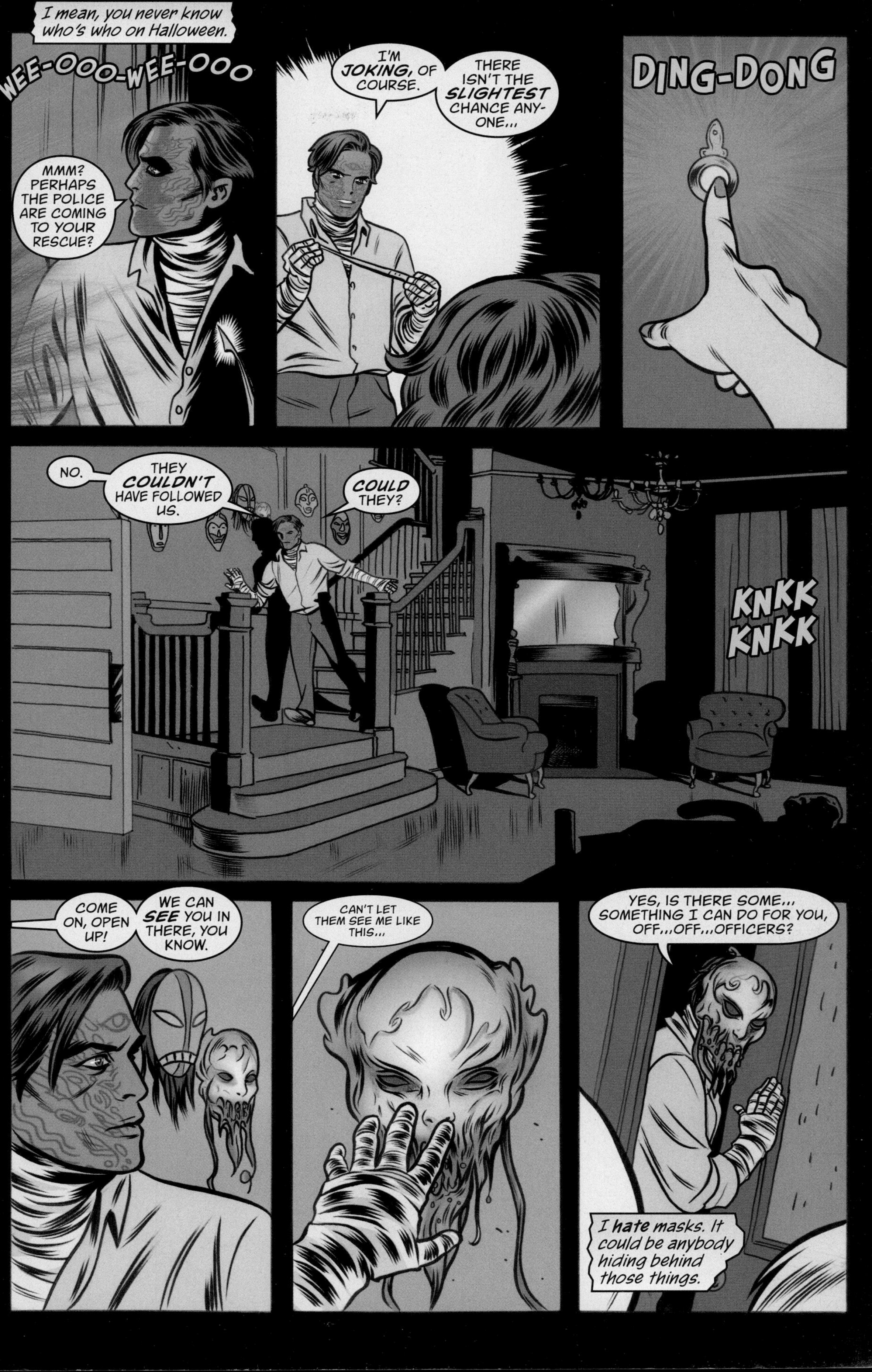
I mean, you never know who's who on Halloween.
WEE-OOO-WEE-OOO
MMM? PERHAPS THE POLICE ARE COMING TO YOUR RESCUE?
I'M JOKING, OF COURSE.
THERE ISN'T THE SLIGHTEST CHANCE ANY-ONE...
DING-DONG
NO.
THEY COULDN'T HAVE FOLLOWED US.
COULD THEY?
KNKK KNKK
COME ON, OPEN UP!
WE CAN SEE YOU IN THERE, YOU KNOW.
CAN'T LET THEM SEE ME LIKE THIS...
YES, IS THERE SOME... SOMETHING I CAN DO FOR YOU, OFF...OFF...OFFICERS?
I hate masks. It could be anybody hiding behind those things.

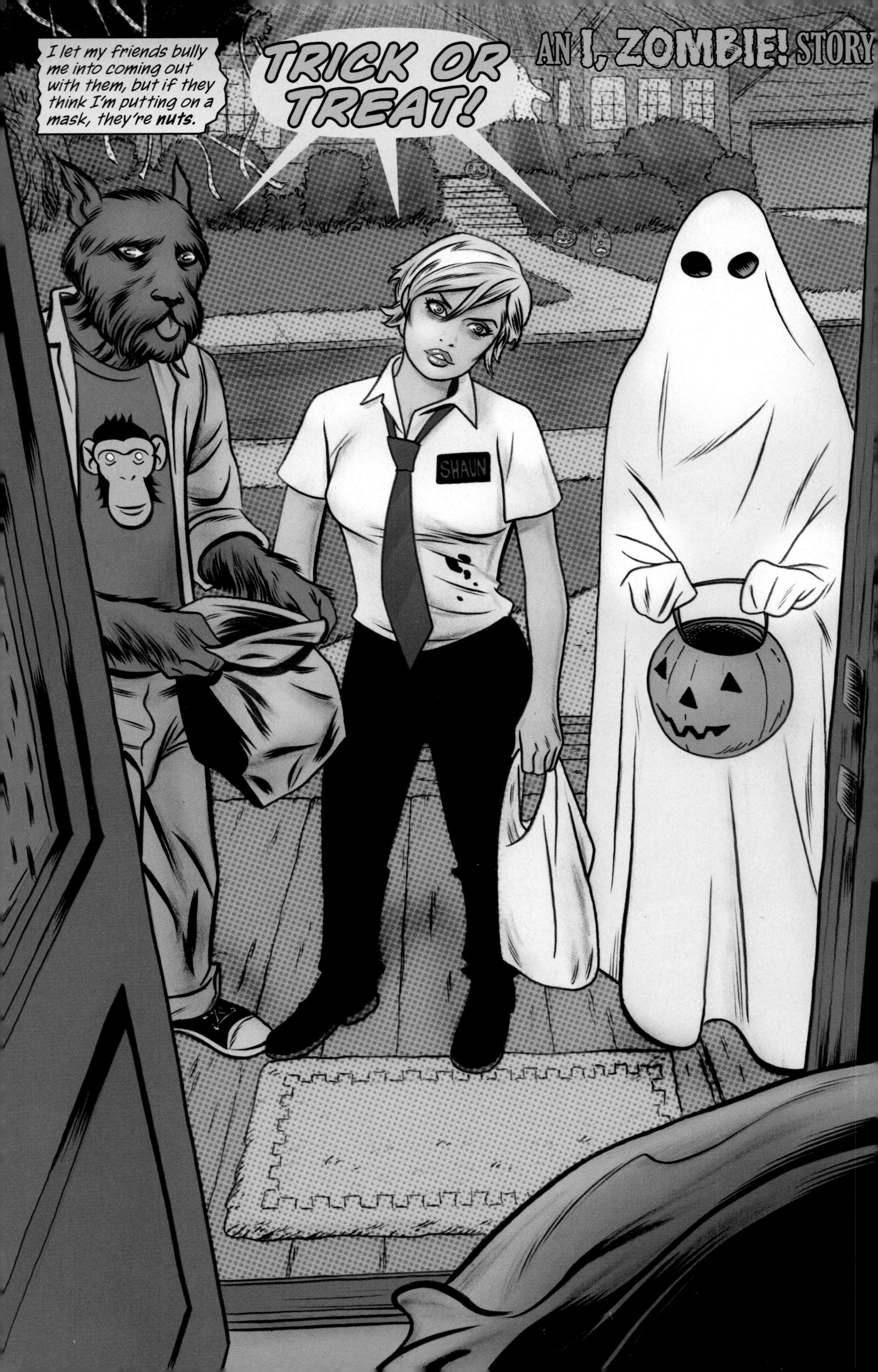
I let my friends bully me into coming out with them, but if they think I'm putting on a mask, they're **nuts**.
TRICK OR TREAT!
AN I, ZOMBIE! STORY
SHAUN

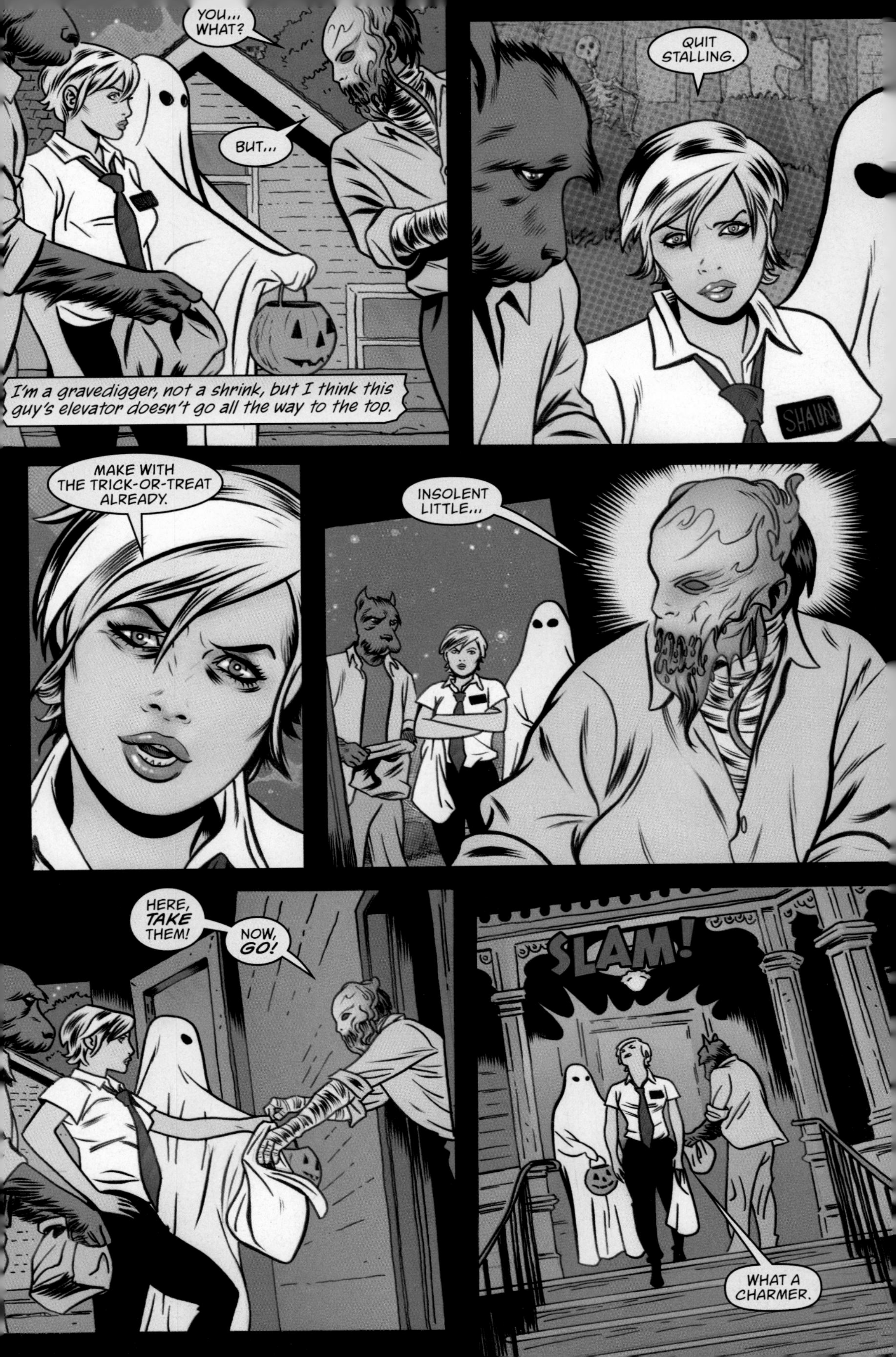
YOU... WHAT?
BUT...
I'm a gravedigger, not a shrink, but I think this guy's elevator doesn't go all the way to the top.
QUIT STALLING.
SHAUN
MAKE WITH THE TRICK-OR-TREAT ALREADY.
INSOLENT LITTLE...
HERE, *TAKE* THEM!
NOW, *GO!*
SLAM!
WHAT A CHARMER.

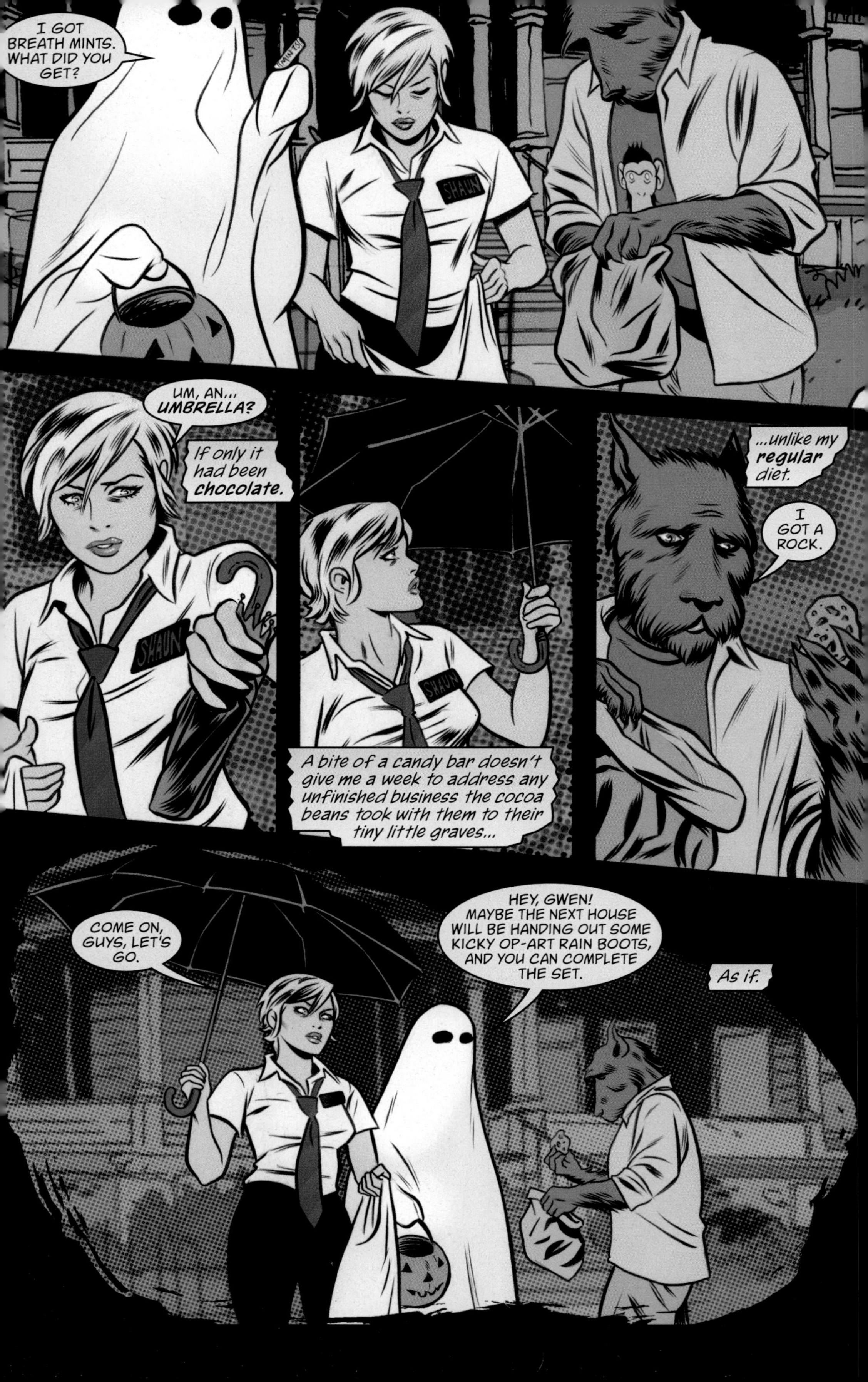

I GOT BREATH MINTS. WHAT DID YOU GET?
MINTS
SHAUN
UM, AN... UMBRELLA?
If only it had been chocolate.
SHAUN
SHAUN
A bite of a candy bar doesn't give me a week to address any unfinished business the cocoa beans took with them to their tiny little graves...
...unlike my regular diet.
I GOT A ROCK.
COME ON, GUYS, LET'S GO.
HEY, GWEN! MAYBE THE NEXT HOUSE WILL BE HANDING OUT SOME KICKY OP-ART RAIN BOOTS, AND YOU CAN COMPLETE THE SET.
As if.

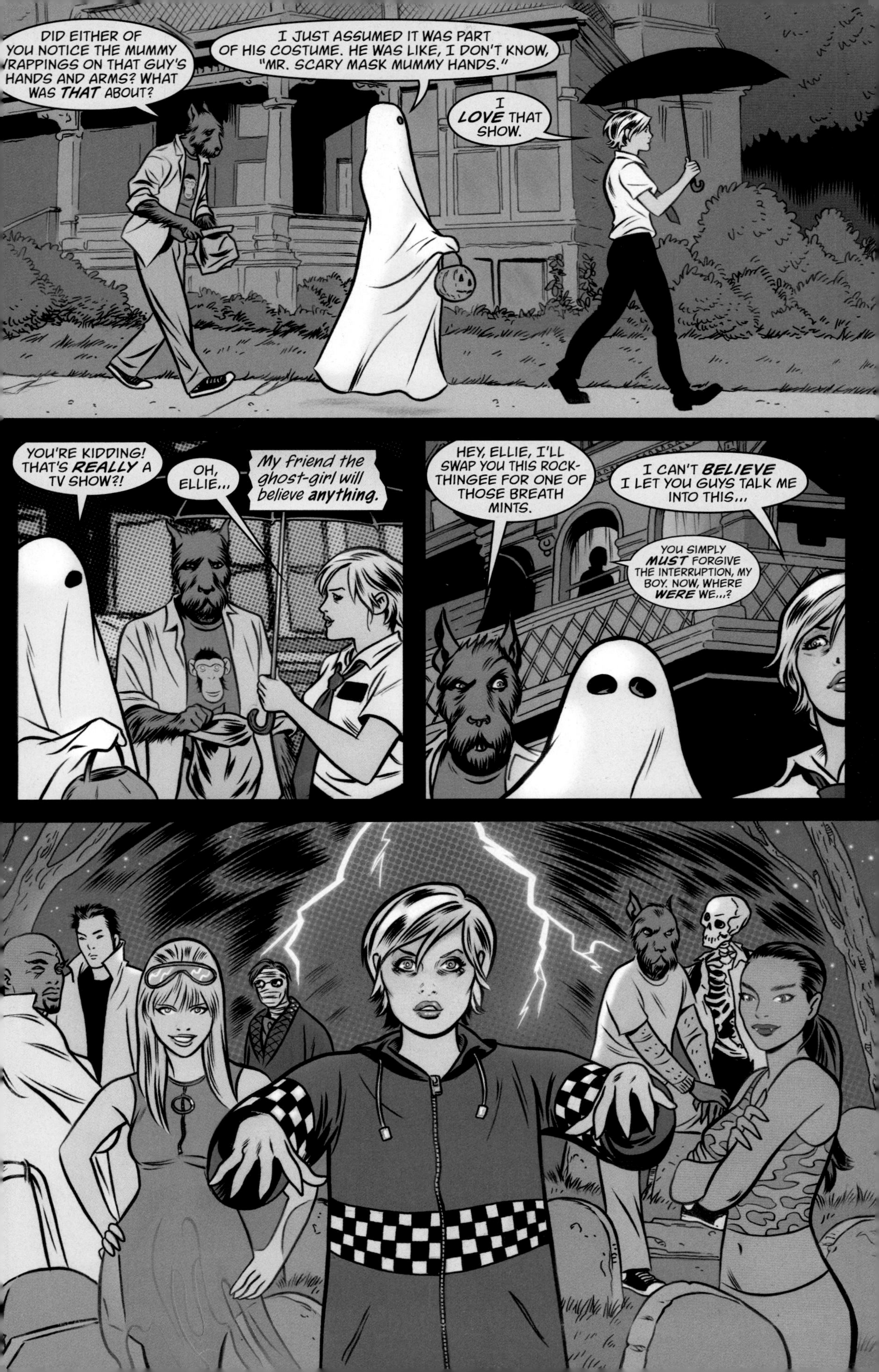
DID EITHER OF YOU NOTICE THE MUMMY WRAPPINGS ON THAT GUY'S HANDS AND ARMS? WHAT WAS THAT ABOUT?
I JUST ASSUMED IT WAS PART OF HIS COSTUME. HE WAS LIKE, I DON'T KNOW, "MR. SCARY MASK MUMMY HANDS."
I LOVE THAT SHOW.
YOU'RE KIDDING! THAT'S REALLY A TV SHOW?!
OH, ELLIE...
My friend the ghost-girl will believe anything.
HEY, ELLIE, I'LL SWAP YOU THIS ROCK-THINGEE FOR ONE OF THOSE BREATH MINTS.
I CAN'T BELIEVE I LET YOU GUYS TALK ME INTO THIS...
YOU SIMPLY MUST FORGIVE THE INTERRUPTION, MY BOY. NOW, WHERE WERE WE...?

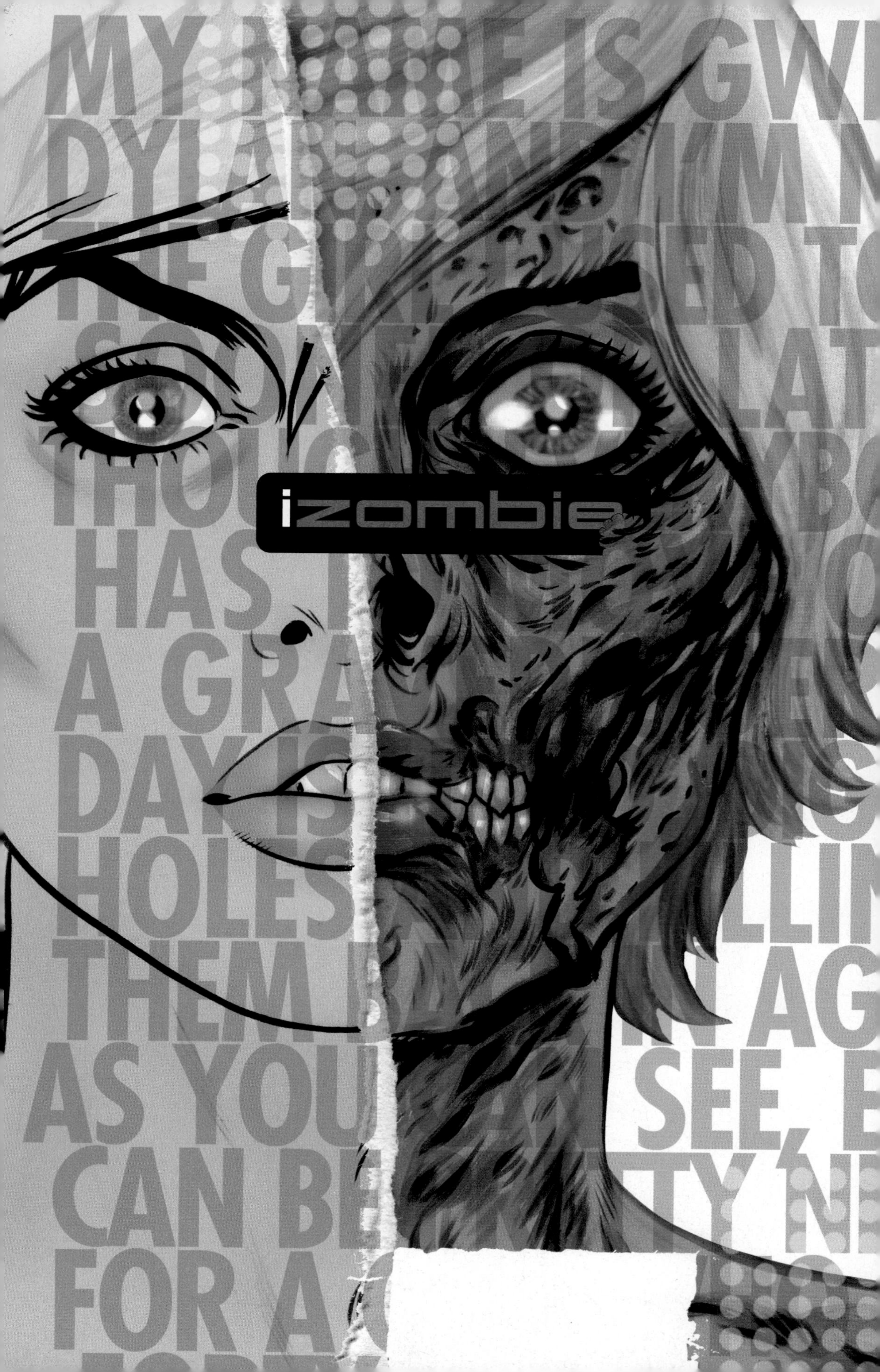
izombie

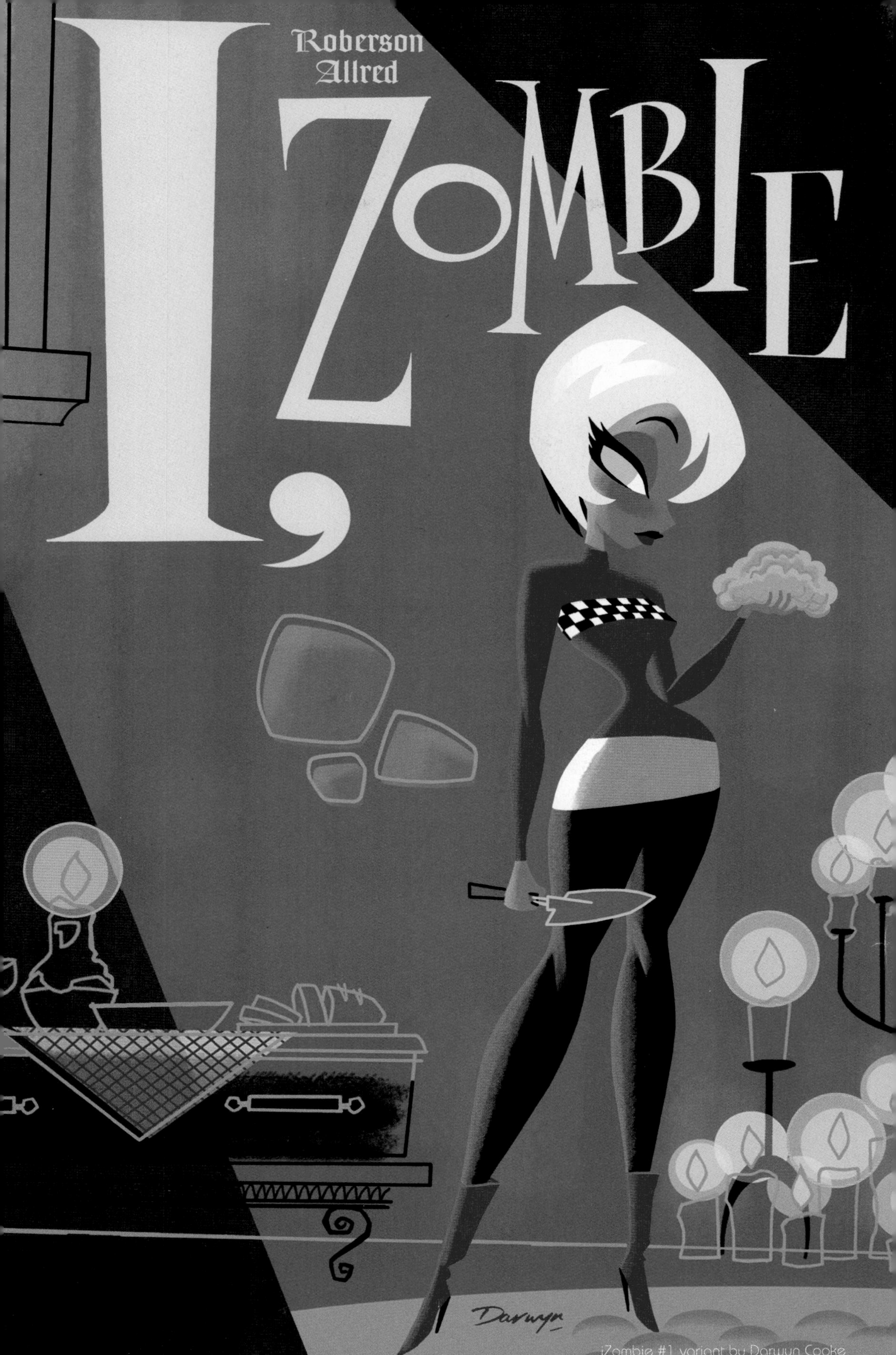
Roberson
Allred
I, ZOMBIE
Darwyn

iZombie #1 variant by Darwyn Cooke

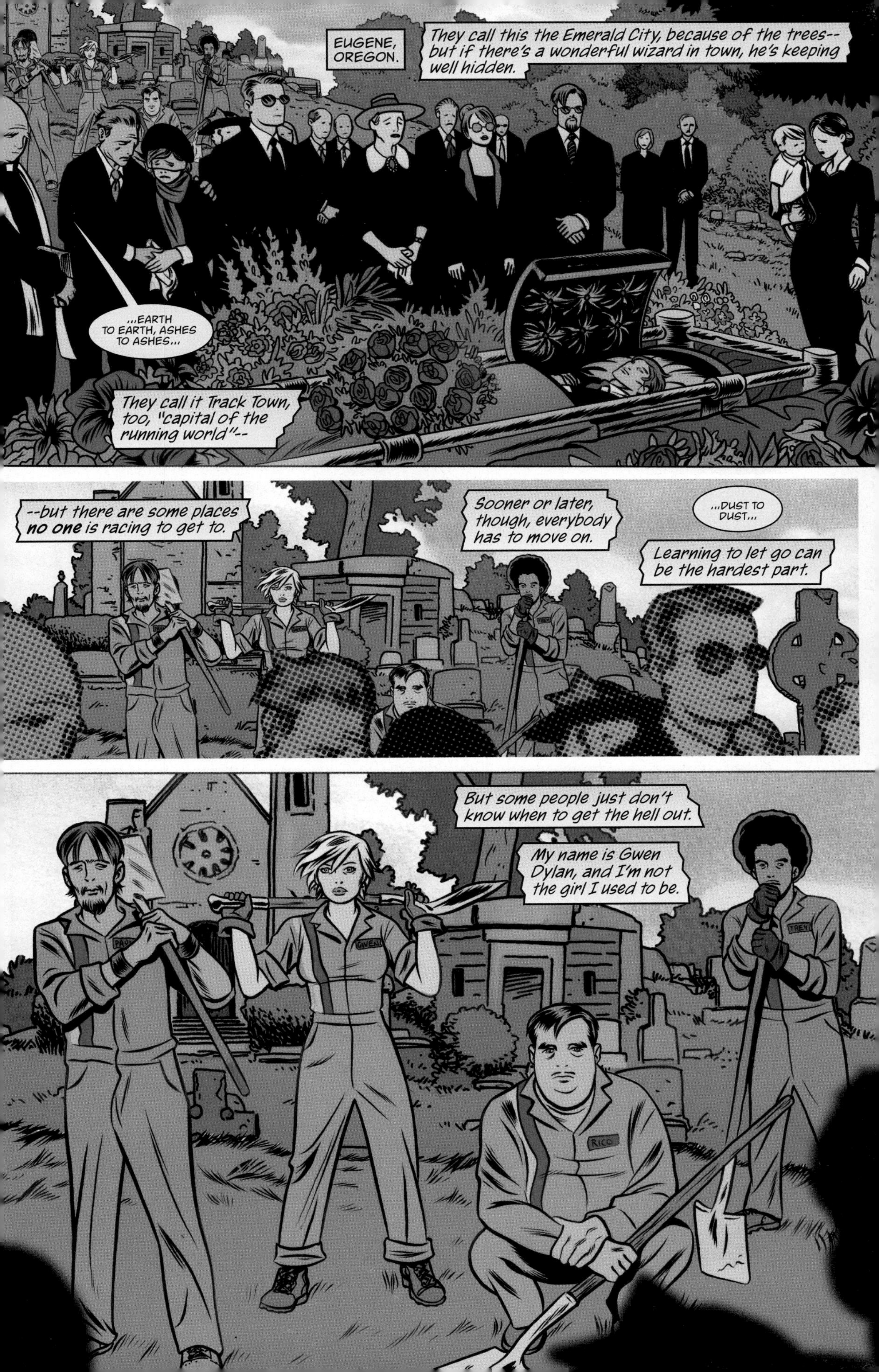
EUGENE, OREGON.
They call this the Emerald City, because of the trees--but if there's a wonderful wizard in town, he's keeping well hidden.
...EARTH TO EARTH, ASHES TO ASHES...
They call it Track Town, too, "capital of the running world"--
--but there are some places **no one** is racing to get to.
Sooner or later, though, everybody has to move on.
...DUST TO DUST...
Learning to let go can be the hardest part.
PAUL
GWEN
TREY
But some people just don't know when to get the hell out.
My name is Gwen Dylan, and I'm not the girl I used to be.
RICO

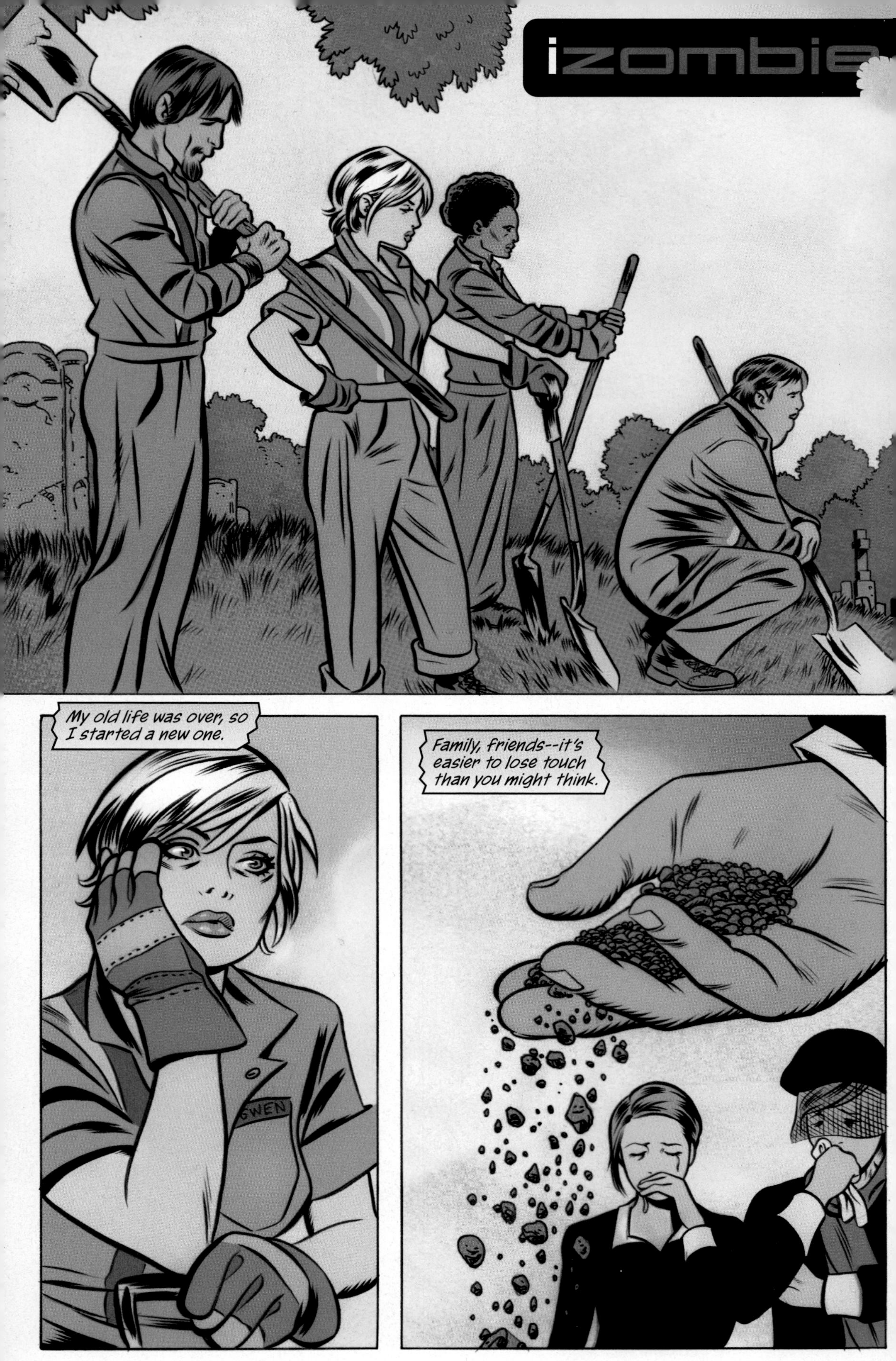
izombie
My old life was over, so I started a new one.
GWEN
Family, friends--it's easier to lose touch than you might think.

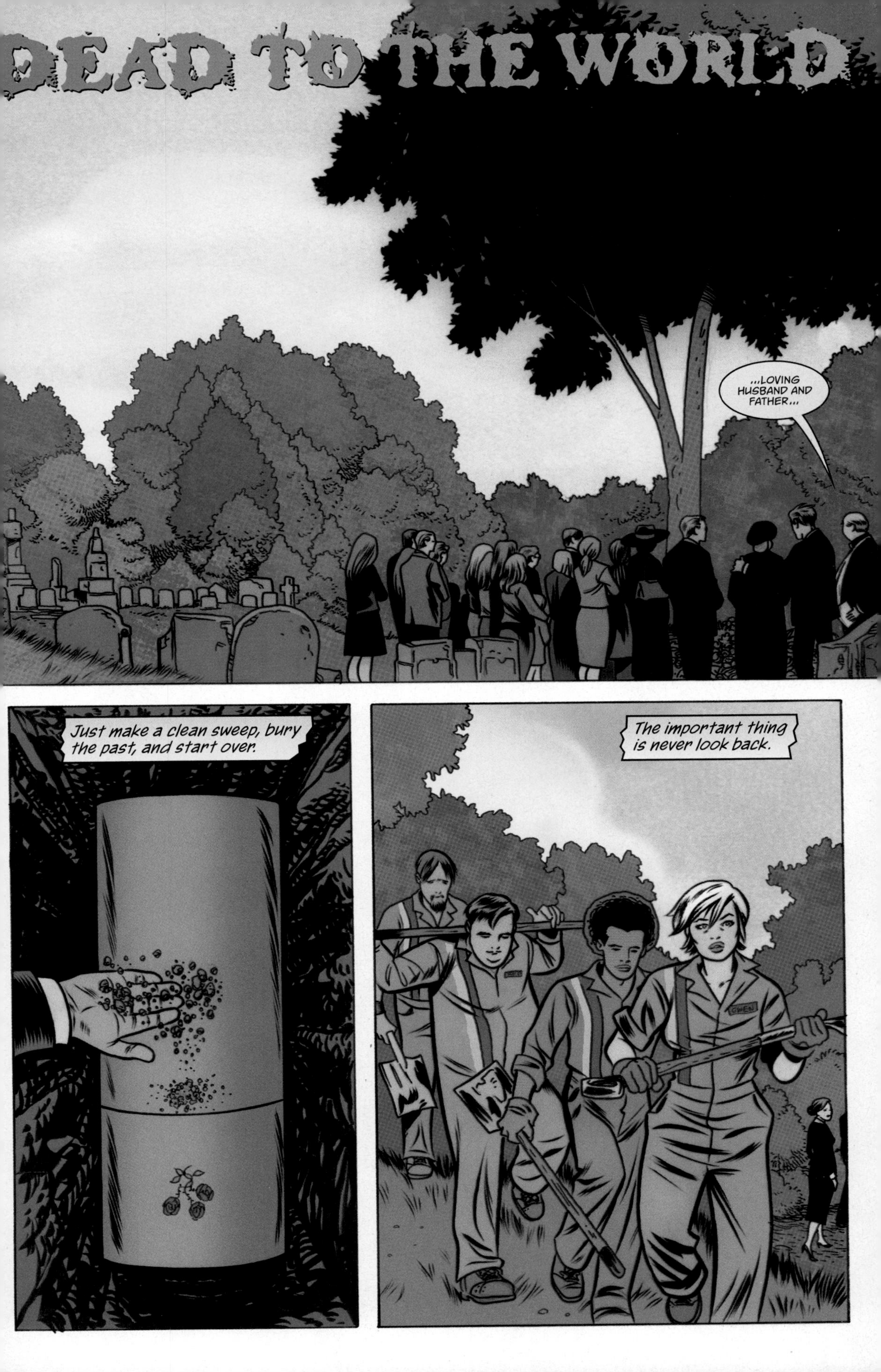
DEAD TO THE WORLD
...LOVING HUSBAND AND FATHER...
Just make a clean sweep, bury the past, and start over.
The important thing is never look back.

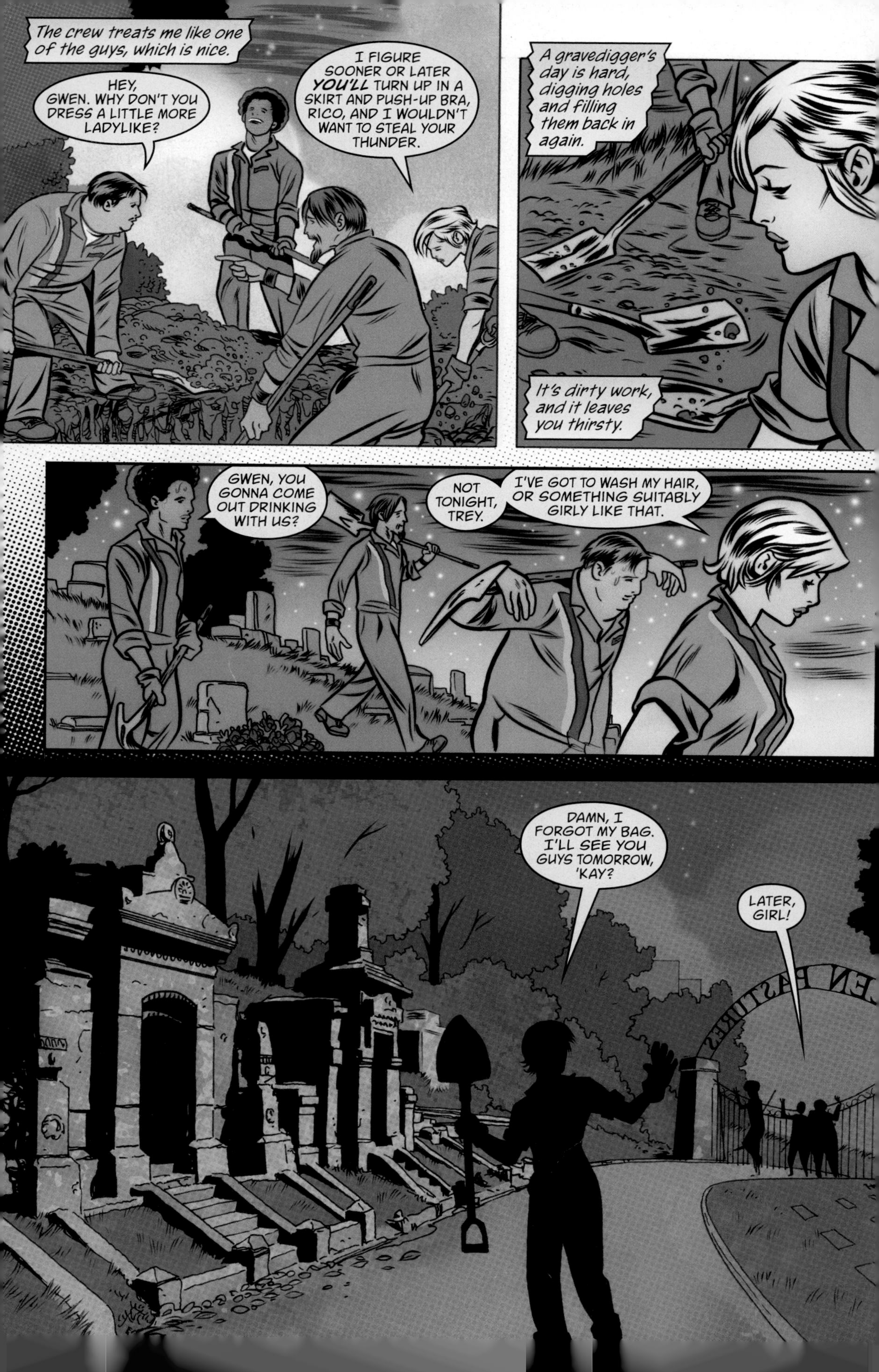
The crew treats me like one of the guys, which is nice.
HEY, GWEN. WHY DON'T YOU DRESS A LITTLE MORE LADYLIKE?
I FIGURE SOONER OR LATER YOU'LL TURN UP IN A SKIRT AND PUSH-UP BRA, RICO, AND I WOULDN'T WANT TO STEAL YOUR THUNDER.
A gravedigger's day is hard, digging holes and filling them back in again.
It's dirty work, and it leaves you thirsty.
GWEN, YOU GONNA COME OUT DRINKING WITH US?
NOT TONIGHT, TREY.
I'VE GOT TO WASH MY HAIR, OR SOMETHING SUITABLY GIRLY LIKE THAT.
DAMN, I FORGOT MY BAG. I'LL SEE YOU GUYS TOMORROW, 'KAY?
LATER, GIRL!

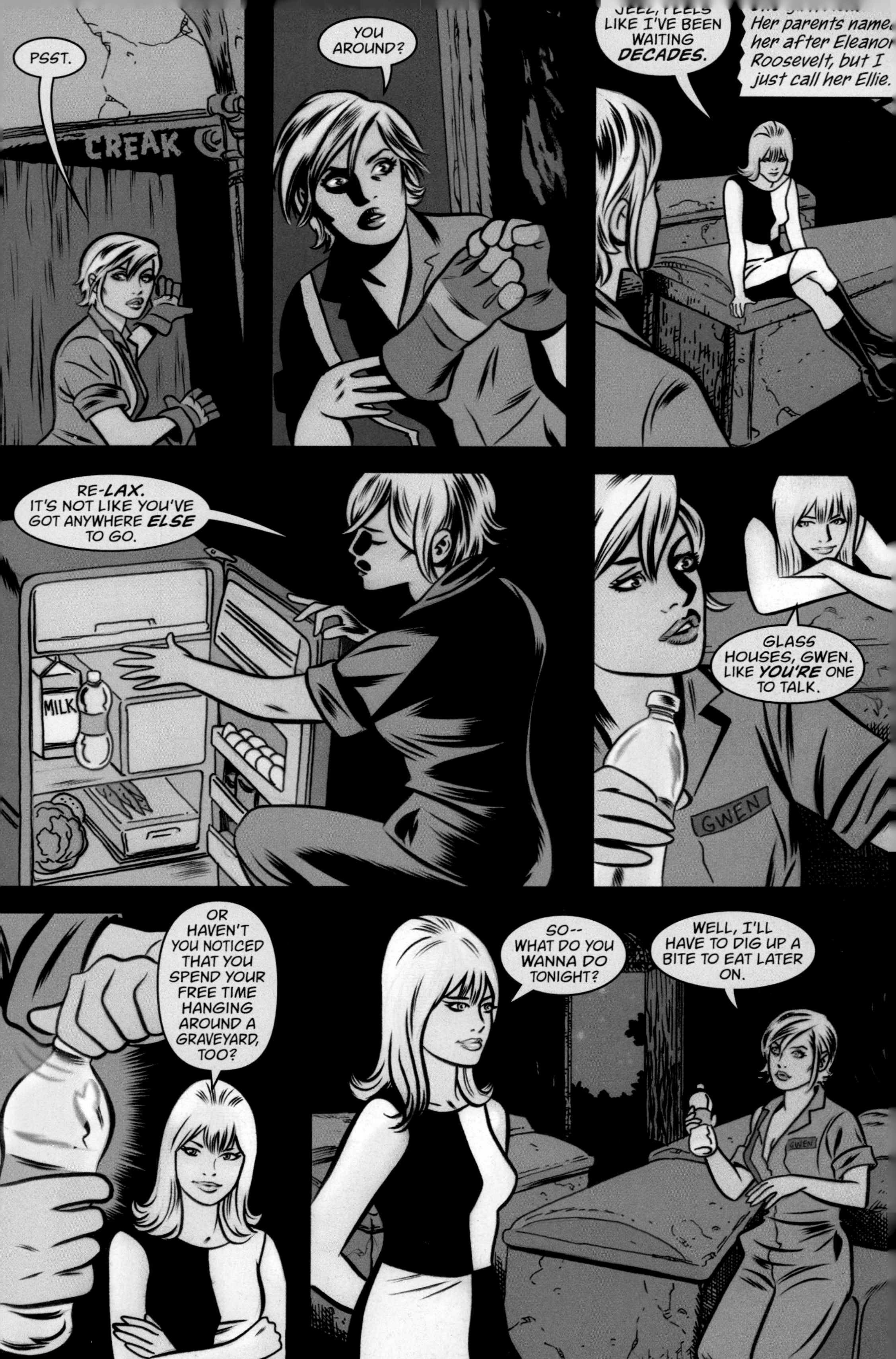
PSST.
CREAK
YOU AROUND?
LIKE I'VE BEEN WAITING DECADES.
Her parents name
her after Eleano
Roosevelt, but I just call her Ellie.
RE-LAX. IT'S NOT LIKE YOU'VE GOT ANYWHERE ELSE TO GO.
MILK
GLASS HOUSES, GWEN. LIKE YOU'RE ONE TO TALK.
GWEN
OR HAVEN'T YOU NOTICED THAT YOU SPEND YOUR FREE TIME HANGING AROUND A GRAVEYARD, TOO?
SO-- WHAT DO YOU WANNA DO TONIGHT?
WELL, I'LL HAVE TO DIG UP A BITE TO EAT LATER ON.

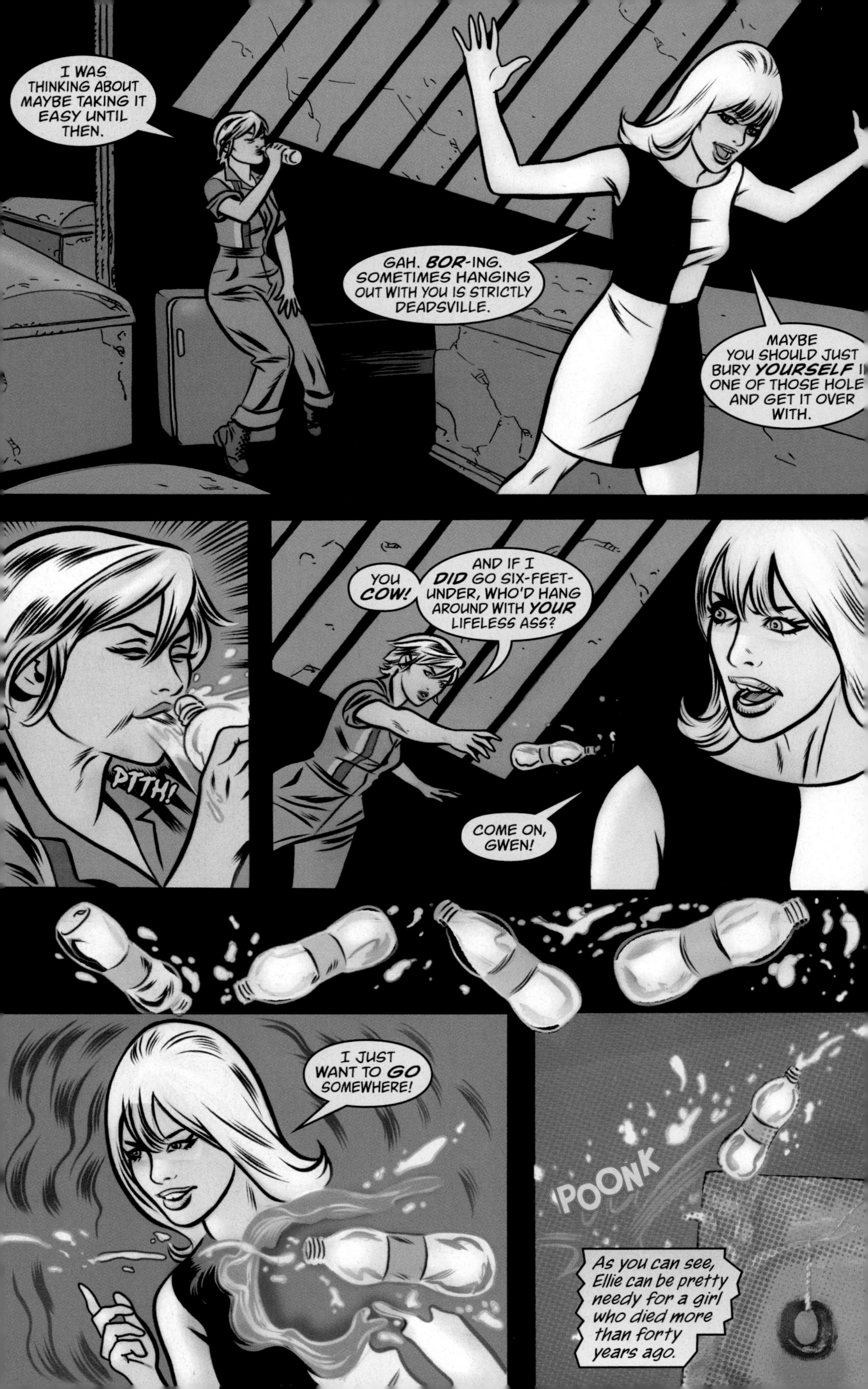
I WAS THINKING ABOUT MAYBE TAKING IT EASY UNTIL THEN.
GAH. BOR-ING. SOMETIMES HANGING OUT WITH YOU IS STRICTLY DEADSVILLE.
MAYBE YOU SHOULD JUST BURY YOURSELF I ONE OF THOSE HOLE AND GET IT OVER WITH.
PTTH!
YOU COW!
AND IF I DID GO SIX-FEET-UNDER, WHO'D HANG AROUND WITH YOUR LIFELESS ASS?
COME ON, GWEN!
I JUST WANT TO GO SOMEWHERE!
POONK
As you can see, Ellie can be pretty needy for a girl who died more than forty years ago.

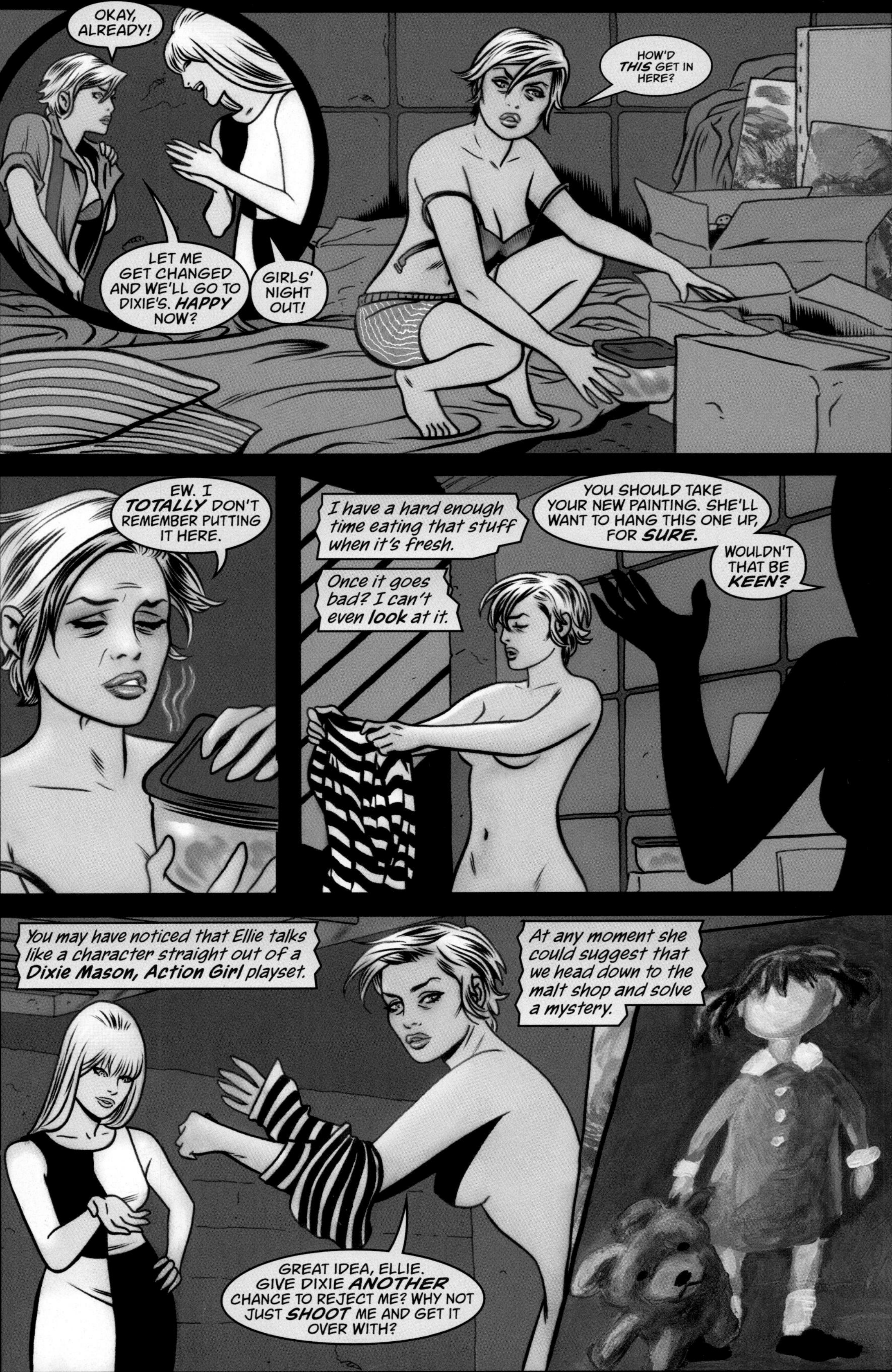
OKAY, ALREADY!
LET ME GET CHANGED AND WE'LL GO TO DIXIE'S. HAPPY NOW?
GIRLS' NIGHT OUT!
HOW'D THIS GET IN HERE?
EW. I TOTALLY DON'T REMEMBER PUTTING IT HERE.
I have a hard enough time eating that stuff when it's fresh.
Once it goes bad? I can't even look at it.
YOU SHOULD TAKE YOUR NEW PAINTING. SHE'LL WANT TO HANG THIS ONE UP, FOR SURE.
WOULDN'T THAT BE KEEN?
You may have noticed that Ellie talks like a character straight out of a Dixie Mason, Action Girl playset.
At any moment she could suggest that we head down to the malt shop and solve a mystery.
GREAT IDEA, ELLIE. GIVE DIXIE ANOTHER CHANCE TO REJECT ME? WHY NOT JUST SHOOT ME AND GET IT OVER WITH?

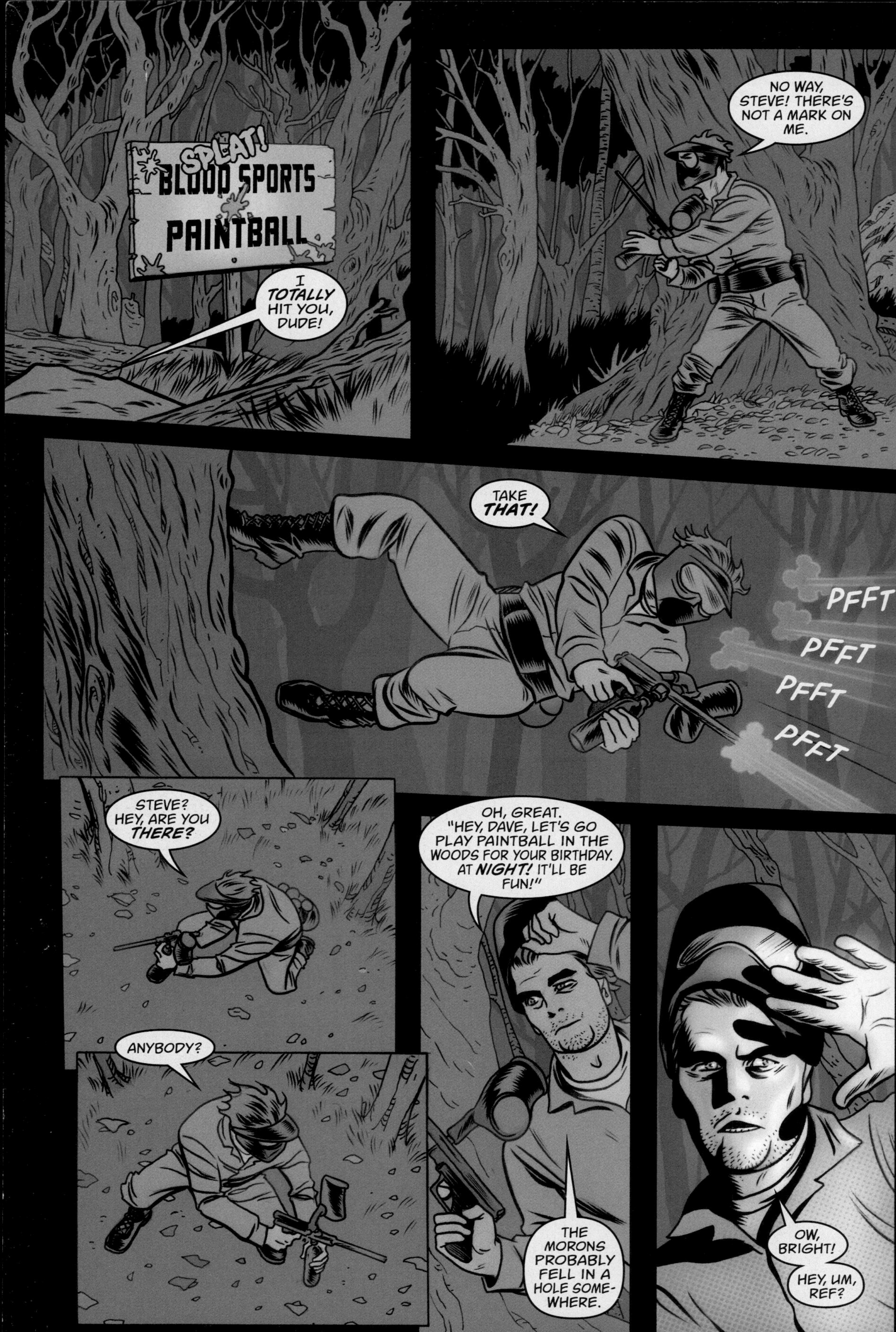
SPLAT!
BLOOD SPORTS
PAINTBALL
I TOTALLY HIT YOU, DUDE!
NO WAY, STEVE! THERE'S NOT A MARK ON ME.
TAKE THAT!
PFFT
PFFT
PFFT
PFFT
STEVE? HEY, ARE YOU THERE?
ANYBODY?
OH, GREAT. "HEY, DAVE, LET'S GO PLAY PAINTBALL IN THE WOODS FOR YOUR BIRTHDAY. AT NIGHT! IT'LL BE FUN!"
THE MORONS PROBABLY FELL IN A HOLE SOME-WHERE.
OW, BRIGHT!
HEY, UM, REF?

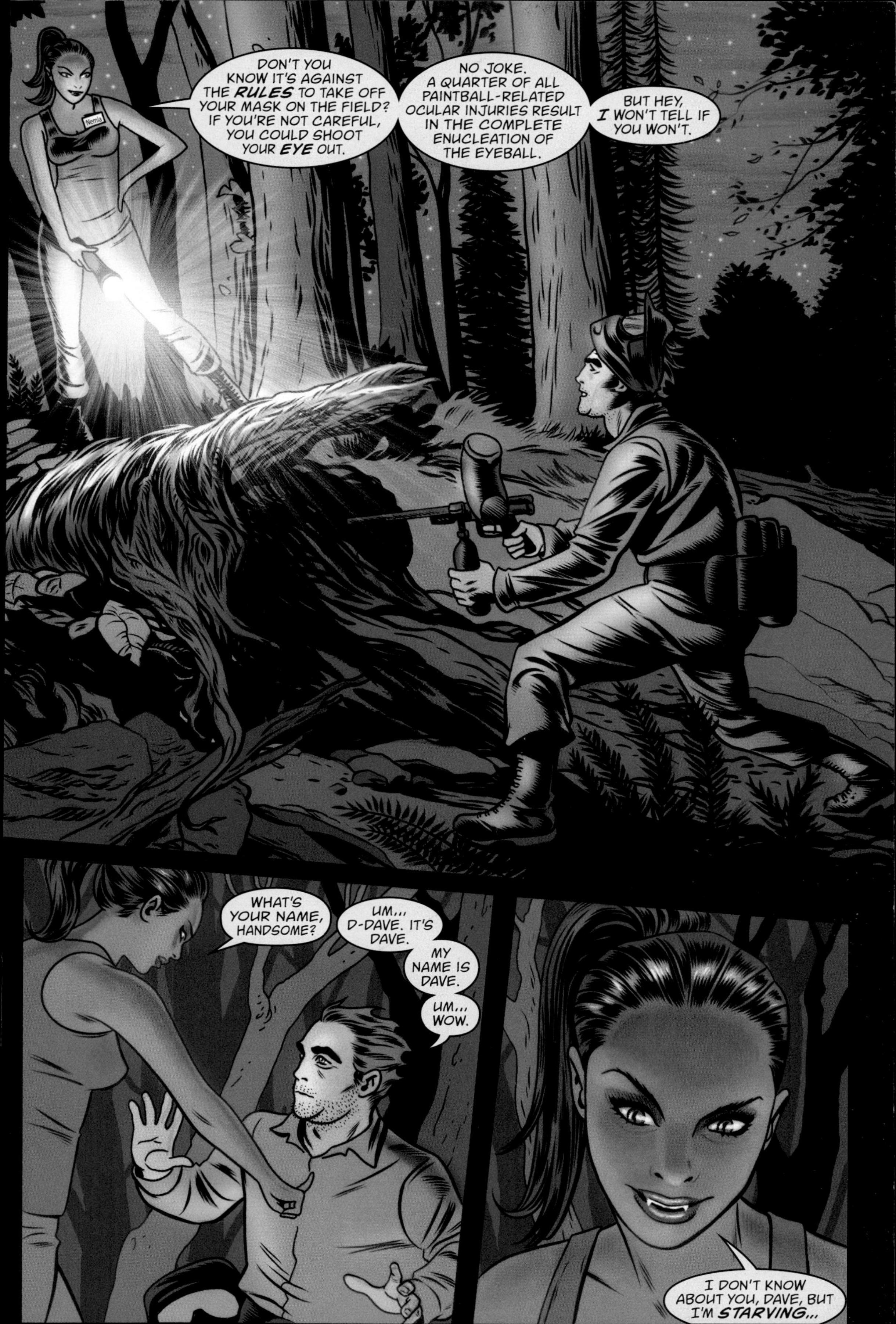
DON'T YOU KNOW IT'S AGAINST THE RULES TO TAKE OFF YOUR MASK ON THE FIELD? IF YOU'RE NOT CAREFUL, YOU COULD SHOOT YOUR EYE OUT.
NO JOKE. A QUARTER OF ALL PAINTBALL-RELATED OCULAR INJURIES RESULT IN THE COMPLETE ENUCLEATION OF THE EYEBALL.
BUT HEY, I WON'T TELL IF YOU WON'T.
Nemia
WHAT'S YOUR NAME, HANDSOME?
UM... D-DAVE. IT'S DAVE.
MY NAME IS DAVE.
UM... WOW.
I DON'T KNOW ABOUT YOU, DAVE, BUT I'M STARVING...

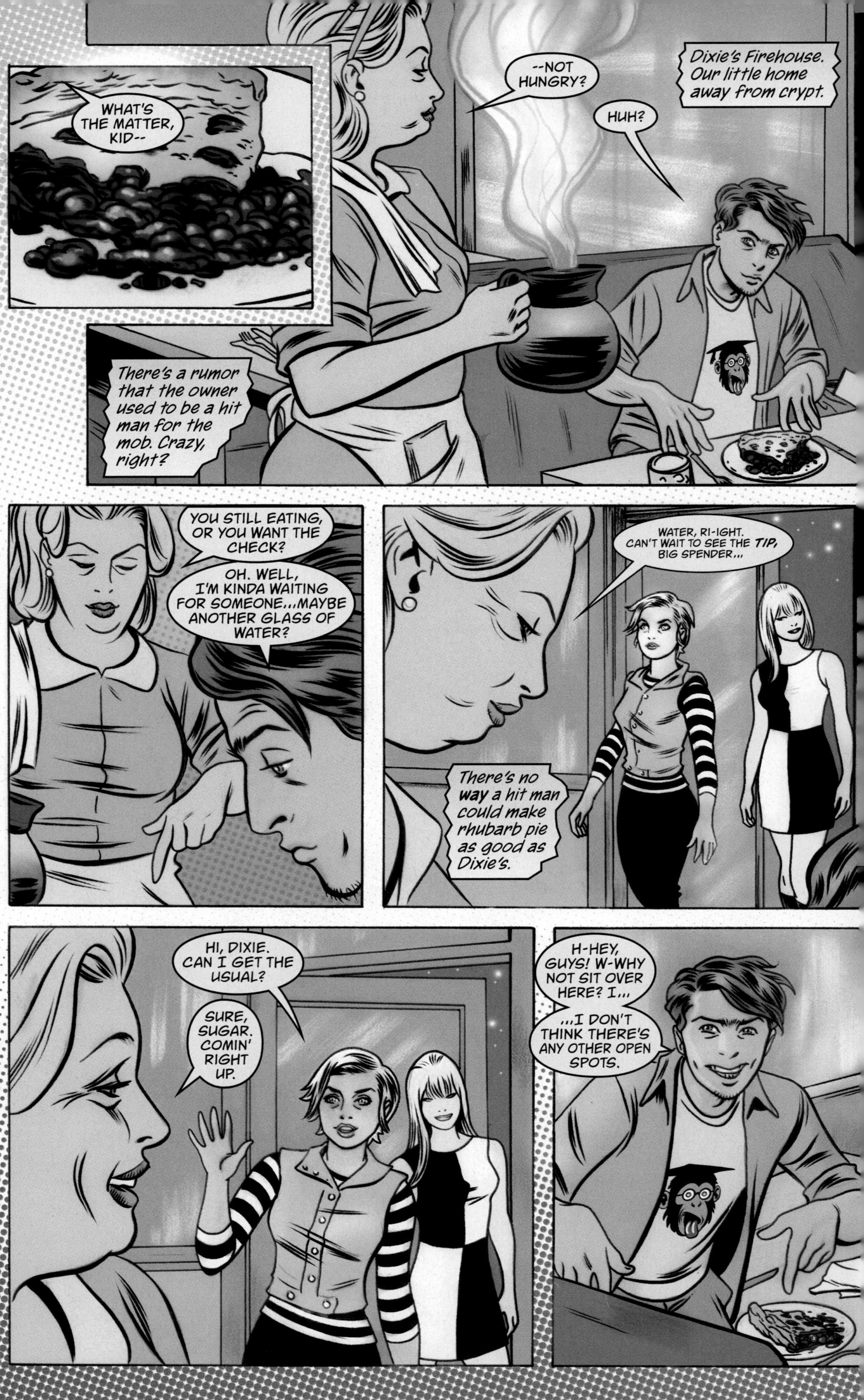
WHAT'S THE MATTER, KID--
--NOT HUNGRY?
Dixie's Firehouse. Our little home away from crypt.
HUH?
There's a rumor that the owner used to be a hit man for the mob. Crazy, right?
YOU STILL EATING, OR YOU WANT THE CHECK?
OH. WELL, I'M KINDA WAITING FOR SOMEONE...MAYBE ANOTHER GLASS OF WATER?
WATER, RI-IGHT. CAN'T WAIT TO SEE THE TIP, BIG SPENDER...
There's no way a hit man could make rhubarb pie as good as Dixie's.
HI, DIXIE. CAN I GET THE USUAL?
SURE, SUGAR. COMIN' RIGHT UP.
H-HEY, GUYS! W-WHY NOT SIT OVER HERE? I...
...I DON'T THINK THERE'S ANY OTHER OPEN SPOTS.

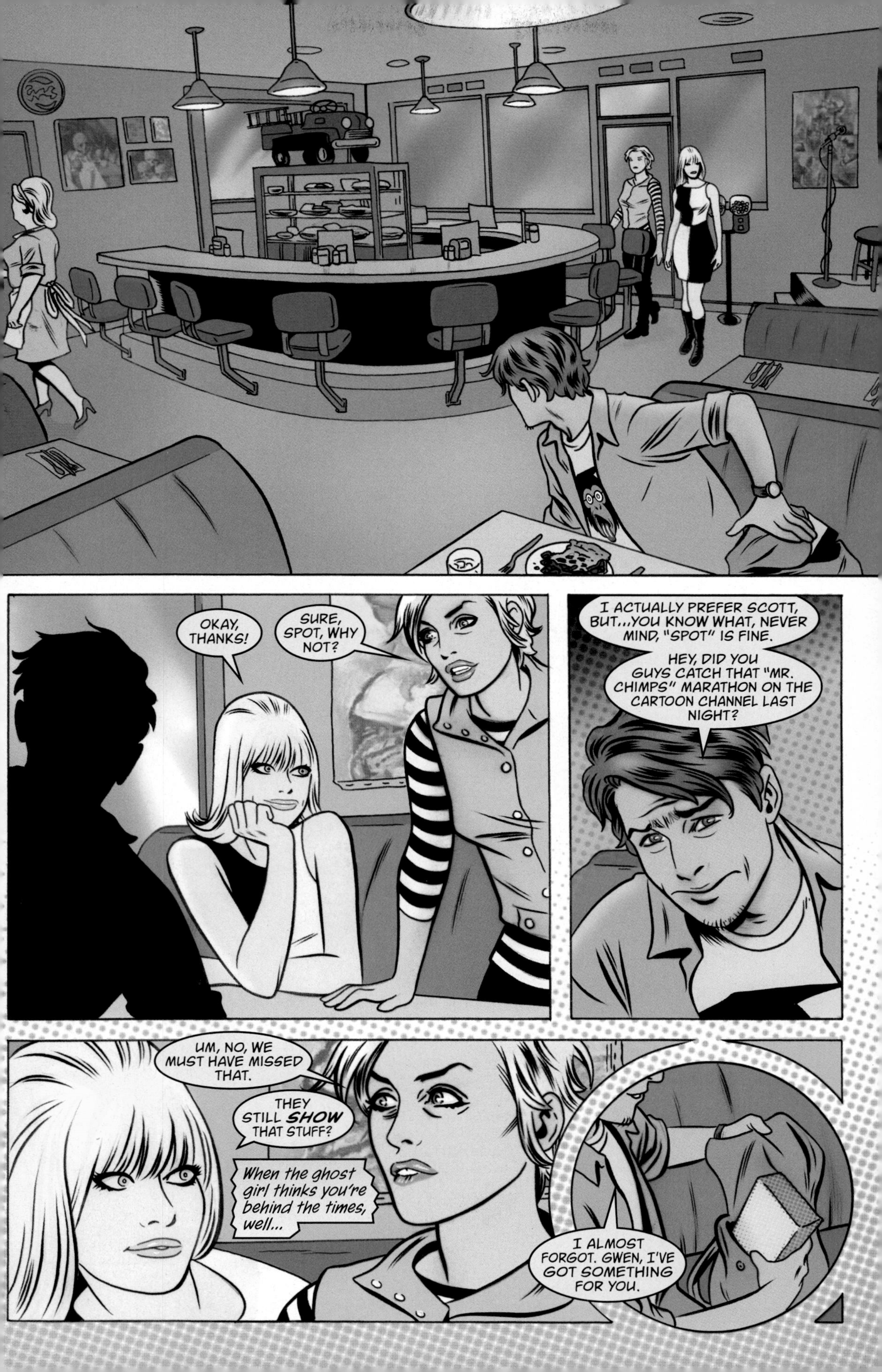
OKAY, THANKS!
SURE, SPOT, WHY NOT?
I ACTUALLY PREFER SCOTT, BUT...YOU KNOW WHAT, NEVER MIND, "SPOT" IS FINE.
HEY, DID YOU GUYS CATCH THAT "MR. CHIMPS" MARATHON ON THE CARTOON CHANNEL LAST NIGHT?
UM, NO, WE MUST HAVE MISSED THAT.
THEY STILL SHOW THAT STUFF?
When the ghost girl thinks you're behind the times, well...
I ALMOST FORGOT. GWEN, I'VE GOT SOMETHING FOR YOU.

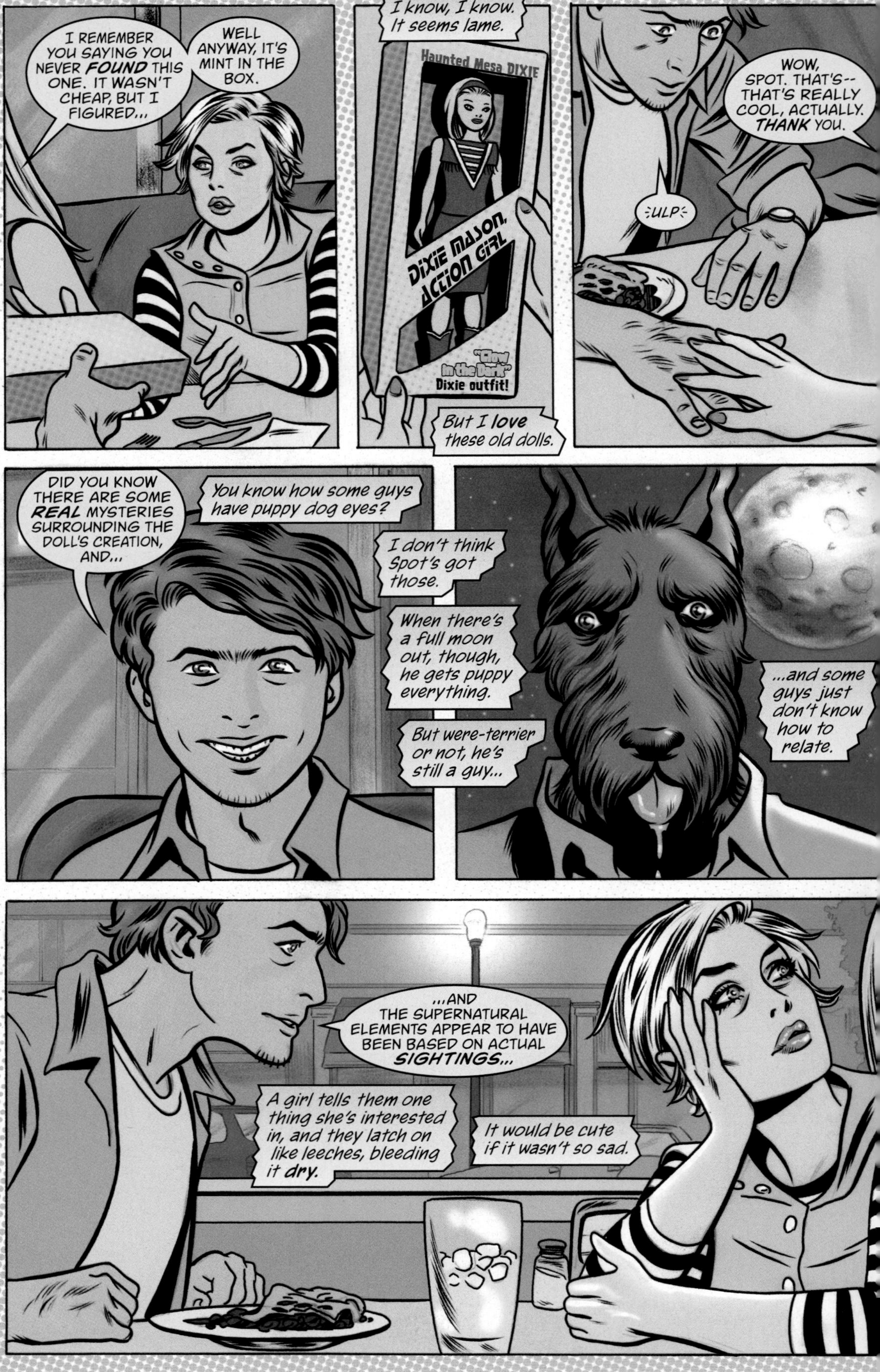
I REMEMBER YOU SAYING YOU NEVER FOUND THIS ONE. IT WASN'T CHEAP, BUT I FIGURED...
WELL ANYWAY, IT'S MINT IN THE BOX.
I know, I know. It seems lame.
Haunted Mesa DIXIE
DIXIE MASON, ACTION GIRL
"Glow in the Dark" Dixie outfit!
But I love these old dolls.
WOW, SPOT. THAT'S-- THAT'S REALLY COOL, ACTUALLY. THANK YOU.
ULP
DID YOU KNOW THERE ARE SOME REAL MYSTERIES SURROUNDING THE DOLL'S CREATION, AND...
You know how some guys have puppy dog eyes?
I don't think Spot's got those.
When there's a full moon out, though, he gets puppy everything.
But were-terrier or not, he's still a guy...
...and some guys just don't know how to relate.
...AND THE SUPERNATURAL ELEMENTS APPEAR TO HAVE BEEN BASED ON ACTUAL SIGHTINGS...
A girl tells them one thing she's interested in, and they latch on like leeches, bleeding it dry.
It would be cute if it wasn't so sad.

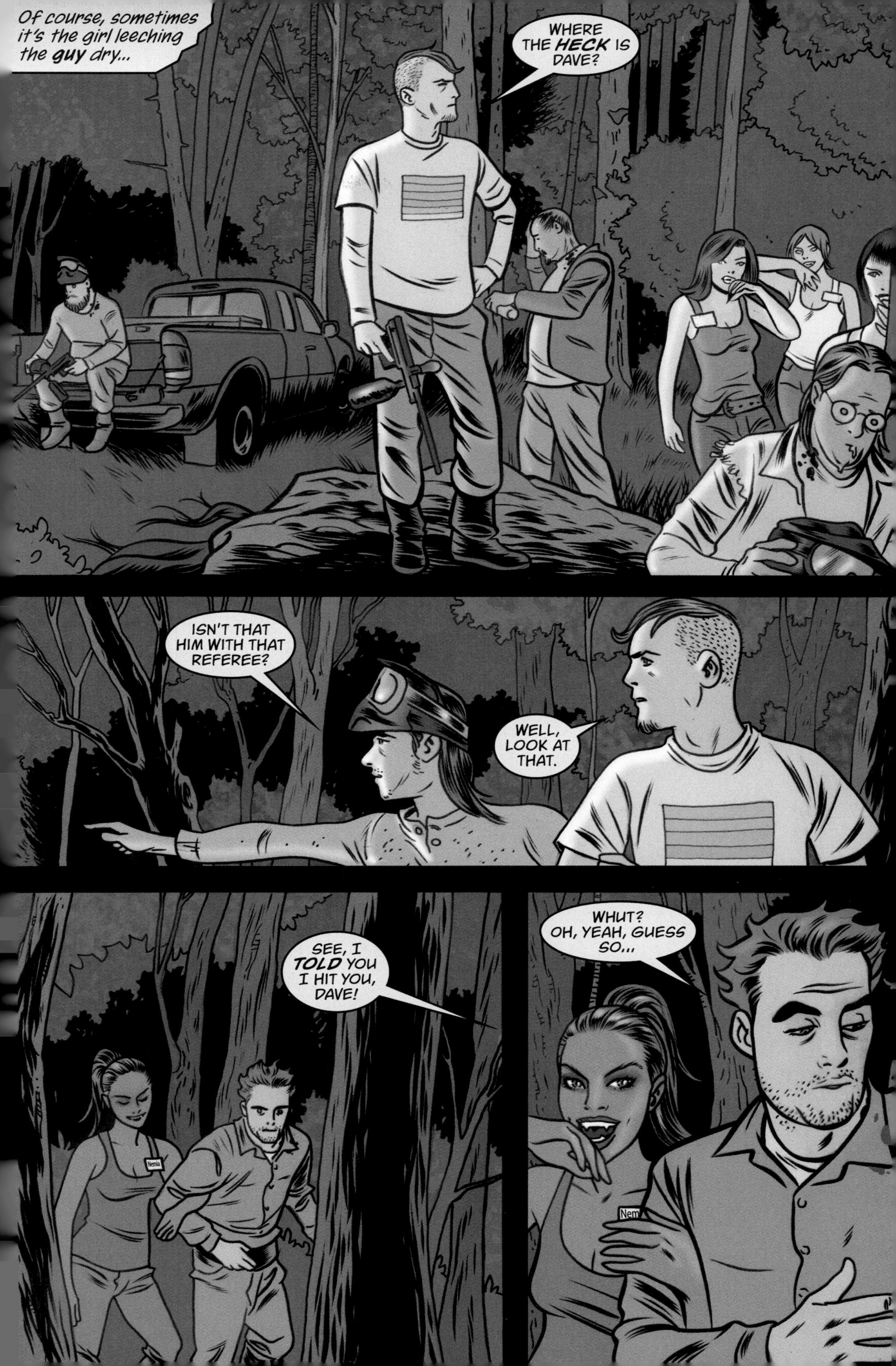
Of course, sometimes it's the girl leeching the **guy** dry...
WHERE THE **HECK** IS DAVE?
ISN'T THAT HIM WITH THAT REFEREE?
WELL, LOOK AT THAT.
SEE, I **TOLD** YOU I HIT YOU, DAVE!
WHUT? OH, YEAH, GUESS SO...

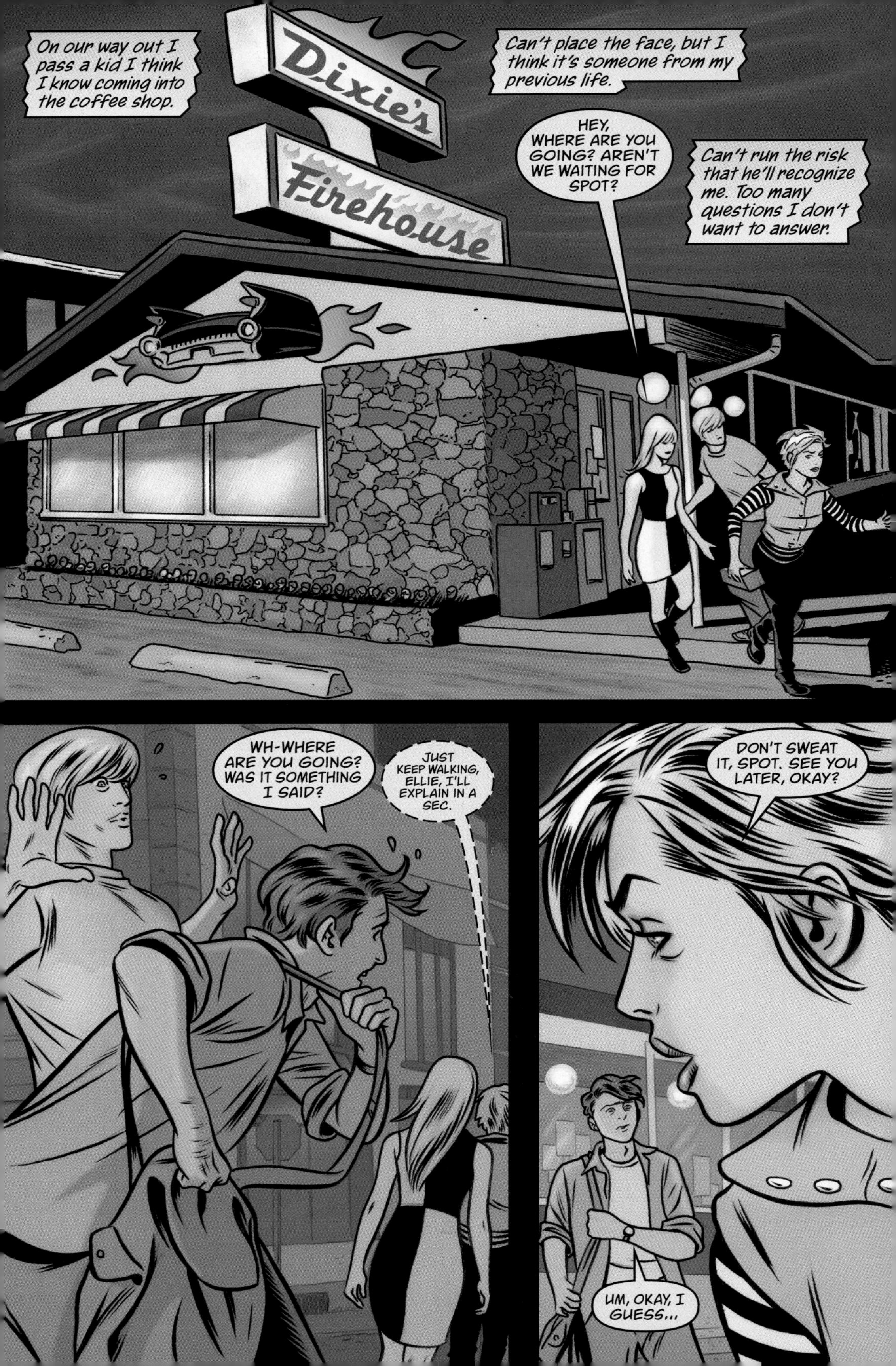
On our way out I pass a kid I think I know coming into the coffee shop.
Dixie's Firehouse
Can't place the face, but I think it's someone from my previous life.
HEY, WHERE ARE YOU GOING? AREN'T WE WAITING FOR SPOT?
Can't run the risk that he'll recognize me. Too many questions I don't want to answer.
WH-WHERE ARE YOU GOING? WAS IT SOMETHING I SAID?
JUST KEEP WALKING, ELLIE, I'LL EXPLAIN IN A SEC.
DON'T SWEAT IT, SPOT. SEE YOU LATER, OKAY?
UM, OKAY, I GUESS...

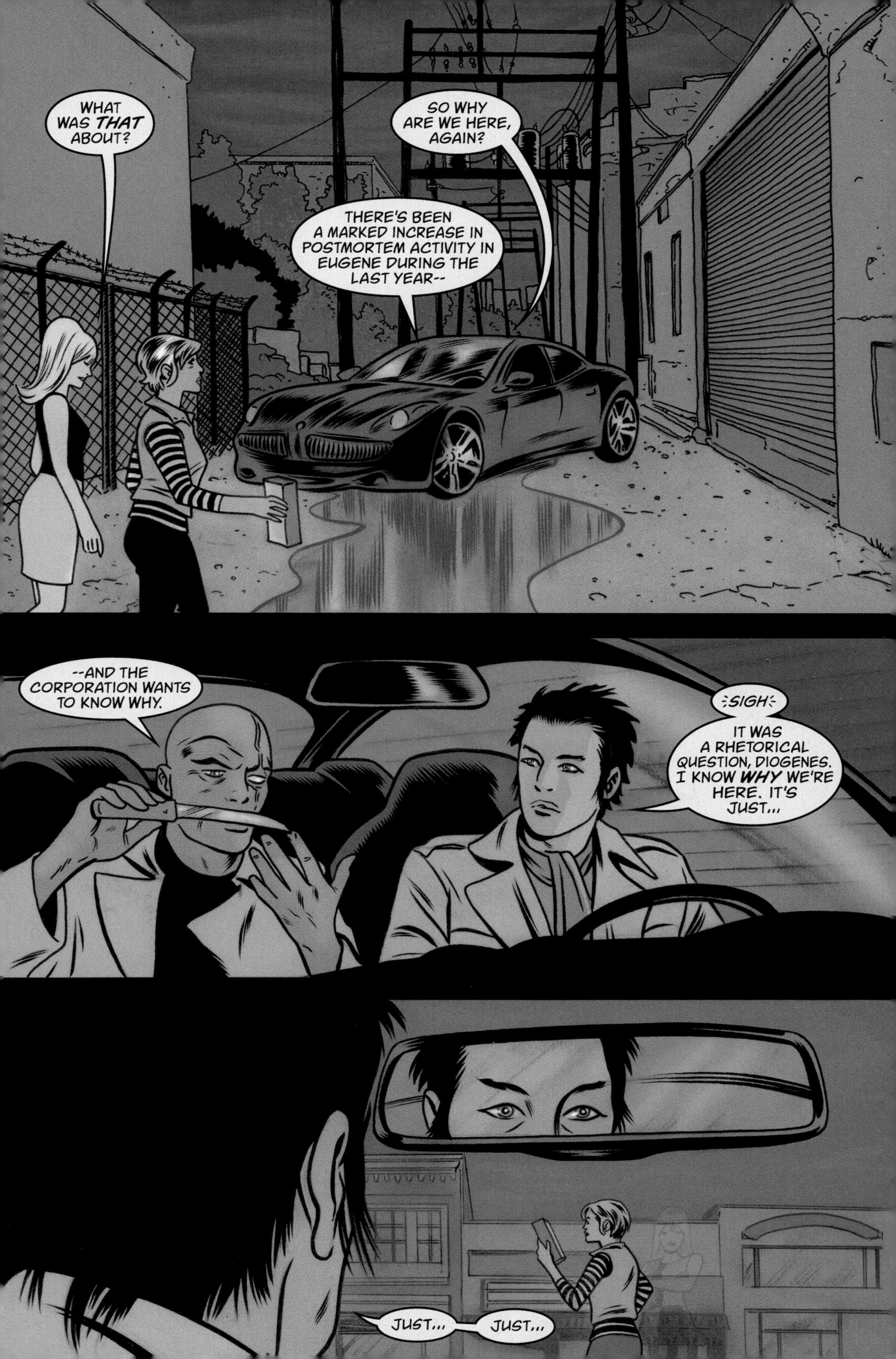
WHAT WAS *THAT* ABOUT?
SO WHY ARE WE HERE, AGAIN?
THERE'S BEEN A MARKED INCREASE IN POSTMORTEM ACTIVITY IN EUGENE DURING THE LAST YEAR--
--AND THE CORPORATION WANTS TO KNOW WHY.
SIGH
IT WAS A RHETORICAL QUESTION, DIOGENES. I KNOW *WHY* WE'RE HERE. IT'S JUST...
JUST...
JUST...

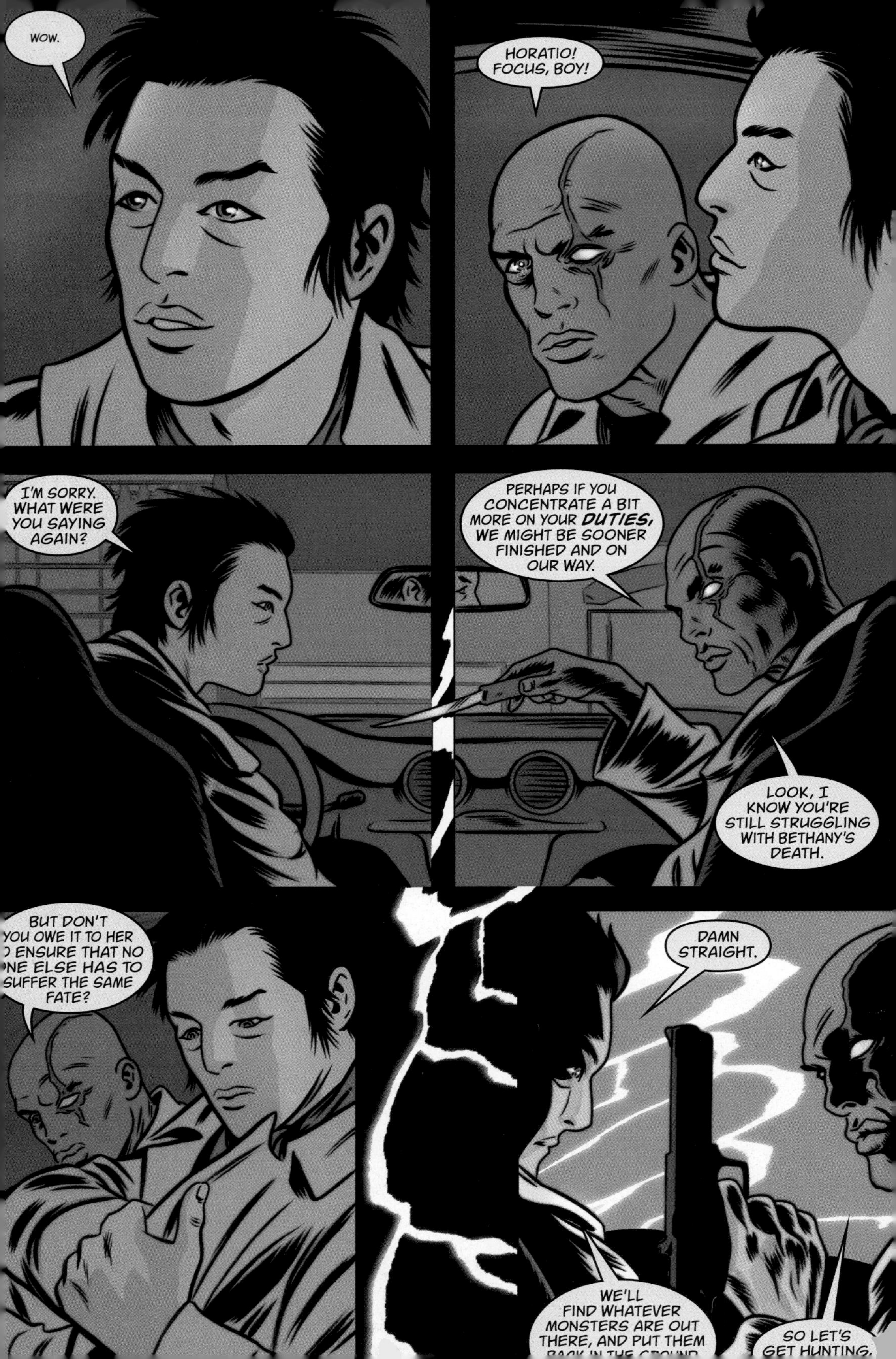
WOW.
HORATIO! FOCUS, BOY!
I'M SORRY. WHAT WERE YOU SAYING AGAIN?
PERHAPS IF YOU CONCENTRATE A BIT MORE ON YOUR *DUTIES*, WE MIGHT BE SOONER FINISHED AND ON OUR WAY.
LOOK, I KNOW YOU'RE STILL STRUGGLING WITH BETHANY'S DEATH.
BUT DON'T YOU OWE IT TO HER ENSURE THAT NO NE ELSE HAS TO SUFFER THE SAME FATE?
DAMN STRAIGHT.
WE'LL FIND WHATEVER MONSTERS ARE OUT THERE, AND PUT THEM
SO LET'S GET HUNTING.

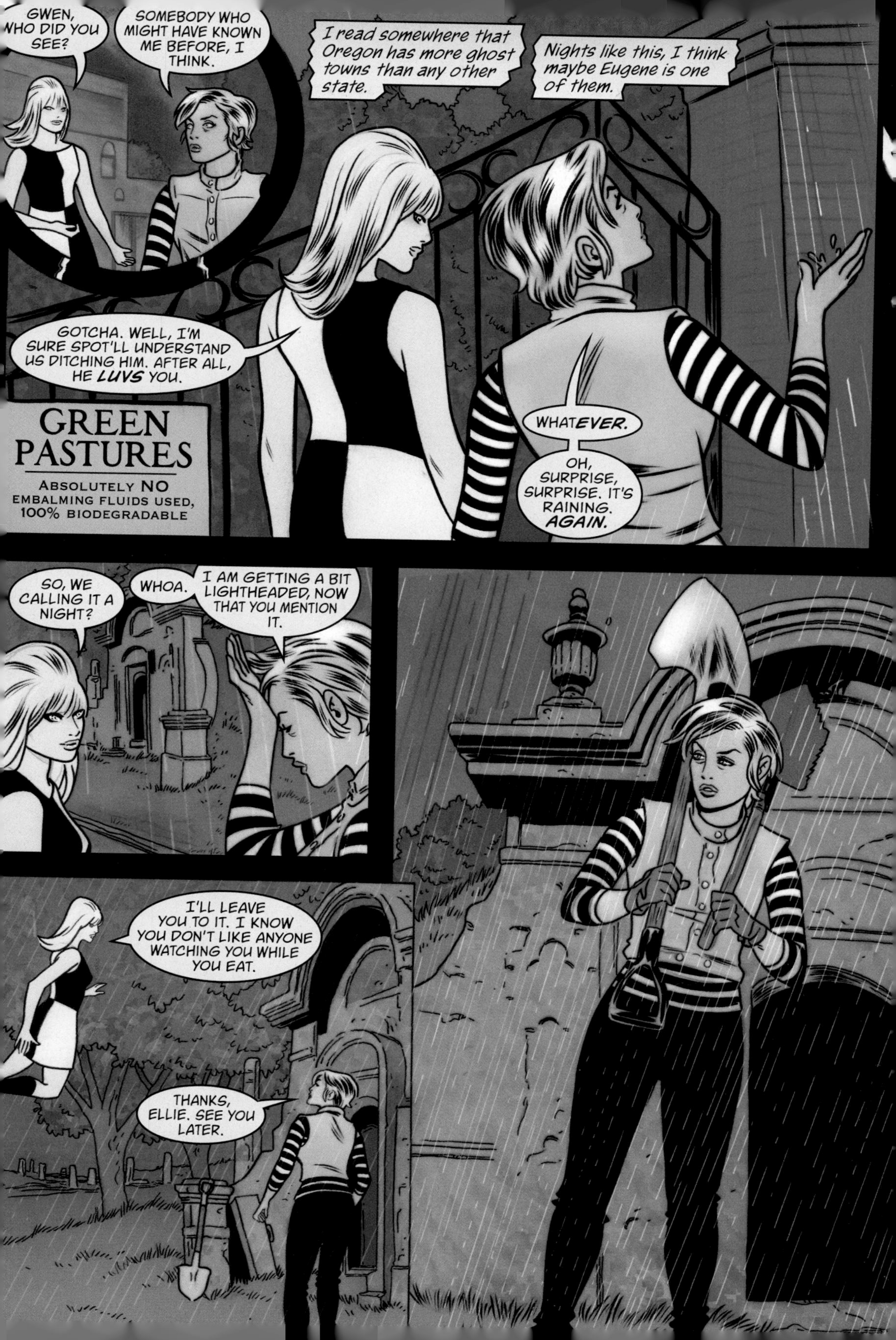
GWEN, WHO DID YOU SEE?
SOMEBODY WHO MIGHT HAVE KNOWN ME BEFORE, I THINK.
I read somewhere that Oregon has more ghost towns than any other state.
Nights like this, I think maybe Eugene is one of them.
GOTCHA. WELL, I'M SURE SPOT'LL UNDERSTAND US DITCHING HIM. AFTER ALL, HE LUVS YOU.
GREEN PASTURES
ABSOLUTELY NO EMBALMING FLUIDS USED, 100% BIODEGRADABLE
WHATEVER.
OH, SURPRISE, SURPRISE. IT'S RAINING. AGAIN.
SO, WE CALLING IT A NIGHT?
WHOA.
I AM GETTING A BIT LIGHTHEADED, NOW THAT YOU MENTION IT.
I'LL LEAVE YOU TO IT. I KNOW YOU DON'T LIKE ANYONE WATCHING YOU WHILE YOU EAT.
THANKS, ELLIE. SEE YOU LATER.

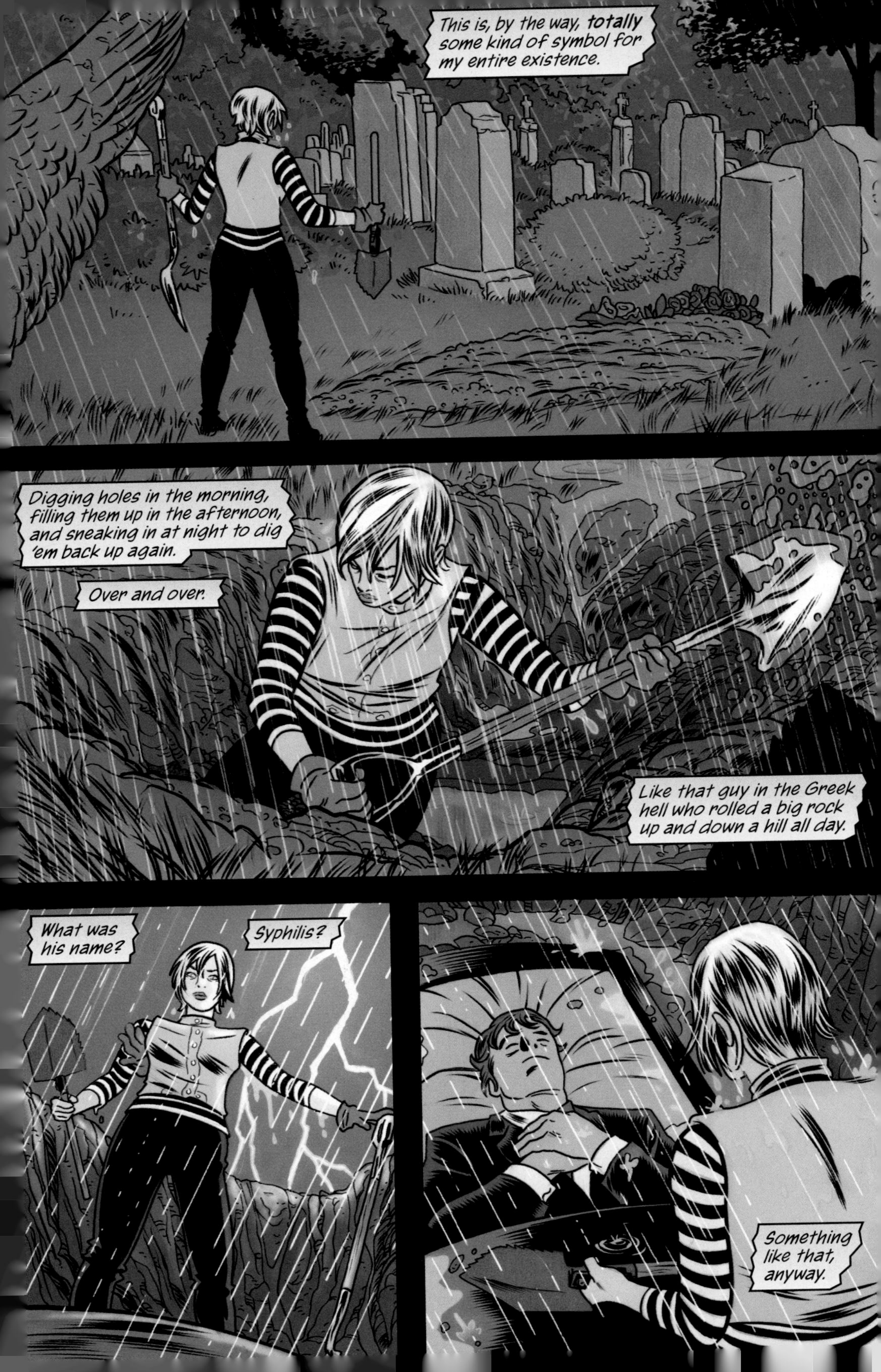
This is, by the way, totally some kind of symbol for my entire existence.
Digging holes in the morning, filling them up in the afternoon, and sneaking in at night to dig 'em back up again.
Over and over.
Like that guy in the Greek hell who rolled a big rock up and down a hill all day.
What was his name?
Syphilis?
Something like that, anyway.

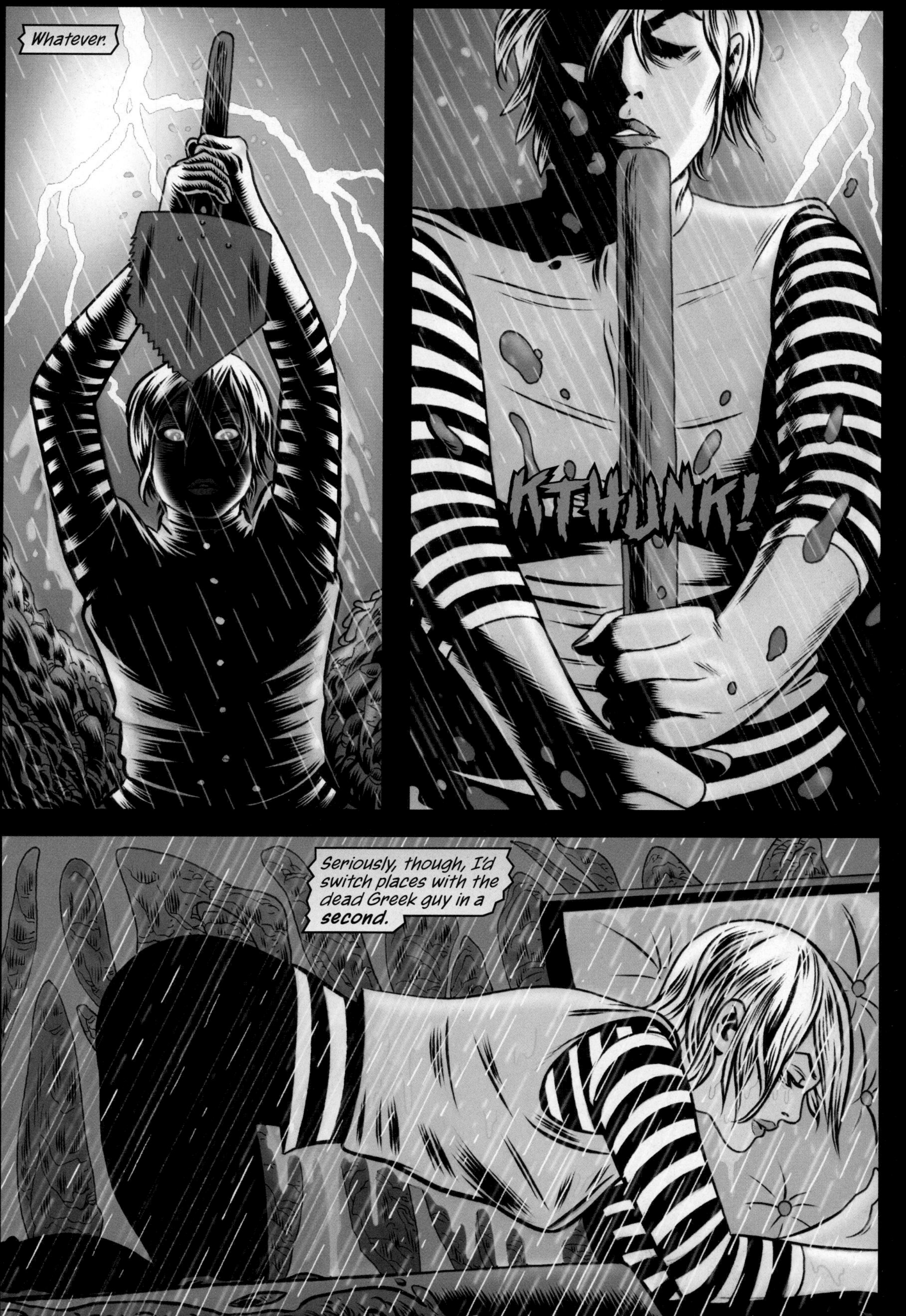
Whatever.
KTHUNK!
Seriously, though, I'd switch places with the dead Greek guy in a **second.**

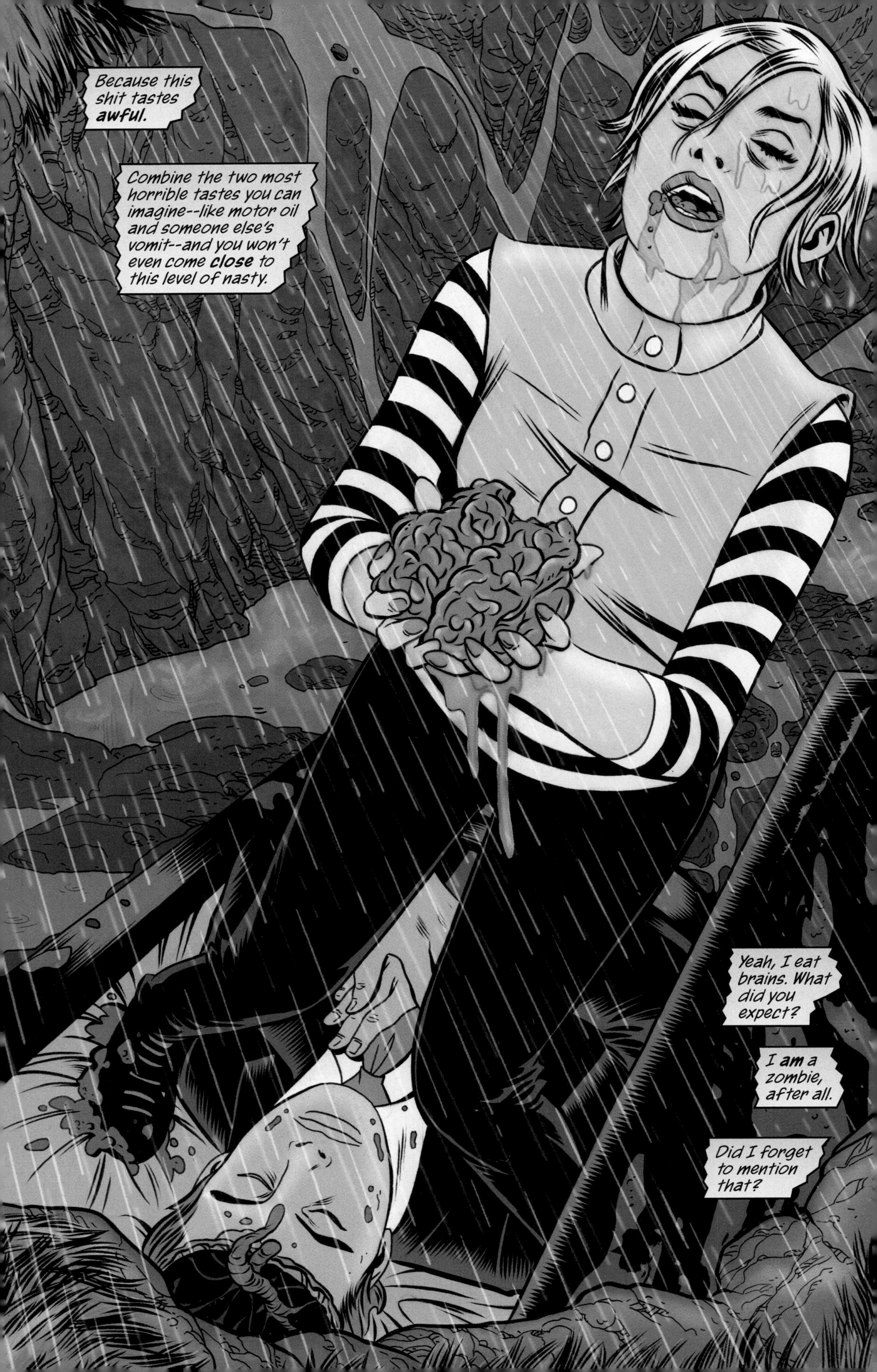
Because this shit tastes **awful.**
Combine the two most horrible tastes you can imagine--like motor oil and someone else's vomit--and you won't even come **close** to this level of nasty.
Yeah, I eat brains. What did you expect?
I **am** a zombie, after all.
Did I forget to mention that?

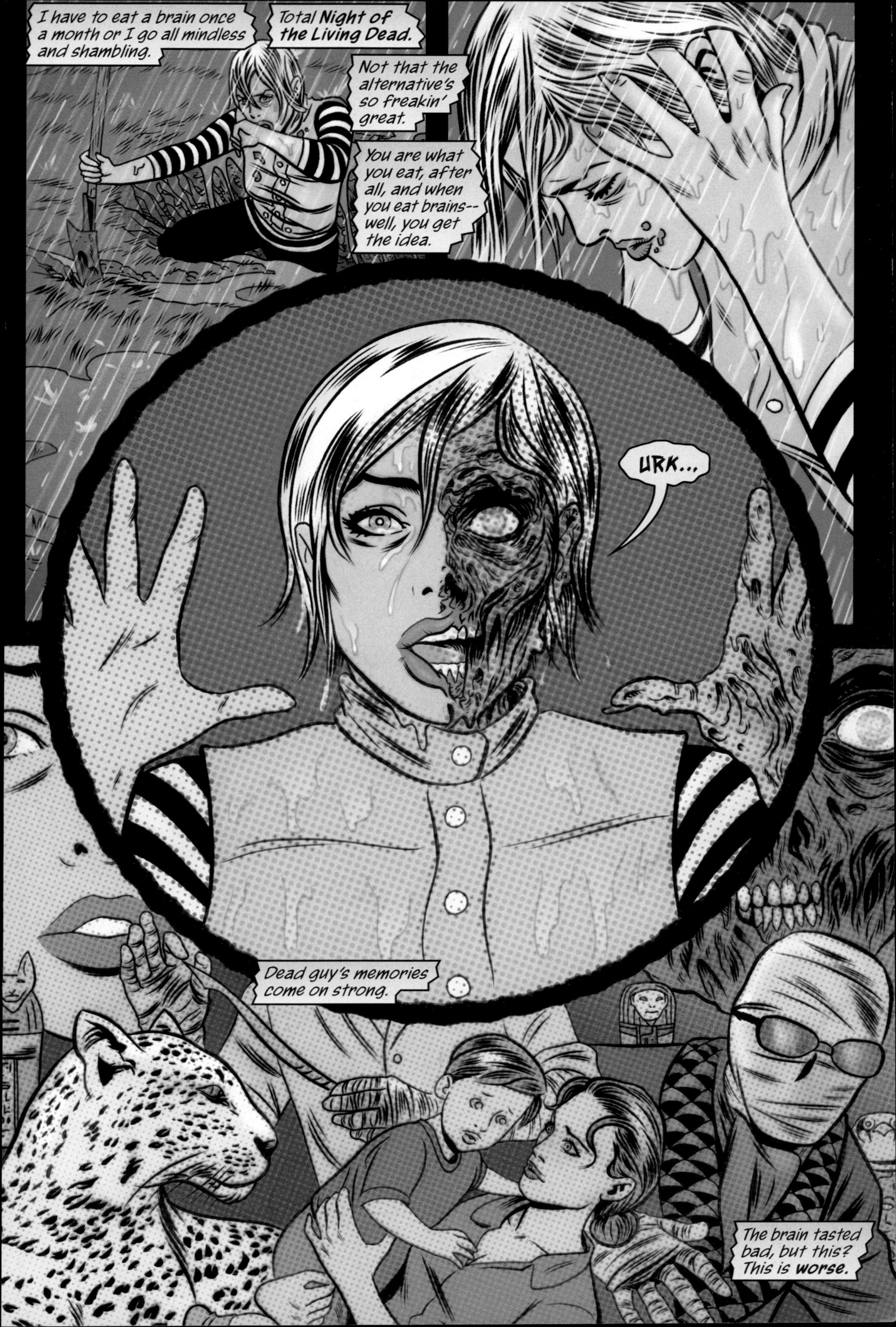
I have to eat a brain once a month or I go all mindless and shambling.
Total Night of the Living Dead.
Not that the alternative's so freakin' great.
You are what you eat, after all, and when you eat brains--well, you get the idea.
URK...
Dead guy's memories come on strong.
The brain tasted bad, but this? This is worse.

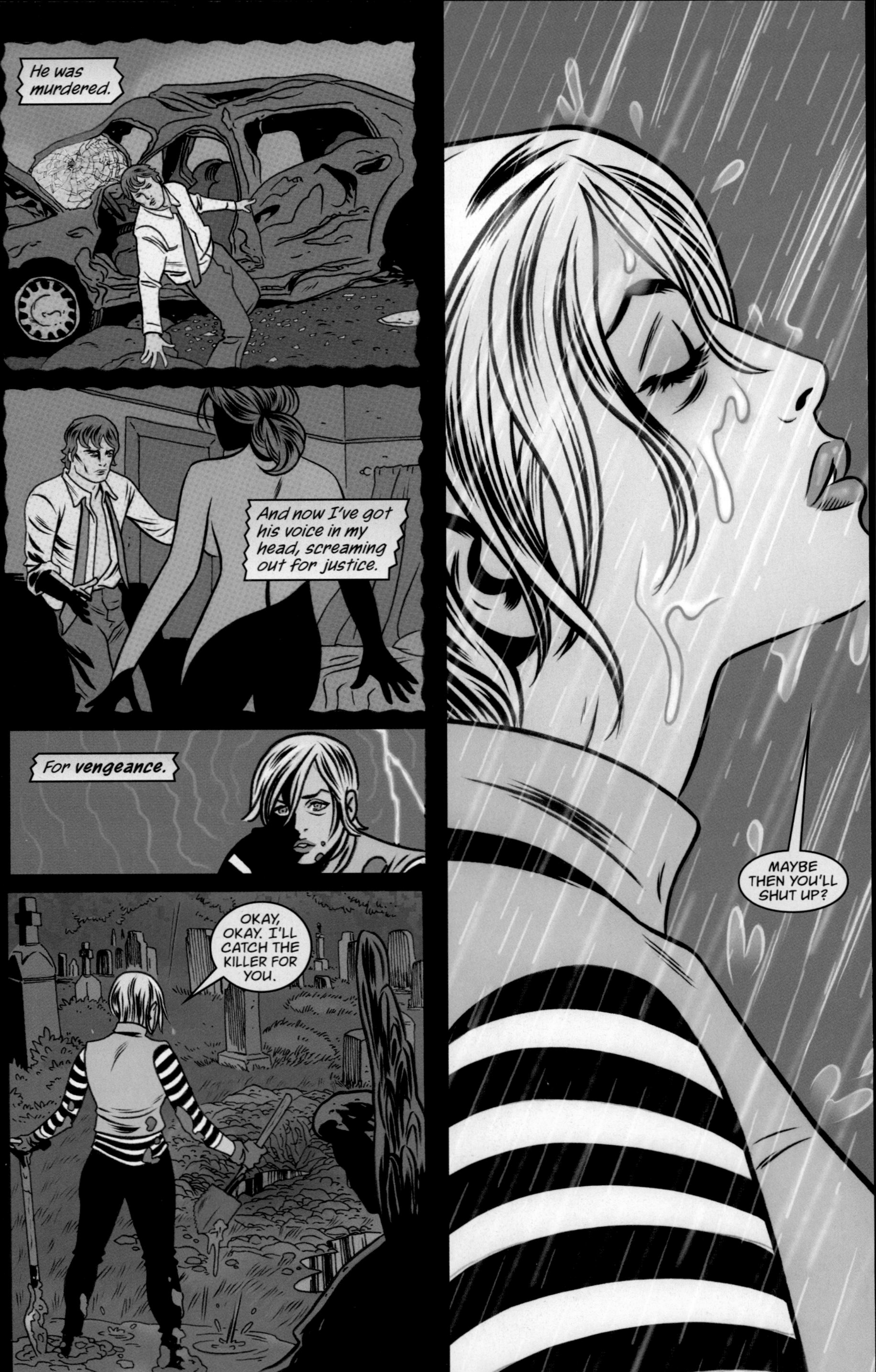
He was murdered.
And now I've got his voice in my head, screaming out for justice.
For vengeance.
OKAY, OKAY. I'LL CATCH THE KILLER FOR YOU.
MAYBE THEN YOU'LL SHUT UP?

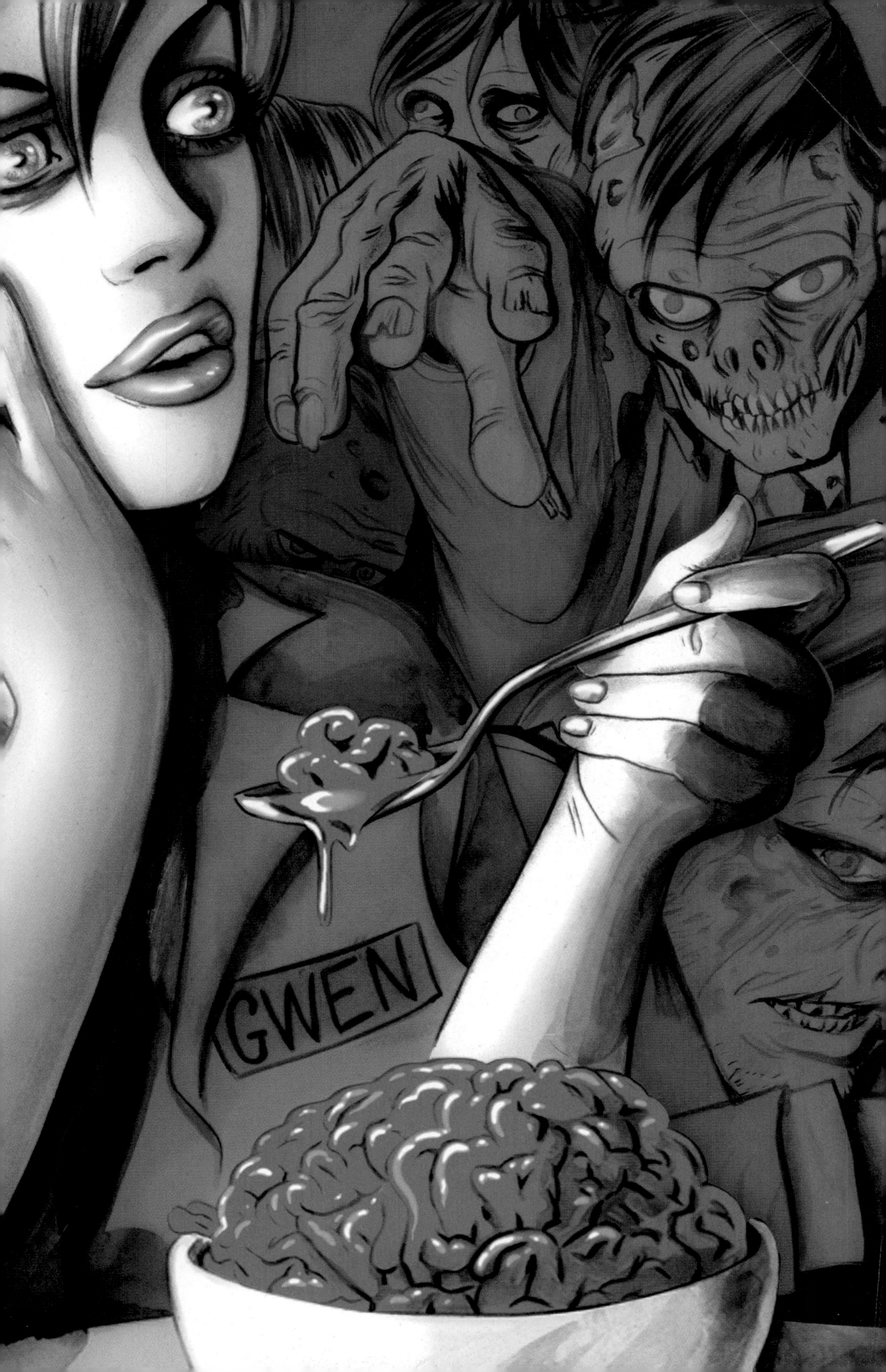
GWEN

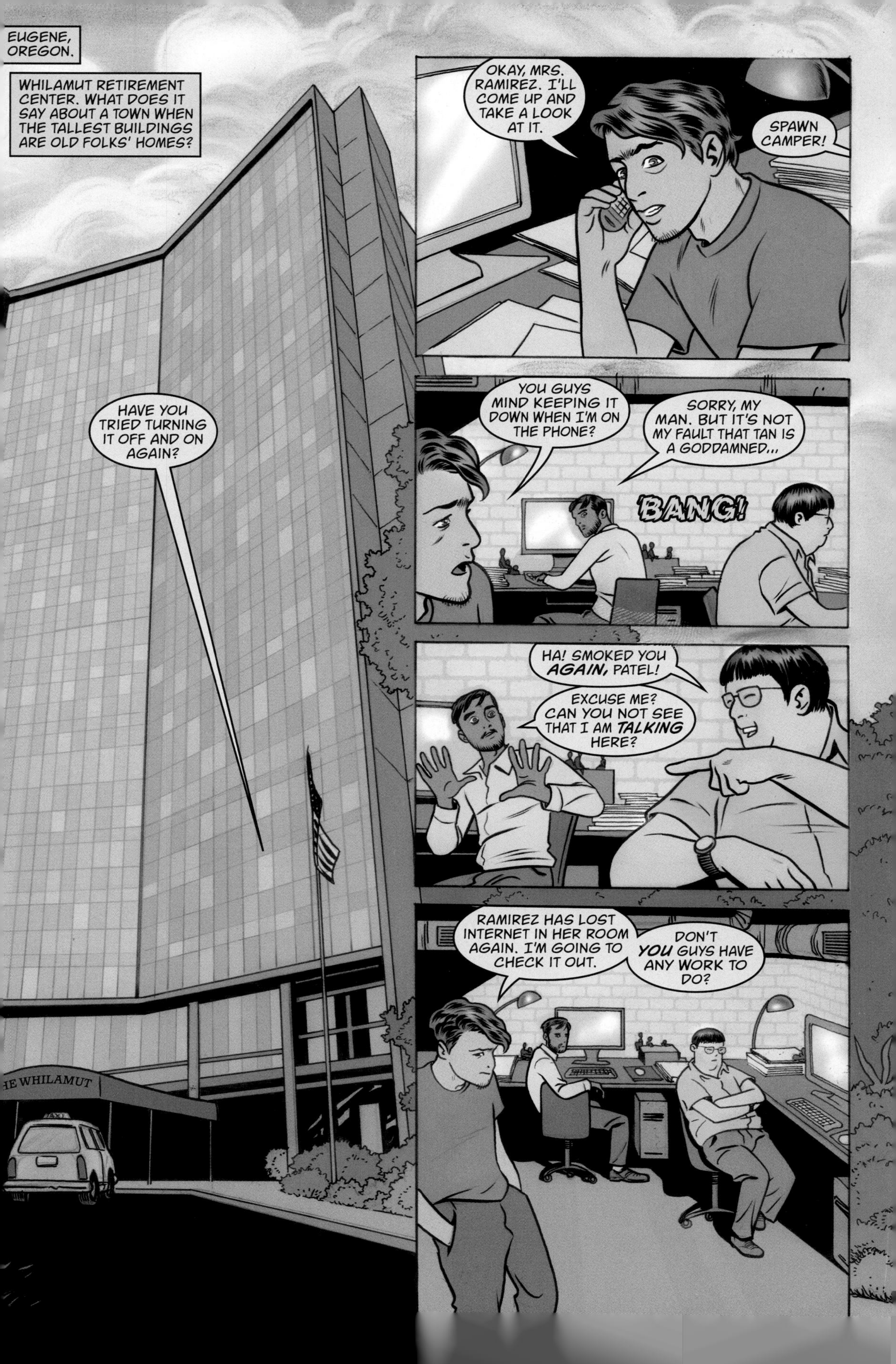
EUGENE, OREGON.
WHILAMUT RETIREMENT CENTER. WHAT DOES IT SAY ABOUT A TOWN WHEN THE TALLEST BUILDINGS ARE OLD FOLKS' HOMES?
HAVE YOU TRIED TURNING IT OFF AND ON AGAIN?
HE WHILAMUT
OKAY, MRS. RAMIREZ. I'LL COME UP AND TAKE A LOOK AT IT.
SPAWN CAMPER!
YOU GUYS MIND KEEPING IT DOWN WHEN I'M ON THE PHONE?
SORRY, MY MAN. BUT IT'S NOT MY FAULT THAT TAN IS A GODDAMNED...
BANG!
HA! SMOKED YOU AGAIN, PATEL!
EXCUSE ME? CAN YOU NOT SEE THAT I AM TALKING HERE?
RAMIREZ HAS LOST INTERNET IN HER ROOM AGAIN. I'M GOING TO CHECK IT OUT.
DON'T YOU GUYS HAVE ANY WORK TO DO?

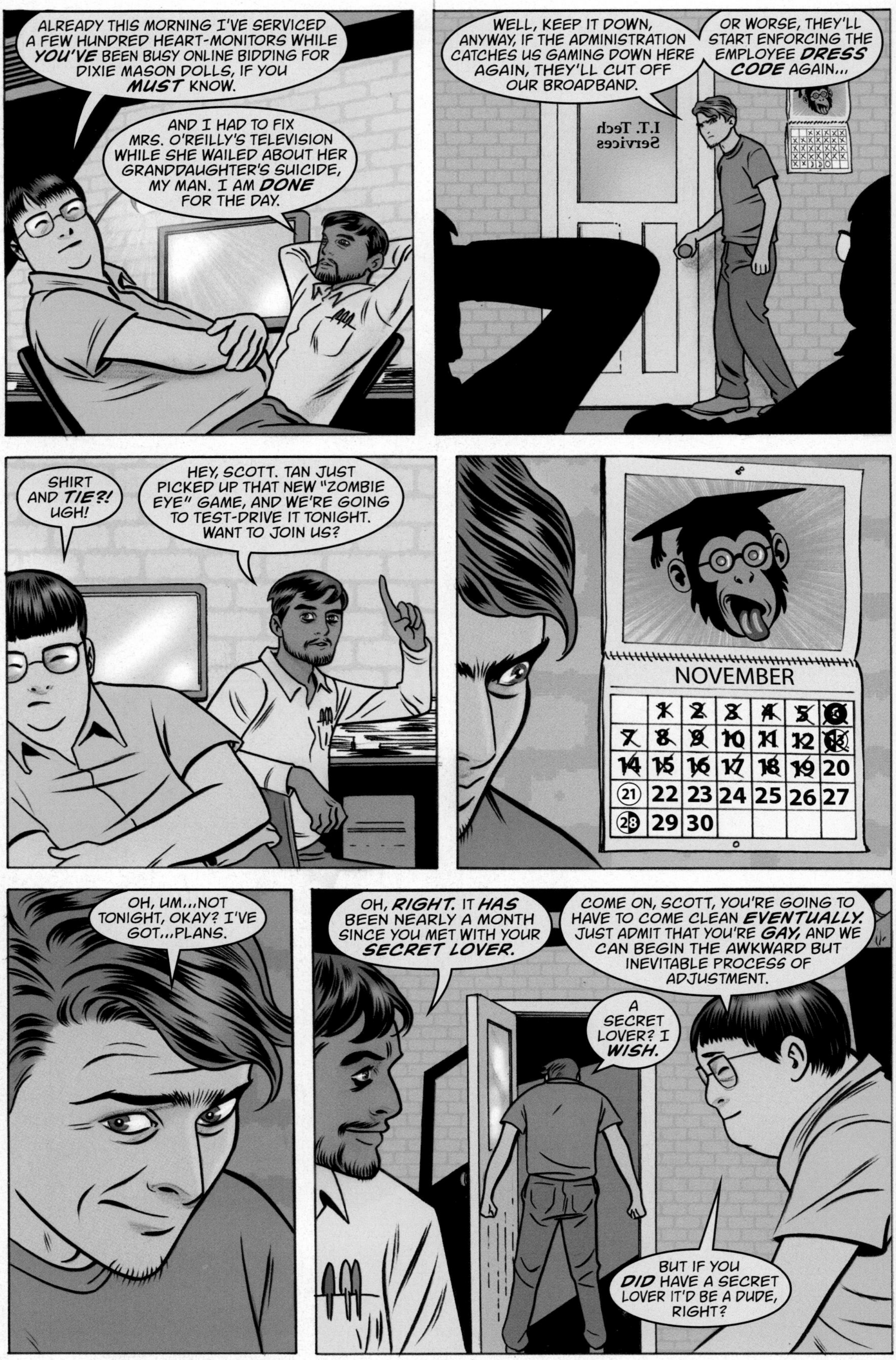
ALREADY THIS MORNING I'VE SERVICED A FEW HUNDRED HEART-MONITORS WHILE YOU'VE BEEN BUSY ONLINE BIDDING FOR DIXIE MASON DOLLS, IF YOU MUST KNOW.
AND I HAD TO FIX MRS. O'REILLY'S TELEVISION WHILE SHE WAILED ABOUT HER GRANDDAUGHTER'S SUICIDE, MY MAN. I AM DONE FOR THE DAY.
WELL, KEEP IT DOWN, ANYWAY, IF THE ADMINISTRATION CATCHES US GAMING DOWN HERE AGAIN, THEY'LL CUT OFF OUR BROADBAND.
OR WORSE, THEY'LL START ENFORCING THE EMPLOYEE DRESS CODE AGAIN...
I.T. Tech Services
SHIRT AND TIE?! UGH!
HEY, SCOTT. TAN JUST PICKED UP THAT NEW "ZOMBIE EYE" GAME, AND WE'RE GOING TO TEST-DRIVE IT TONIGHT. WANT TO JOIN US?
NOVEMBER
1 2 3 4 5 6
7 8 9 10 11 12 13
14 15 16 17 18 19 20
21 22 23 24 25 26 27
28 29 30
OH, UM...NOT TONIGHT, OKAY? I'VE GOT...PLANS.
OH, RIGHT. IT HAS BEEN NEARLY A MONTH SINCE YOU MET WITH YOUR SECRET LOVER.
COME ON, SCOTT, YOU'RE GOING TO HAVE TO COME CLEAN EVENTUALLY. JUST ADMIT THAT YOU'RE GAY, AND WE CAN BEGIN THE AWKWARD BUT INEVITABLE PROCESS OF ADJUSTMENT.
A SECRET LOVER? I WISH.
BUT IF YOU DID HAVE A SECRET LOVER IT'D BE A DUDE, RIGHT?

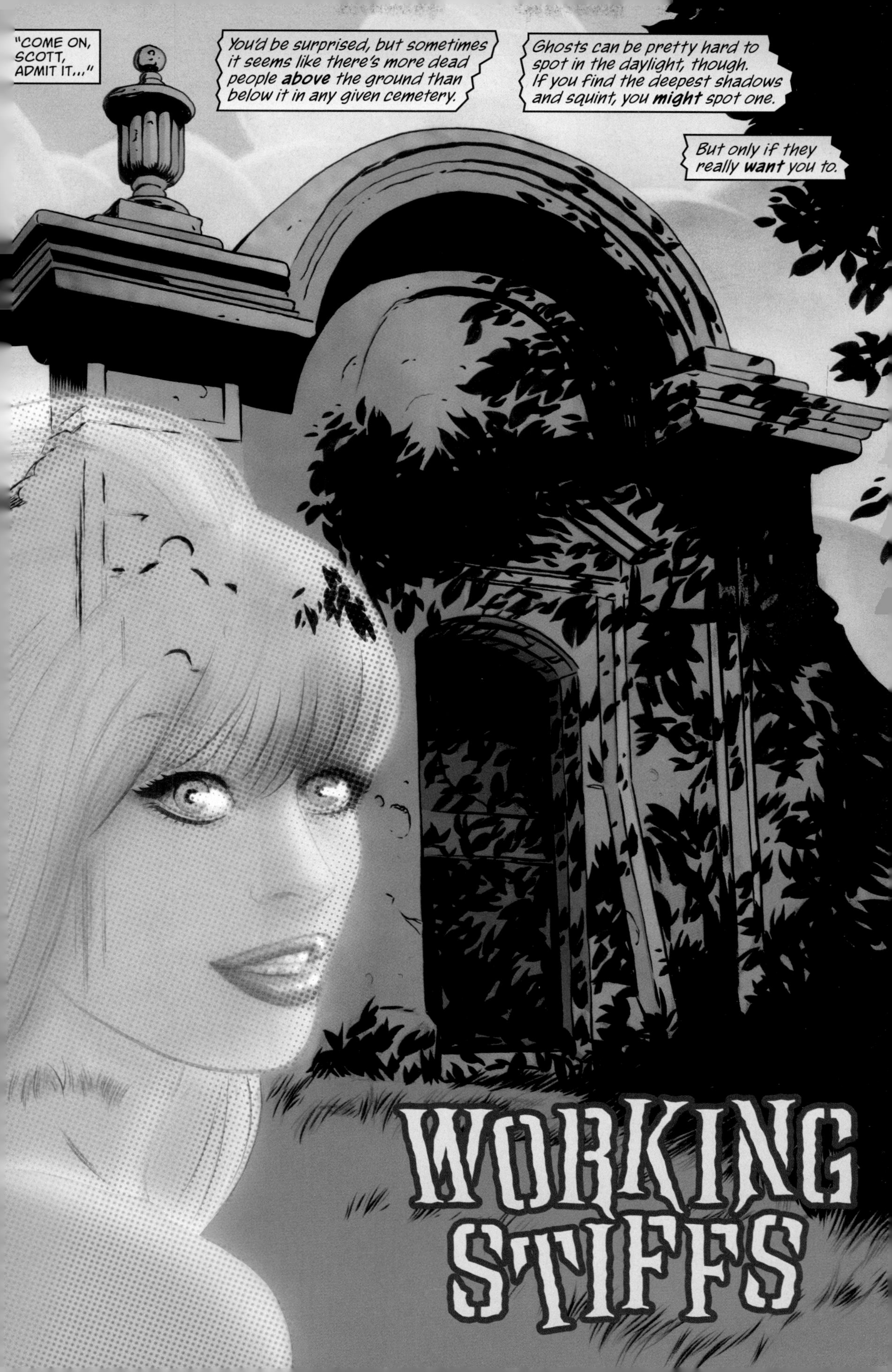
"COME ON, SCOTT, ADMIT IT..."
You'd be surprised, but sometimes it seems like there's more dead people above the ground than below it in any given cemetery.
Ghosts can be pretty hard to spot in the daylight, though. If you find the deepest shadows and squint, you might spot one.
But only if they really want you to.
WORKING STIFFS

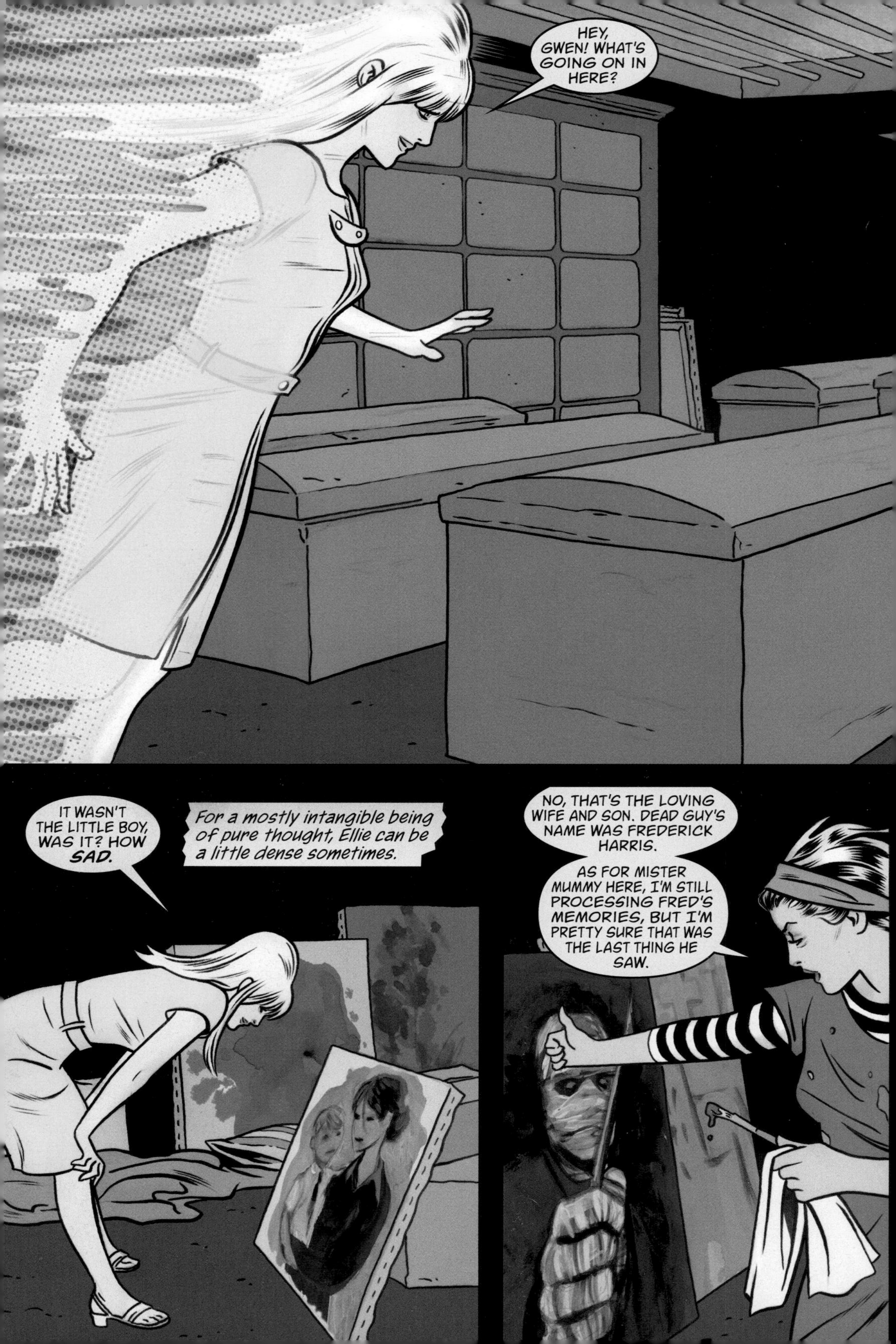
HEY, GWEN! WHAT'S GOING ON IN HERE?
IT WASN'T THE LITTLE BOY, WAS IT? HOW **SAD**.
For a mostly intangible being of pure thought, Ellie can be a little dense sometimes.
NO, THAT'S THE LOVING WIFE AND SON. DEAD GUY'S NAME WAS FREDERICK HARRIS.
AS FOR MISTER MUMMY HERE, I'M STILL PROCESSING FRED'S MEMORIES, BUT I'M PRETTY SURE THAT WAS THE LAST THING HE SAW.

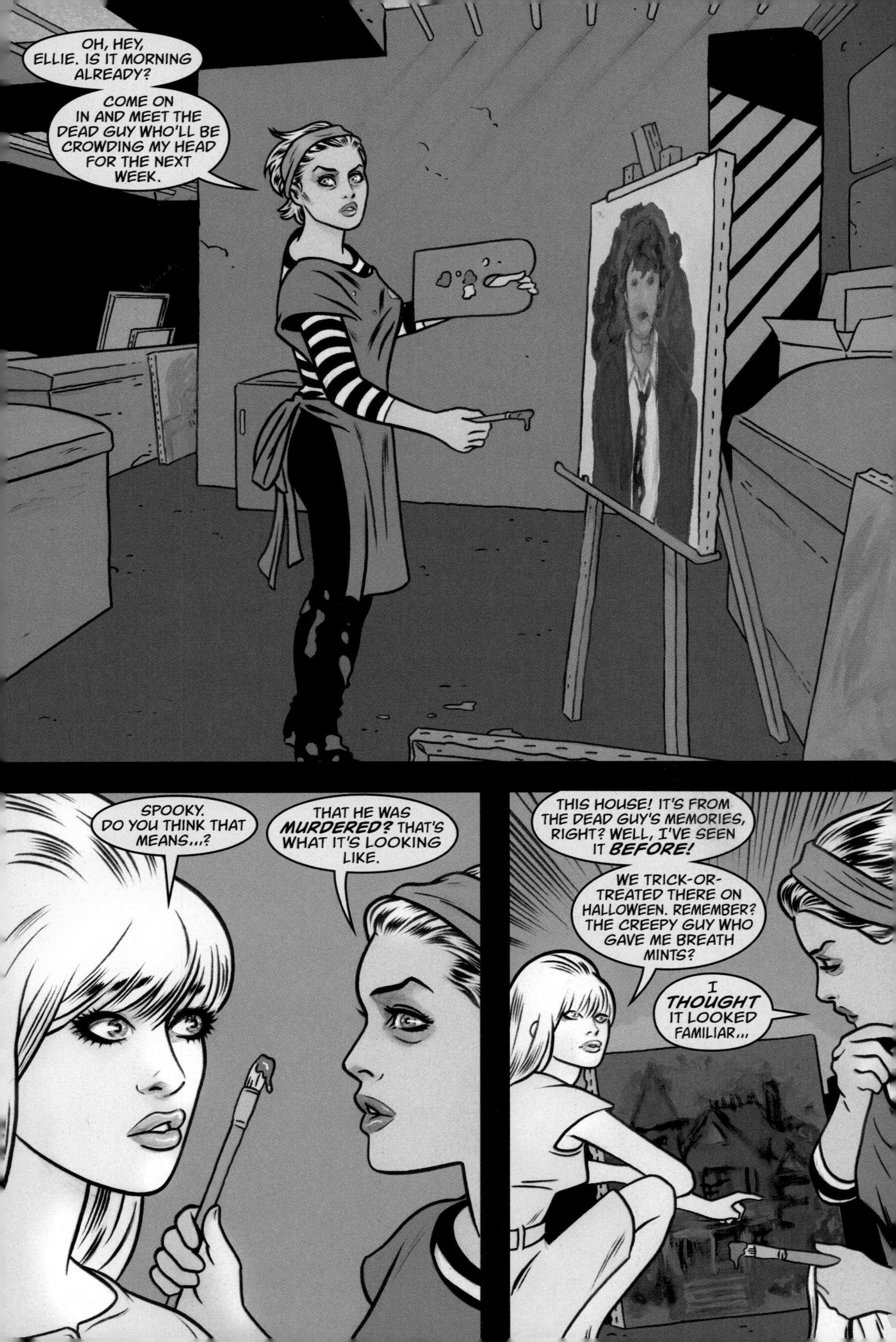
OH, HEY, ELLIE. IS IT MORNING ALREADY?
COME ON IN AND MEET THE DEAD GUY WHO'LL BE CROWDING MY HEAD FOR THE NEXT WEEK.
SPOOKY. DO YOU THINK THAT MEANS...?
THAT HE WAS MURDERED? THAT'S WHAT IT'S LOOKING LIKE.
THIS HOUSE! IT'S FROM THE DEAD GUY'S MEMORIES, RIGHT? WELL, I'VE SEEN IT BEFORE!
WE TRICK-OR-TREATED THERE ON HALLOWEEN. REMEMBER? THE CREEPY GUY WHO GAVE ME BREATH MINTS?
I THOUGHT IT LOOKED FAMILIAR...

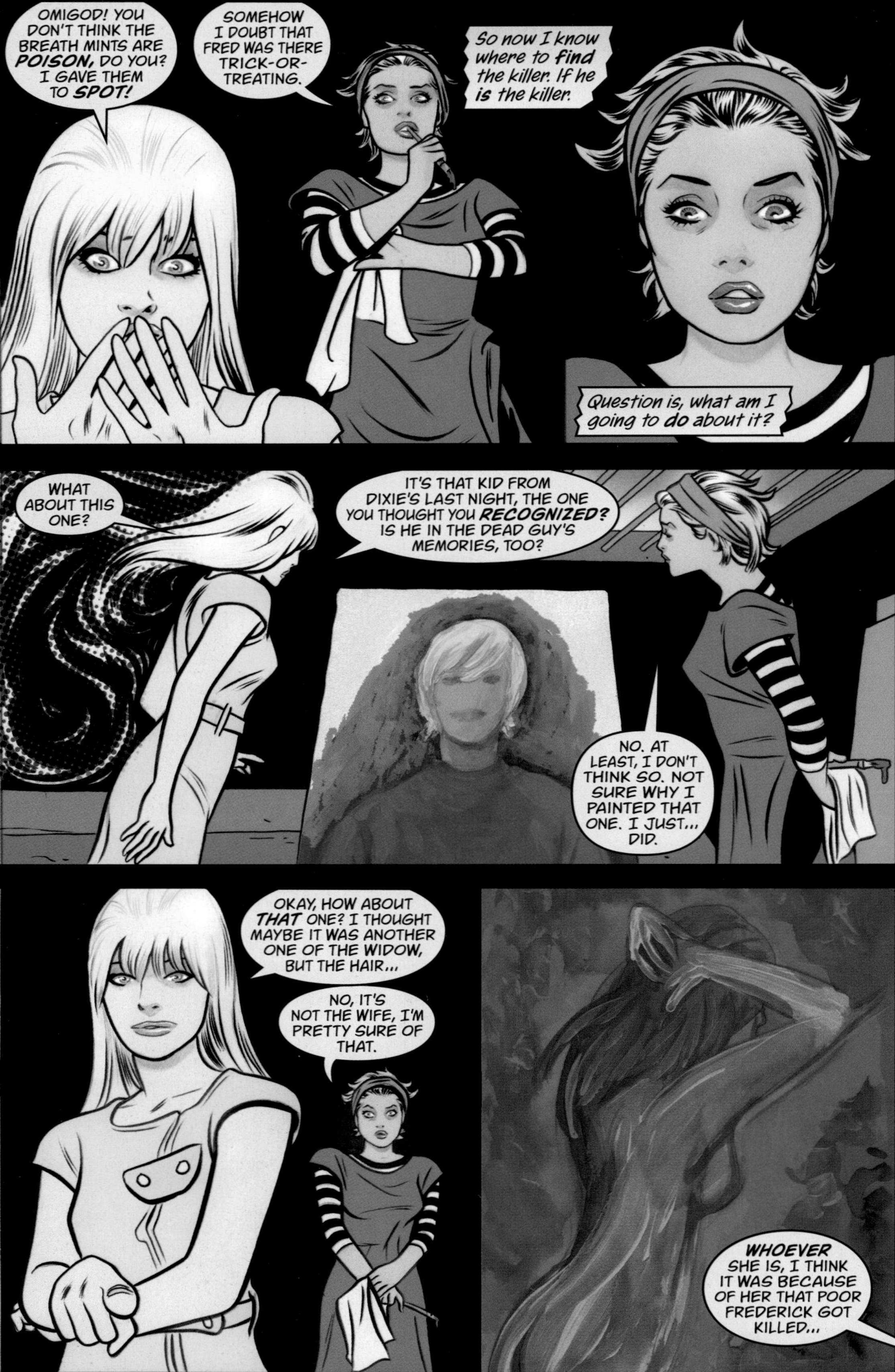
OMIGOD! YOU DON'T THINK THE BREATH MINTS ARE POISON, DO YOU? I GAVE THEM TO SPOT!
SOMEHOW I DOUBT THAT FRED WAS THERE TRICK-OR-TREATING.
So now I know where to find the killer. If he is the killer.
Question is, what am I going to do about it?
WHAT ABOUT THIS ONE?
IT'S THAT KID FROM DIXIE'S LAST NIGHT, THE ONE YOU THOUGHT YOU RECOGNIZED? IS HE IN THE DEAD GUY'S MEMORIES, TOO?
NO. AT LEAST, I DON'T THINK SO. NOT SURE WHY I PAINTED THAT ONE. I JUST... DID.
OKAY, HOW ABOUT THAT ONE? I THOUGHT MAYBE IT WAS ANOTHER ONE OF THE WIDOW, BUT THE HAIR...
NO, IT'S NOT THE WIFE, I'M PRETTY SURE OF THAT.
WHOEVER SHE IS, I THINK IT WAS BECAUSE OF HER THAT POOR FREDERICK GOT KILLED...

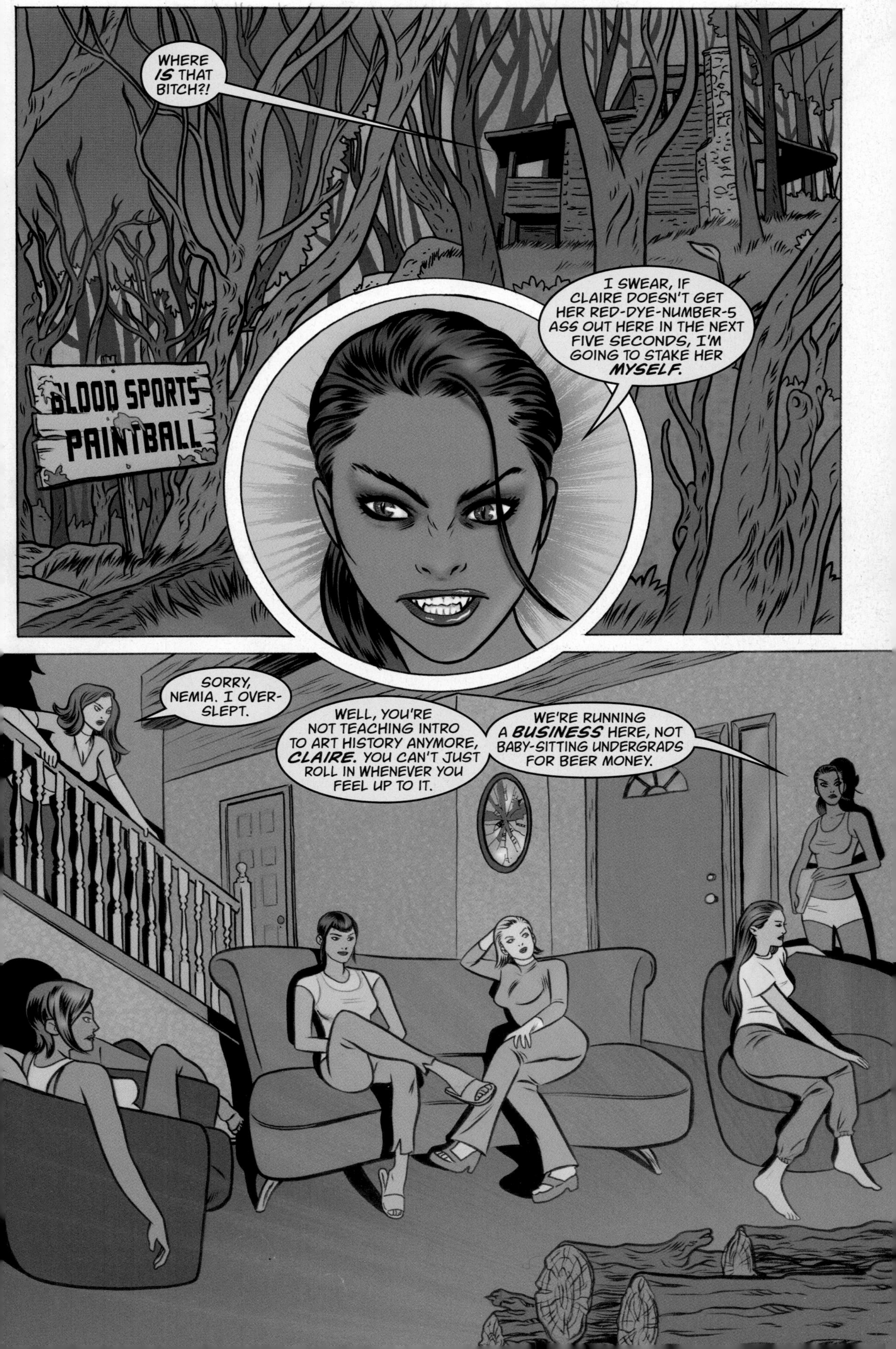
WHERE IS THAT BITCH?!
BLOOD SPORTS PAINTBALL
I SWEAR, IF CLAIRE DOESN'T GET HER RED-DYE-NUMBER-5 ASS OUT HERE IN THE NEXT FIVE SECONDS, I'M GOING TO STAKE HER MYSELF.
SORRY, NEMIA. I OVER-SLEPT.
WELL, YOU'RE NOT TEACHING INTRO TO ART HISTORY ANYMORE, CLAIRE. YOU CAN'T JUST ROLL IN WHENEVER YOU FEEL UP TO IT.
WE'RE RUNNING A BUSINESS HERE, NOT BABY-SITTING UNDERGRADS FOR BEER MONEY.

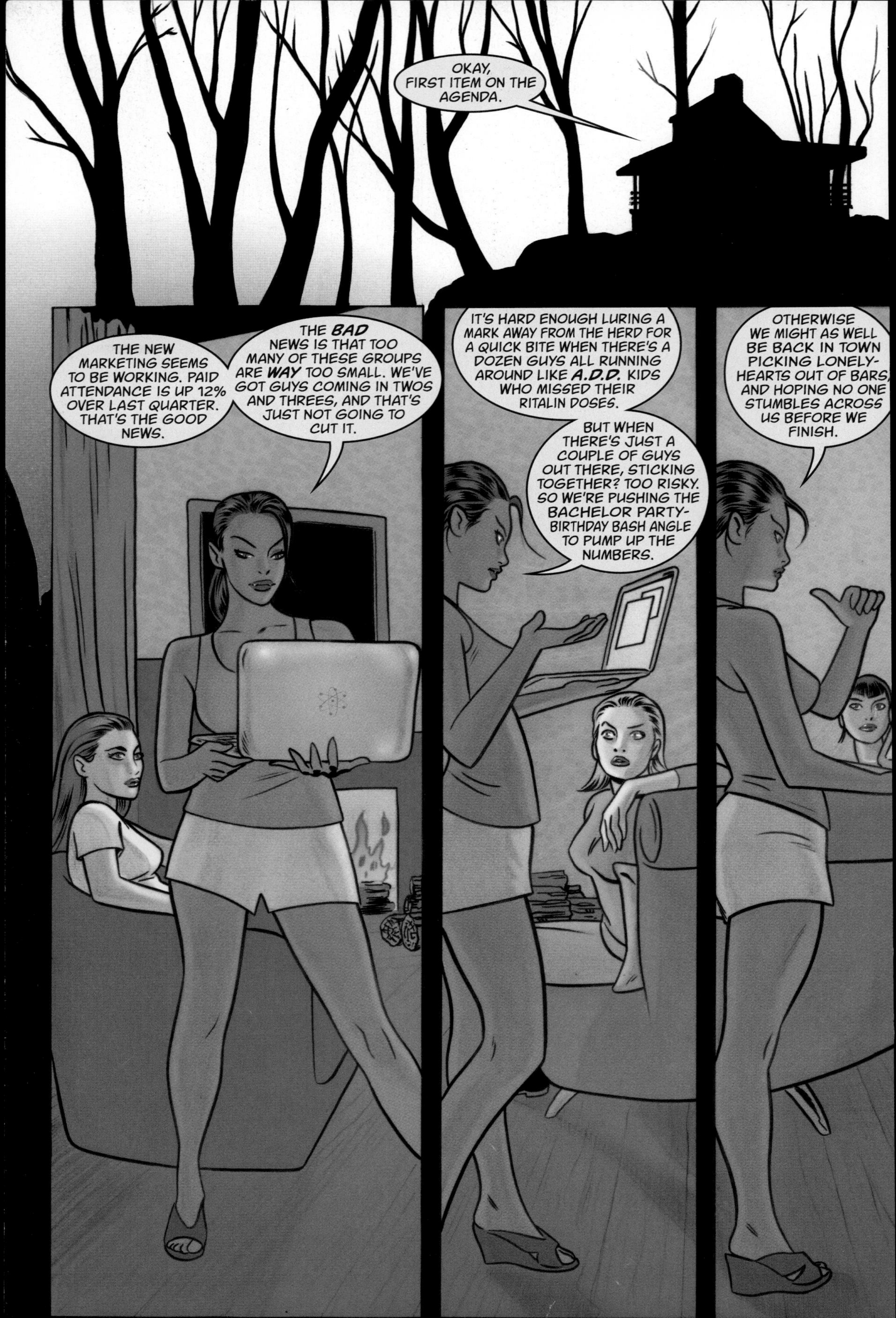
OKAY, FIRST ITEM ON THE AGENDA.
THE NEW MARKETING SEEMS TO BE WORKING. PAID ATTENDANCE IS UP 12% OVER LAST QUARTER. THAT'S THE GOOD NEWS.
THE BAD NEWS IS THAT TOO MANY OF THESE GROUPS ARE WAY TOO SMALL. WE'VE GOT GUYS COMING IN TWOS AND THREES, AND THAT'S JUST NOT GOING TO CUT IT.
IT'S HARD ENOUGH LURING A MARK AWAY FROM THE HERD FOR A QUICK BITE WHEN THERE'S A DOZEN GUYS ALL RUNNING AROUND LIKE A.D.D. KIDS WHO MISSED THEIR RITALIN DOSES.
BUT WHEN THERE'S JUST A COUPLE OF GUYS OUT THERE, STICKING TOGETHER? TOO RISKY. SO WE'RE PUSHING THE BACHELOR PARTY-BIRTHDAY BASH ANGLE TO PUMP UP THE NUMBERS.
OTHERWISE WE MIGHT AS WELL BE BACK IN TOWN PICKING LONELY-HEARTS OUT OF BARS, AND HOPING NO ONE STUMBLES ACROSS US BEFORE WE FINISH.

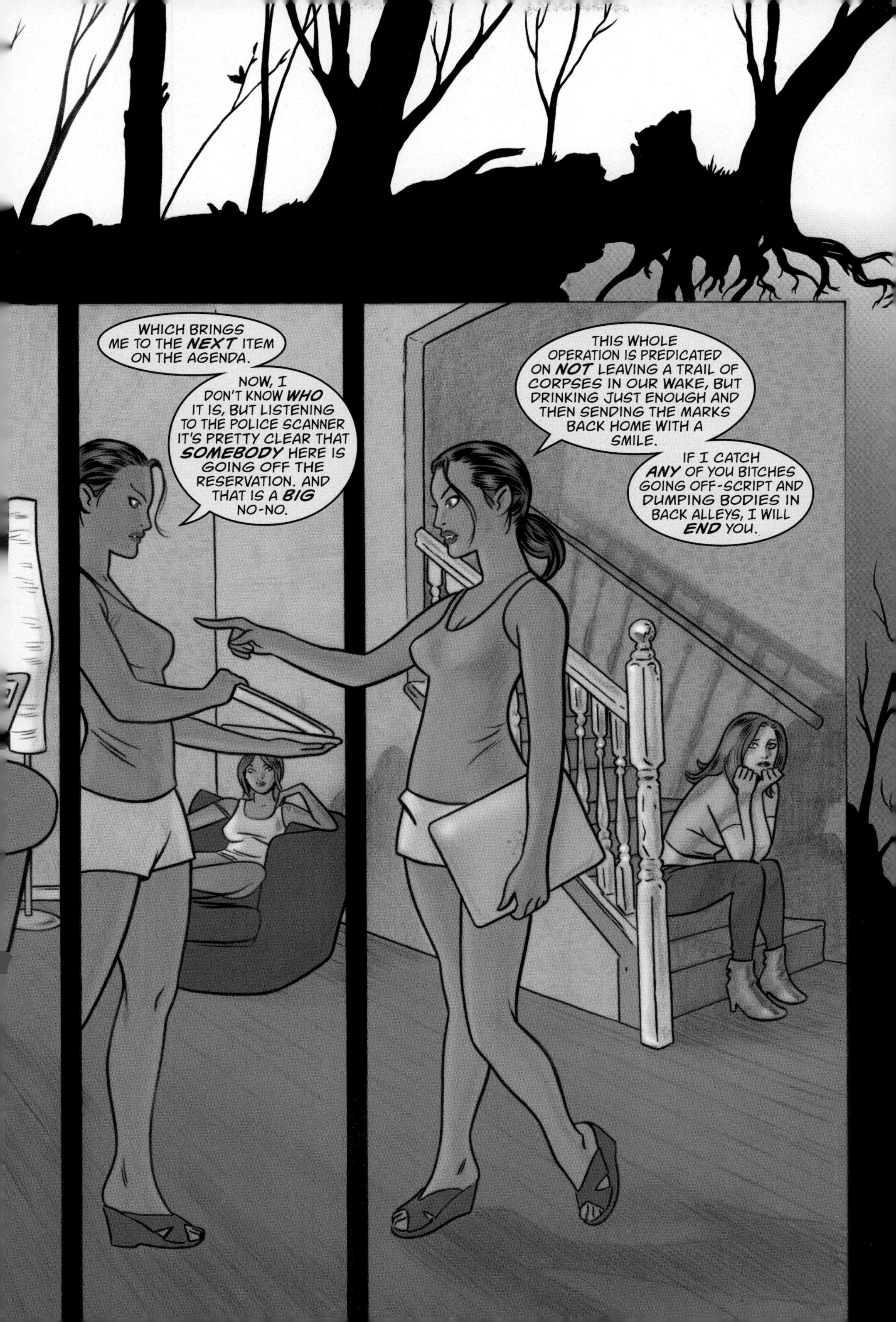

WHICH BRINGS ME TO THE ***NEXT*** ITEM ON THE AGENDA.
NOW, I DON'T KNOW ***WHO*** IT IS, BUT LISTENING TO THE POLICE SCANNER IT'S PRETTY CLEAR THAT ***SOMEBODY*** HERE IS GOING OFF THE RESERVATION. AND THAT IS A ***BIG*** NO-NO.
THIS WHOLE OPERATION IS PREDICATED ON ***NOT*** LEAVING A TRAIL OF CORPSES IN OUR WAKE, BUT DRINKING JUST ENOUGH AND THEN SENDING THE MARKS BACK HOME WITH A SMILE.
IF I CATCH ***ANY*** OF YOU BITCHES GOING OFF-SCRIPT AND DUMPING BODIES IN BACK ALLEYS, I WILL ***END*** YOU.

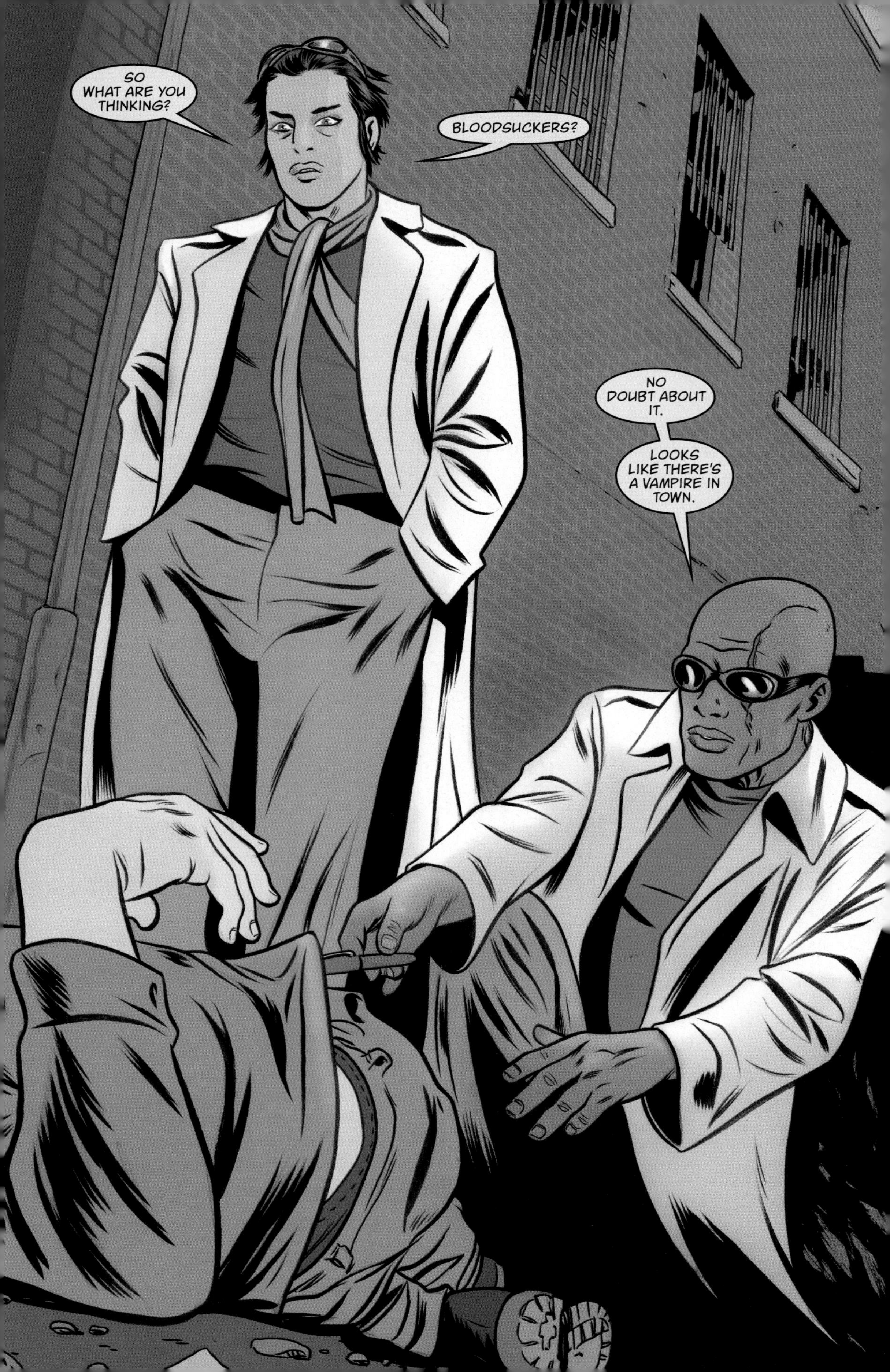
SO WHAT ARE YOU THINKING?
BLOODSUCKERS?
NO DOUBT ABOUT IT.
LOOKS LIKE THERE'S A VAMPIRE IN TOWN.

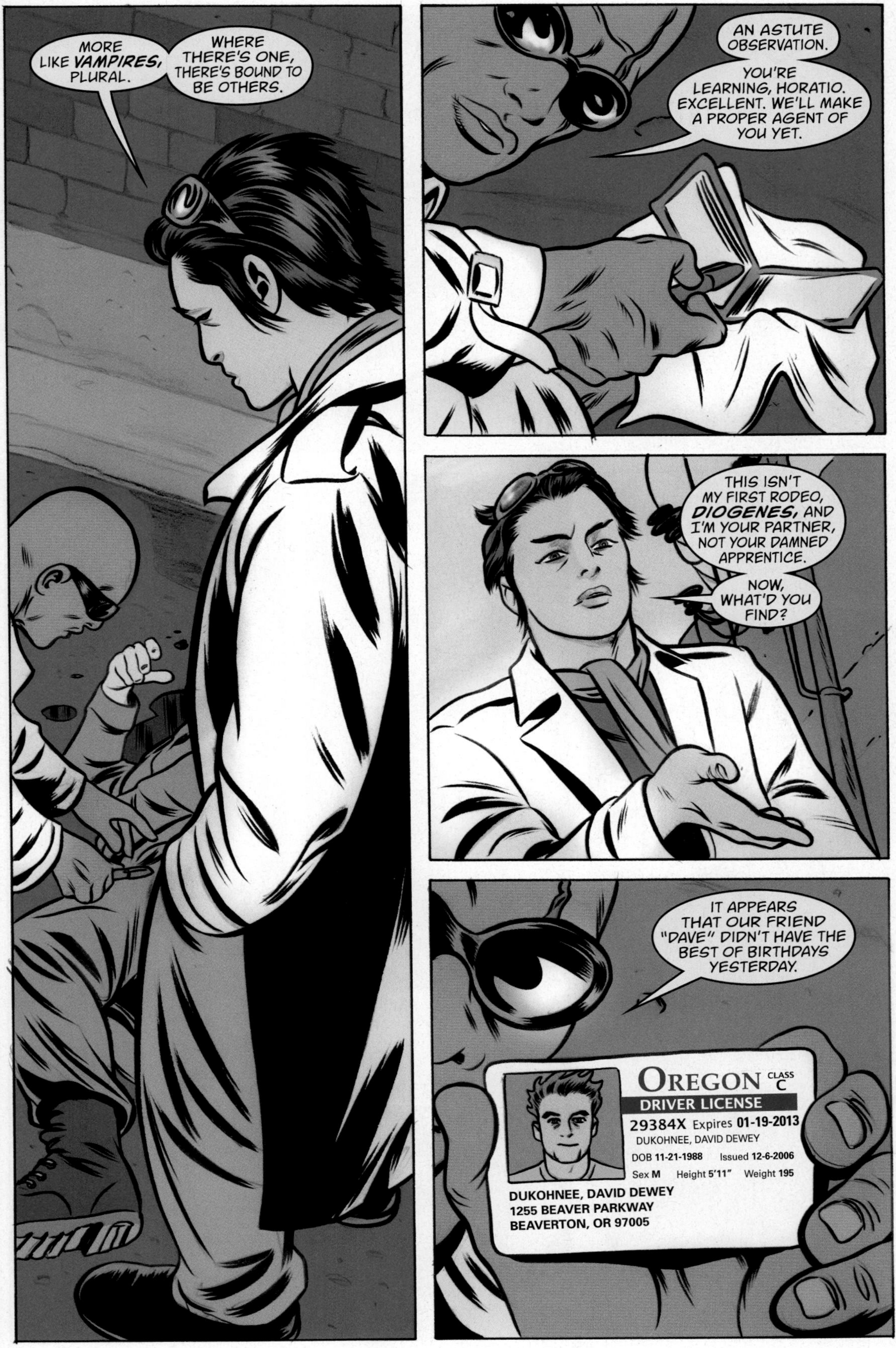
MORE LIKE VAMPIRES, PLURAL.
WHERE THERE'S ONE, THERE'S BOUND TO BE OTHERS.
AN ASTUTE OBSERVATION.
YOU'RE LEARNING, HORATIO. EXCELLENT. WE'LL MAKE A PROPER AGENT OF YOU YET.
THIS ISN'T MY FIRST RODEO, DIOGENES, AND I'M YOUR PARTNER, NOT YOUR DAMNED APPRENTICE.
NOW, WHAT'D YOU FIND?
IT APPEARS THAT OUR FRIEND "DAVE" DIDN'T HAVE THE BEST OF BIRTHDAYS YESTERDAY.
OREGON CLASS C
DRIVER LICENSE
29384X Expires 01-19-2013
DUKOHNEE, DAVID DEWEY
DOB 11-21-1988 Issued 12-6-2006
Sex M Height 5'11" Weight 195
DUKOHNEE, DAVID DEWEY
1255 BEAVER PARKWAY
BEAVERTON, OR 97005

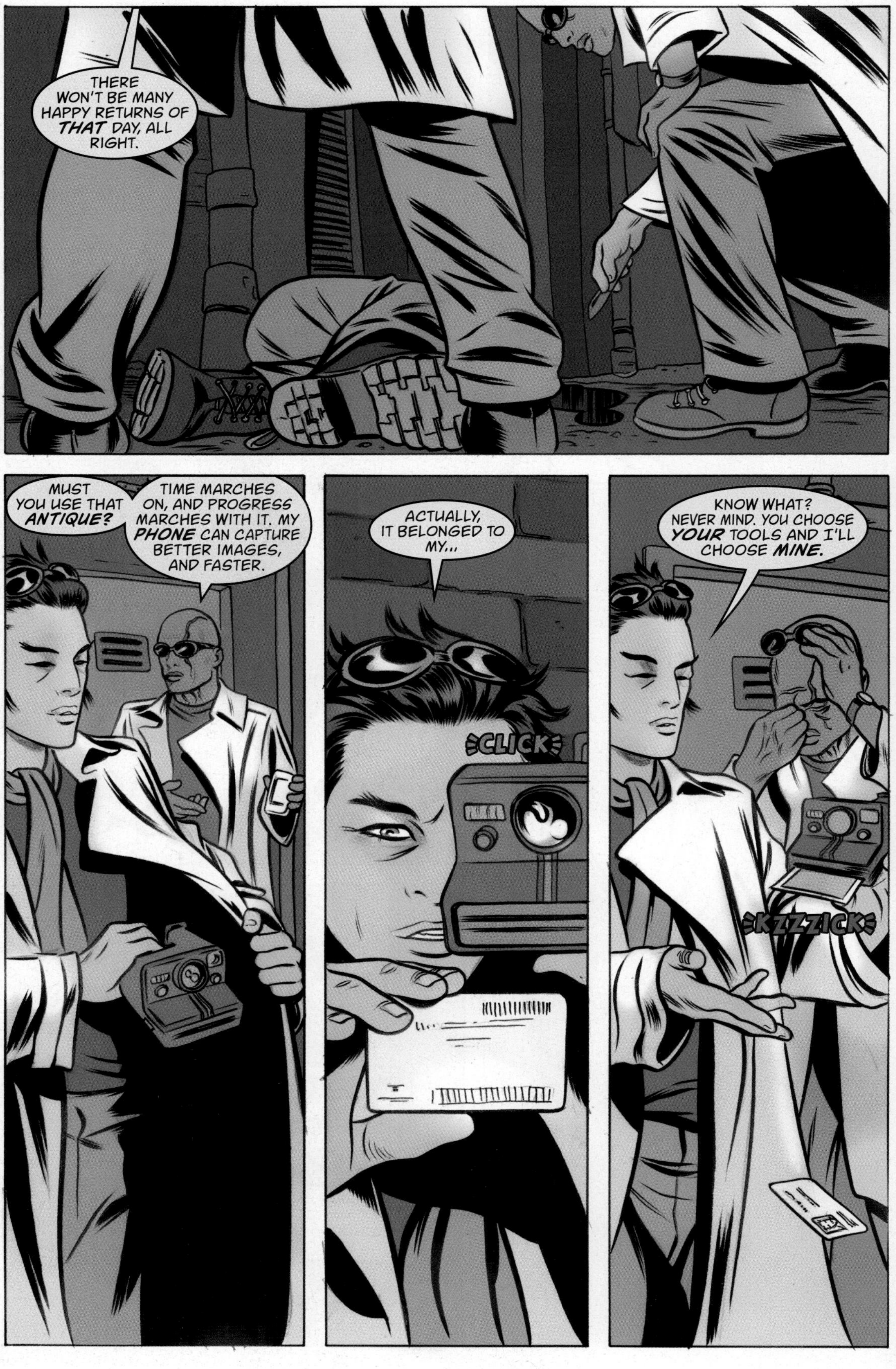
THERE WON'T BE MANY HAPPY RETURNS OF *THAT* DAY, ALL RIGHT.
MUST YOU USE THAT *ANTIQUE?*
TIME MARCHES ON, AND PROGRESS MARCHES WITH IT. MY *PHONE* CAN CAPTURE BETTER IMAGES, AND FASTER.
ACTUALLY, IT BELONGED TO MY...
CLICK
KNOW WHAT? NEVER MIND. YOU CHOOSE *YOUR* TOOLS AND I'LL CHOOSE *MINE.*
KZZZICK

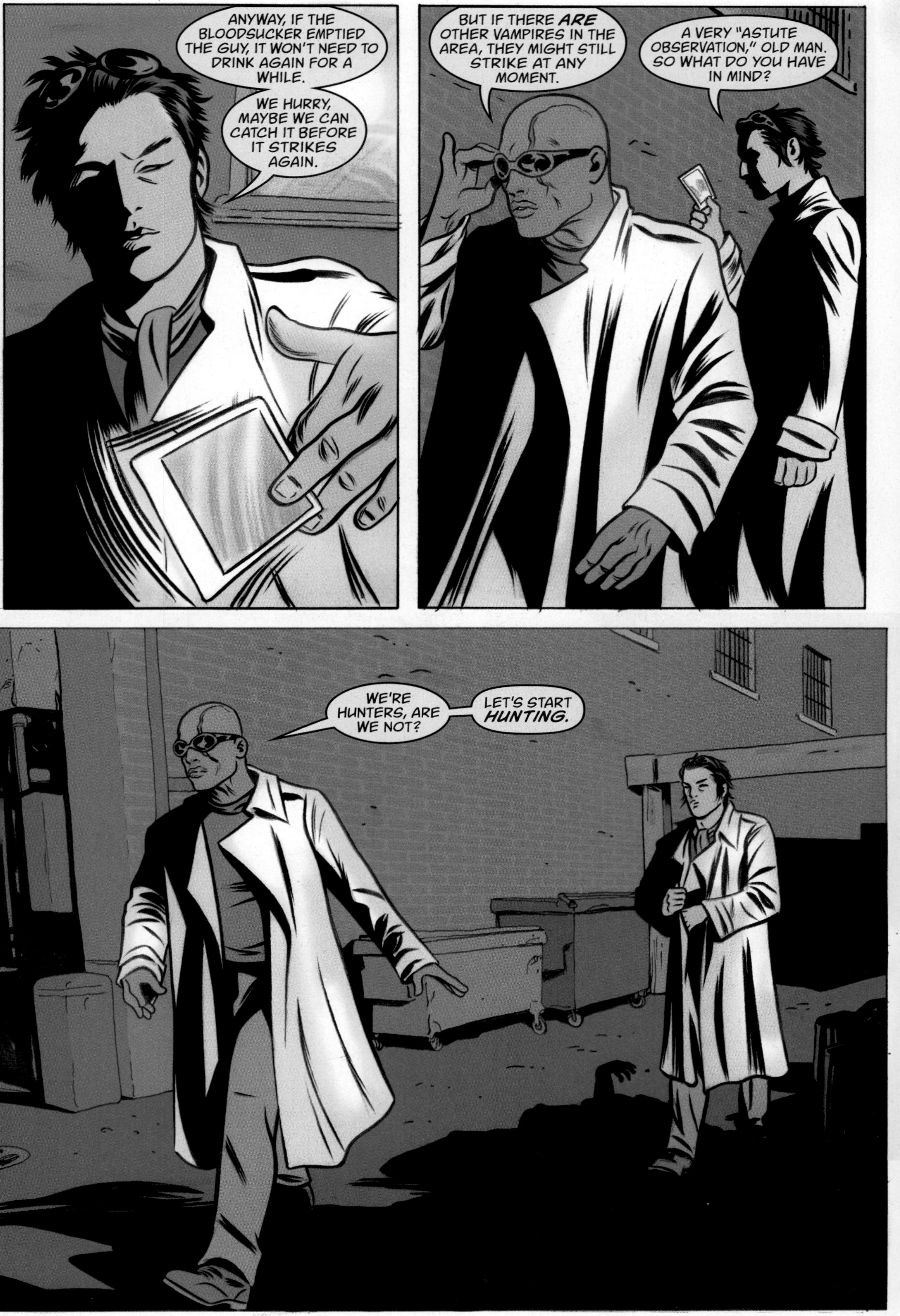
ANYWAY, IF THE BLOODSUCKER EMPTIED THE GUY, IT WON'T NEED TO DRINK AGAIN FOR A WHILE.
WE HURRY, MAYBE WE CAN CATCH IT BEFORE IT STRIKES AGAIN.
BUT IF THERE ARE OTHER VAMPIRES IN THE AREA, THEY MIGHT STILL STRIKE AT ANY MOMENT.
A VERY "ASTUTE OBSERVATION," OLD MAN. SO WHAT DO YOU HAVE IN MIND?
WE'RE HUNTERS, ARE WE NOT?
LET'S START HUNTING.

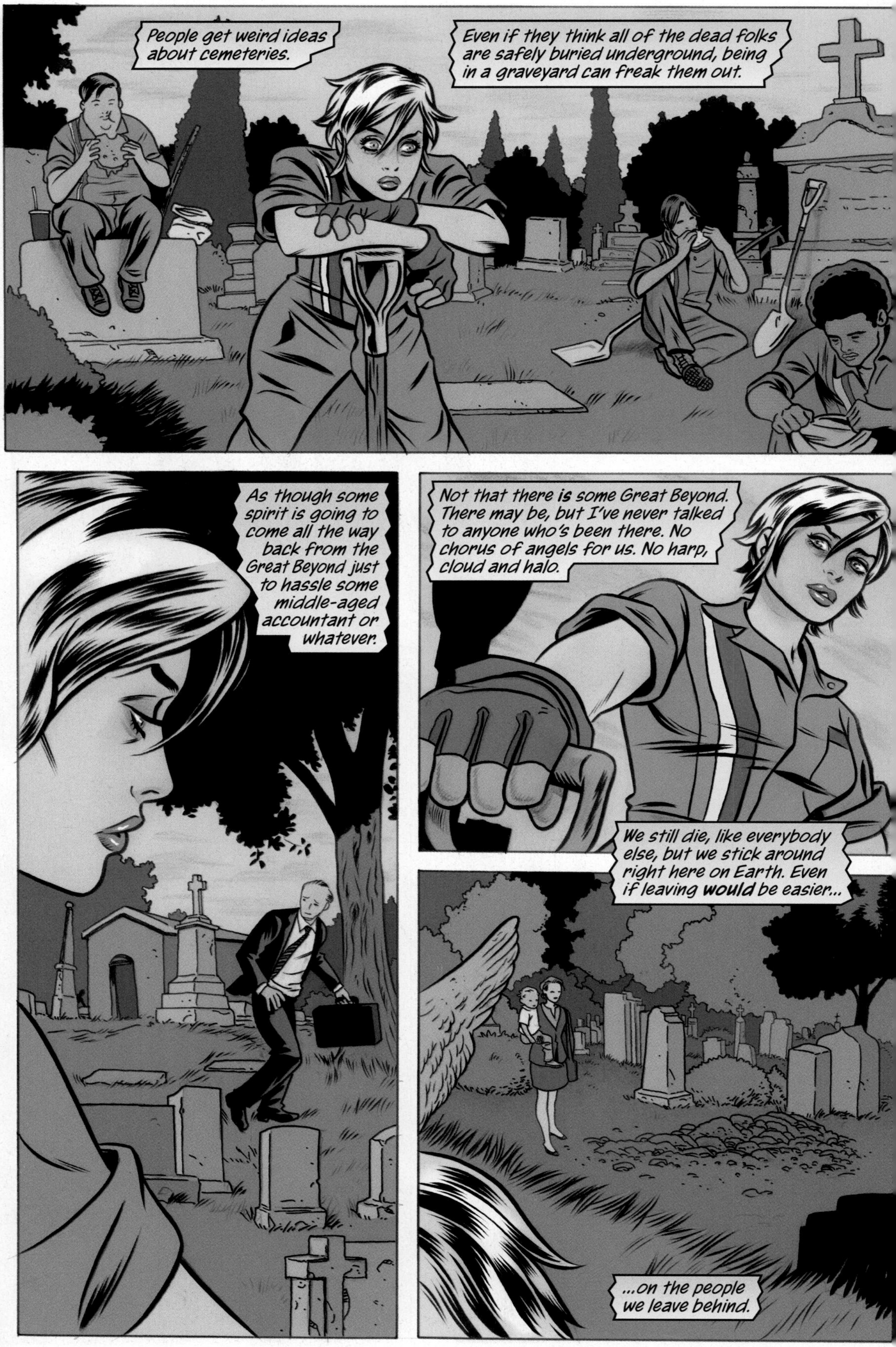
People get weird ideas about cemeteries.
Even if they think all of the dead folks are safely buried underground, being in a graveyard can freak them out.
As though some spirit is going to come all the way back from the Great Beyond just to hassle some middle-aged accountant or whatever.
Not that there is some Great Beyond. There may be, but I've never talked to anyone who's been there. No chorus of angels for us. No harp, cloud and halo.
We still die, like everybody else, but we stick around right here on Earth. Even if leaving would be easier...
...on the people we leave behind.

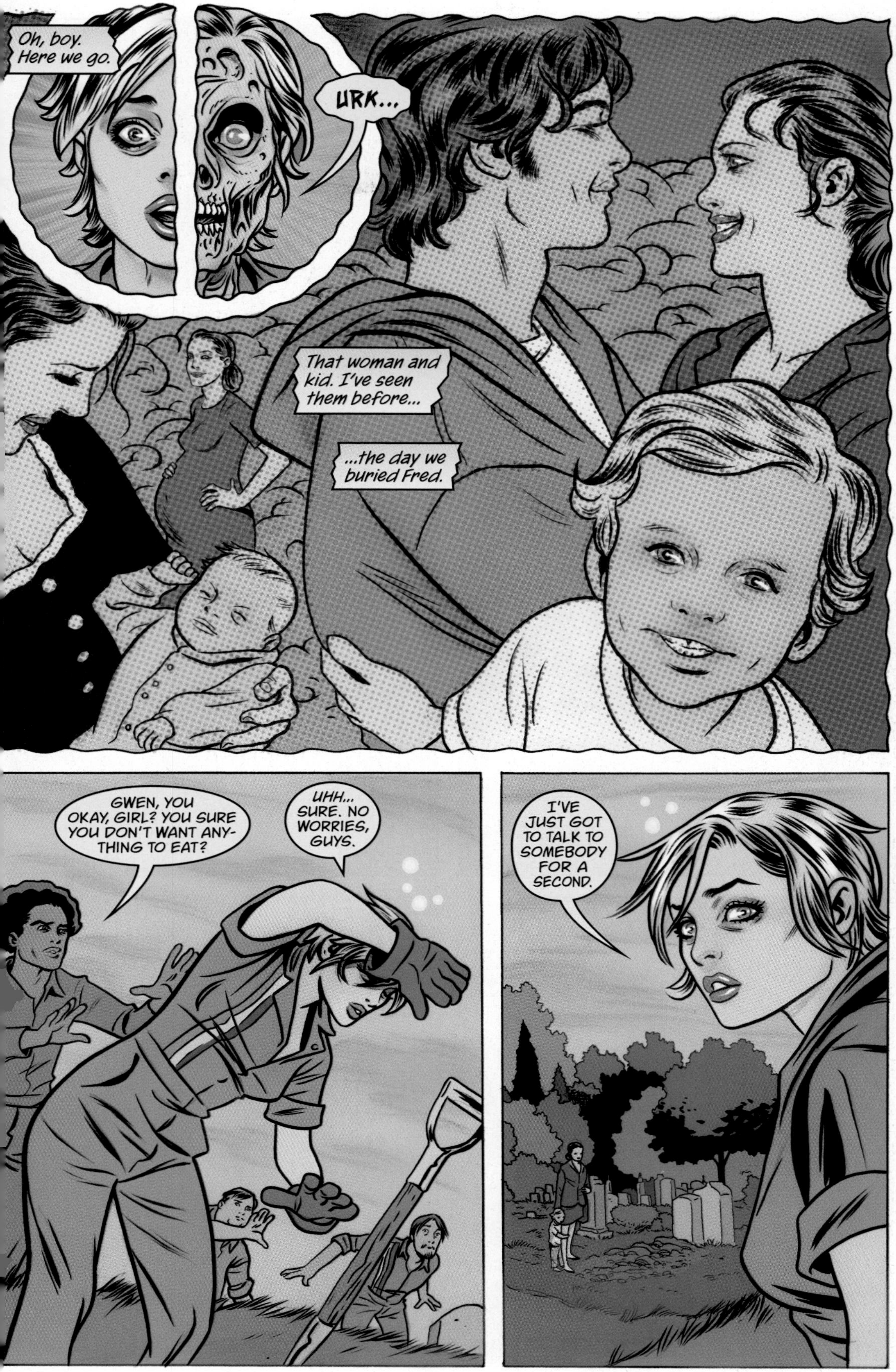
Oh, boy. Here we go.
URK...
That woman and kid. I've seen them before...
...the day we buried Fred.
GWEN, YOU OKAY, GIRL? YOU SURE YOU DON'T WANT ANY-THING TO EAT?
UHH... SURE. NO WORRIES, GUYS.
I'VE JUST GOT TO TALK TO SOMEBODY FOR A SECOND.

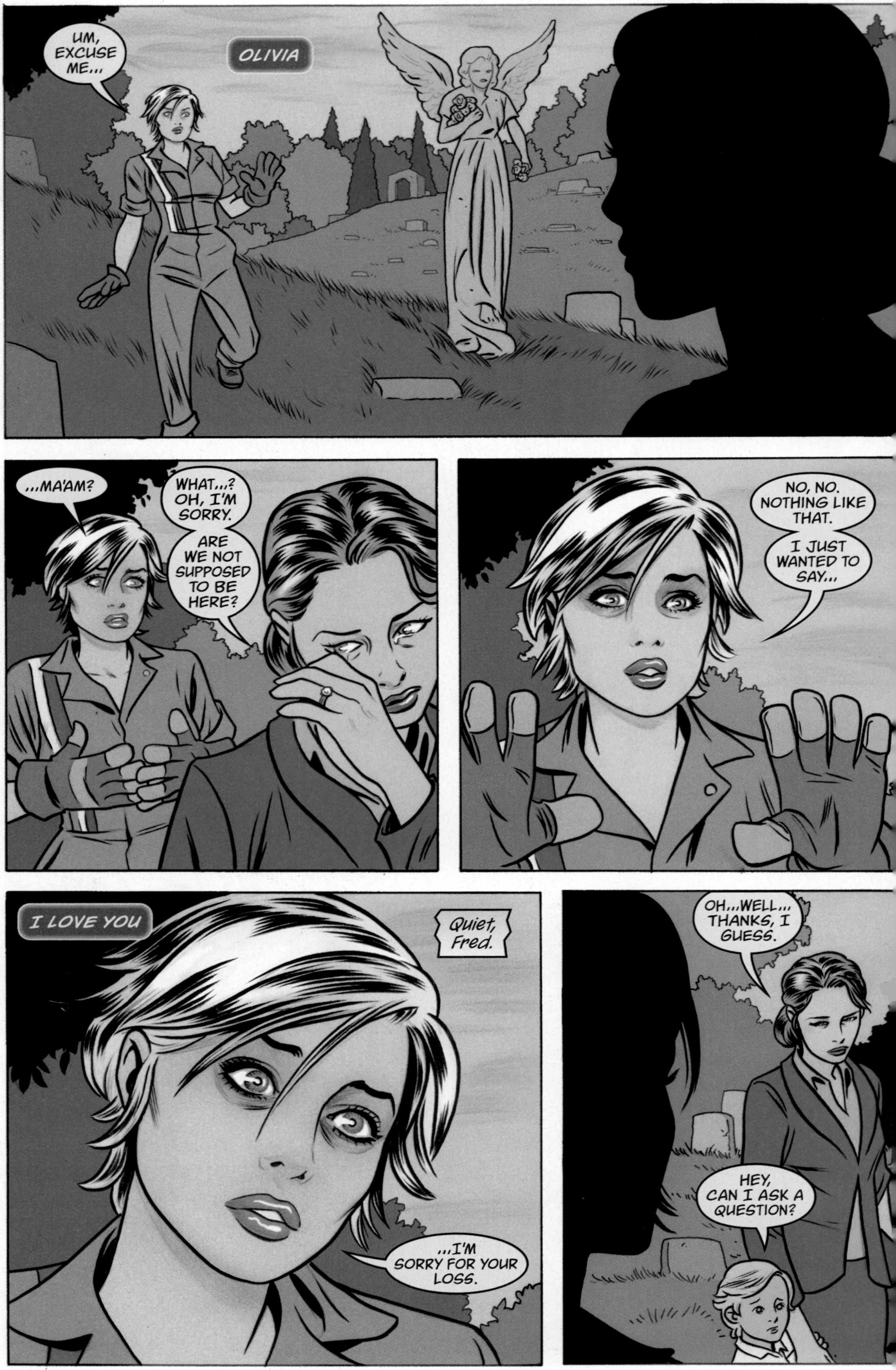
UM, EXCUSE ME...
OLIVIA
...MA'AM?
WHAT...? OH, I'M SORRY.
ARE WE NOT SUPPOSED TO BE HERE?
NO, NO. NOTHING LIKE THAT.
I JUST WANTED TO SAY...
I LOVE YOU
Quiet, Fred.
...I'M SORRY FOR YOUR LOSS.
OH...WELL... THANKS, I GUESS.
HEY, CAN I ASK A QUESTION?

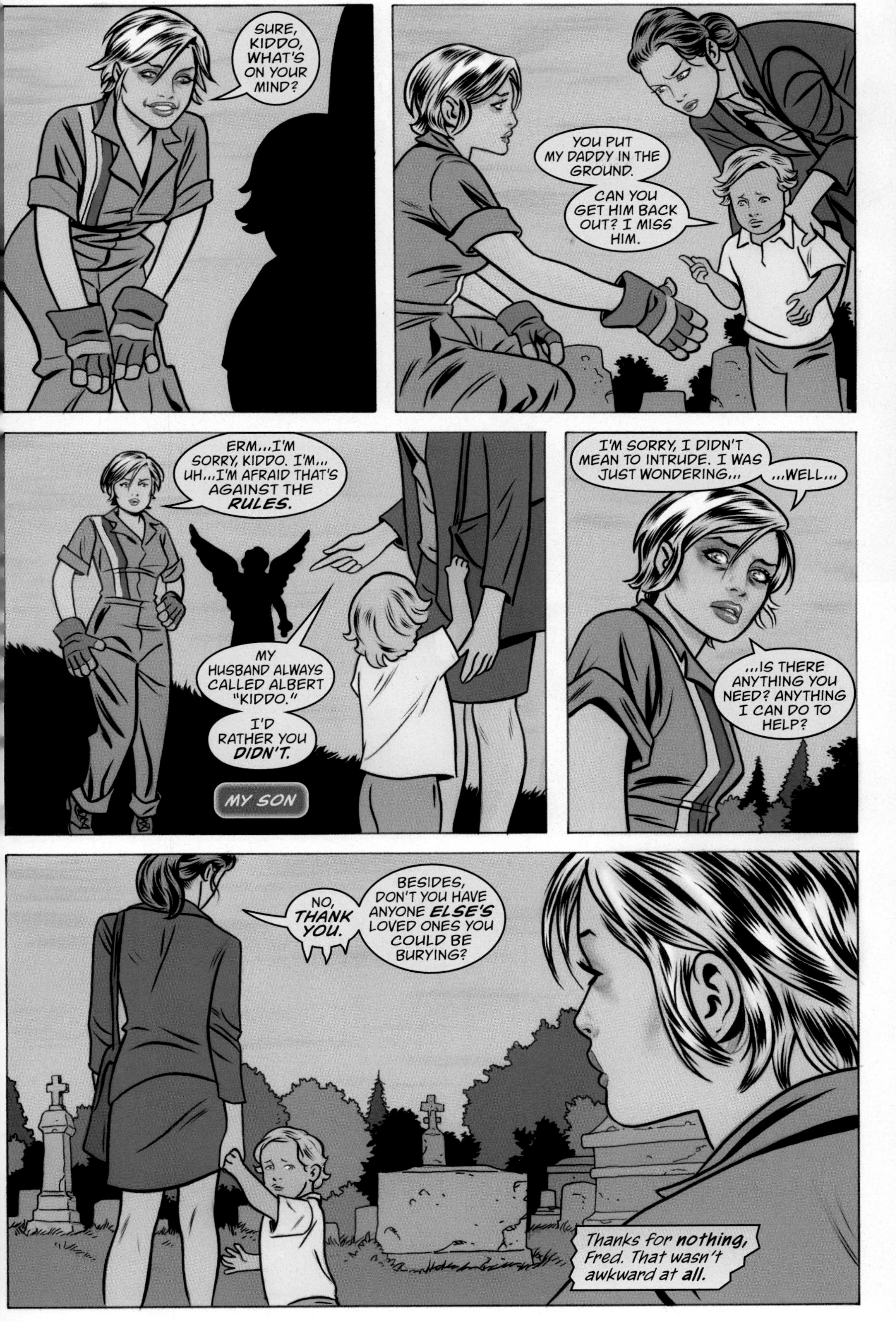
SURE, KIDDO, WHAT'S ON YOUR MIND?
YOU PUT MY DADDY IN THE GROUND.
CAN YOU GET HIM BACK OUT? I MISS HIM.
ERM...I'M SORRY, KIDDO. I'M... UH...I'M AFRAID THAT'S AGAINST THE RULES.
MY HUSBAND ALWAYS CALLED ALBERT "KIDDO."
I'D RATHER YOU DIDN'T.
MY SON
I'M SORRY, I DIDN'T MEAN TO INTRUDE. I WAS JUST WONDERING...
...WELL...
...IS THERE ANYTHING YOU NEED? ANYTHING I CAN DO TO HELP?
NO, THANK YOU.
BESIDES, DON'T YOU HAVE ANYONE ELSE'S LOVED ONES YOU COULD BE BURYING?
Thanks for nothing, Fred. That wasn't awkward at all.

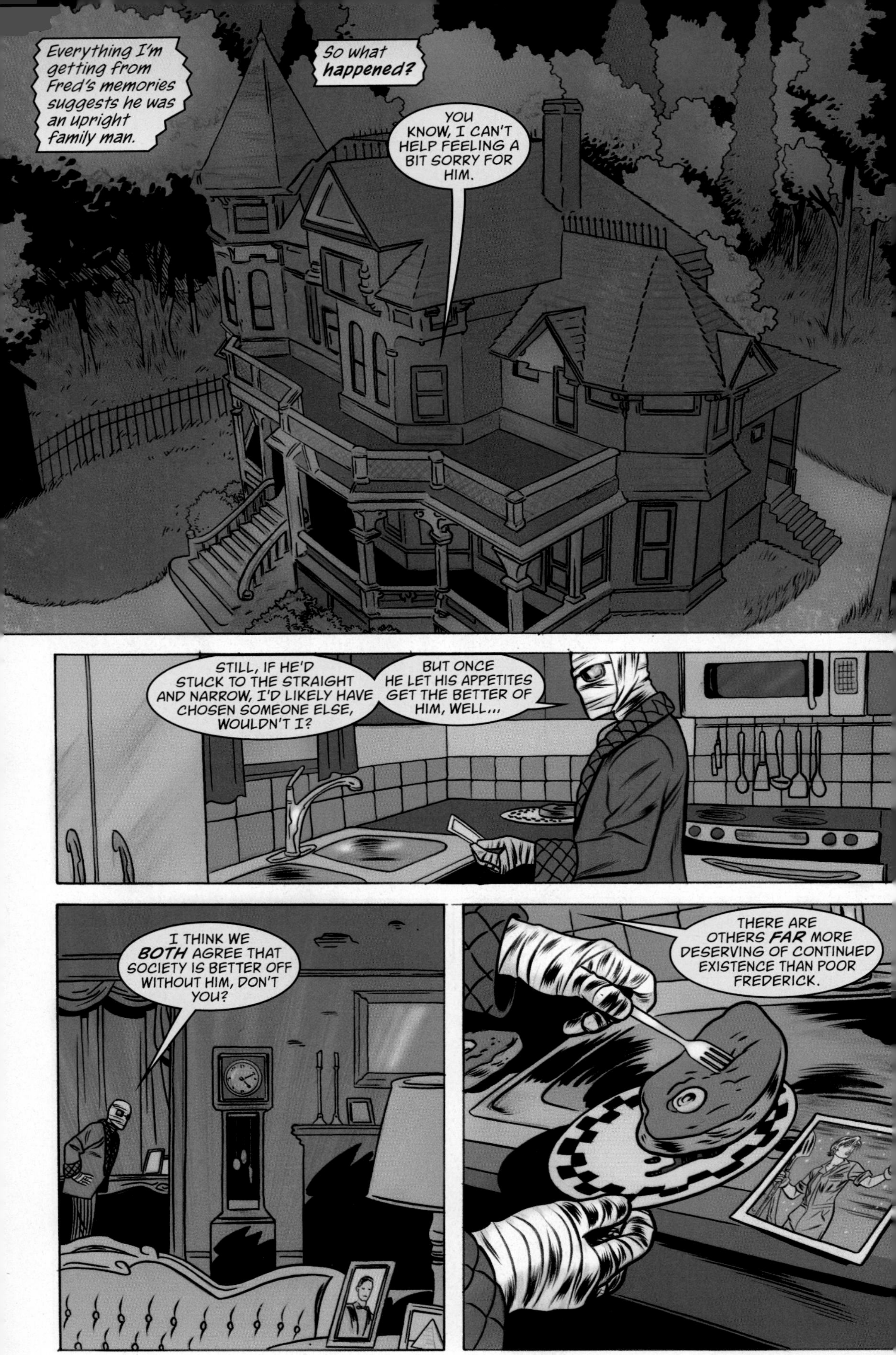
Everything I'm getting from Fred's memories suggests he was an upright family man.
So what happened?
YOU KNOW, I CAN'T HELP FEELING A BIT SORRY FOR HIM.
STILL, IF HE'D STUCK TO THE STRAIGHT AND NARROW, I'D LIKELY HAVE CHOSEN SOMEONE ELSE, WOULDN'T I?
BUT ONCE HE LET HIS APPETITES GET THE BETTER OF HIM, WELL...
I THINK WE BOTH AGREE THAT SOCIETY IS BETTER OFF WITHOUT HIM, DON'T YOU?
THERE ARE OTHERS FAR MORE DESERVING OF CONTINUED EXISTENCE THAN POOR FREDERICK.

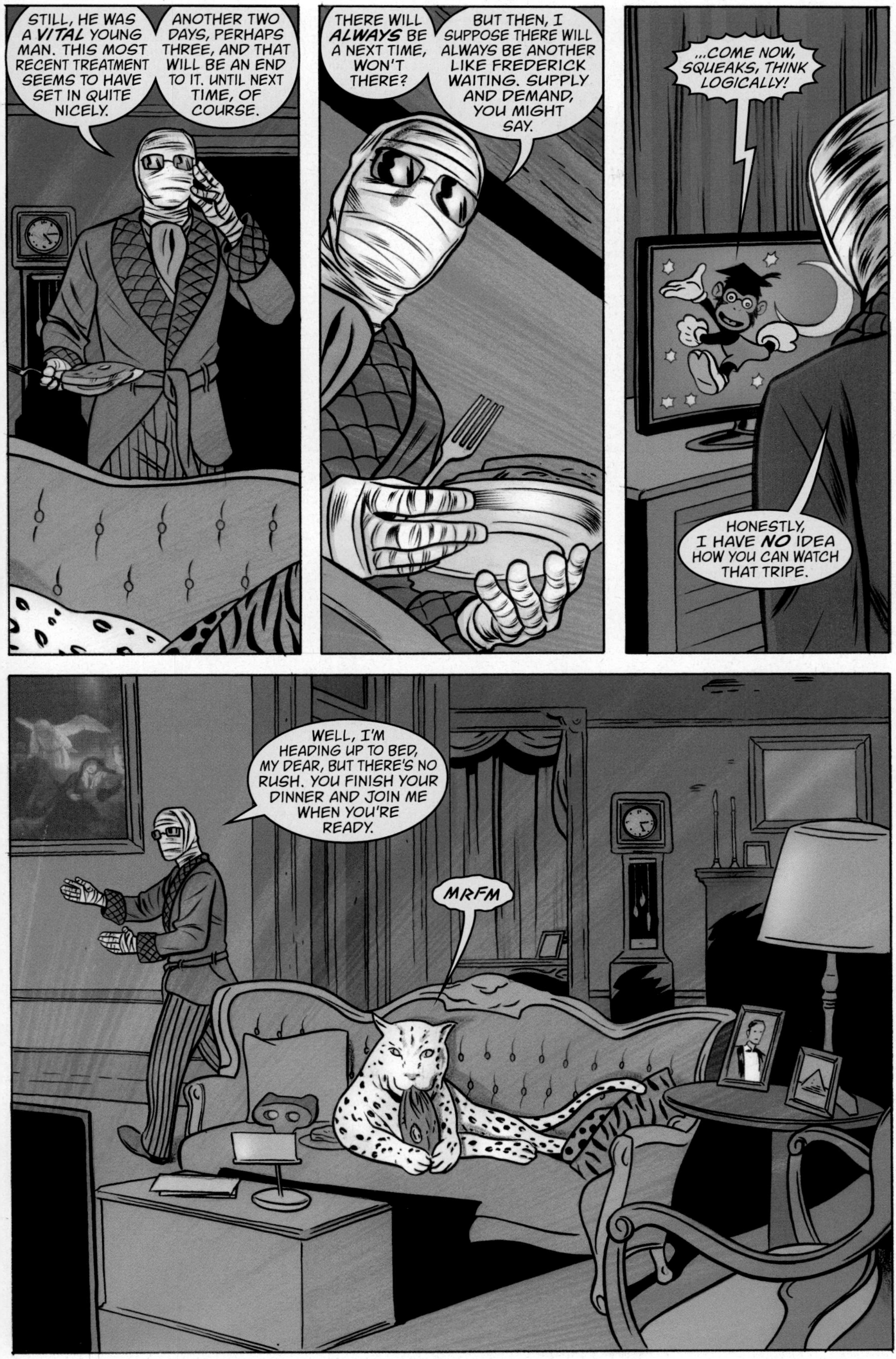
STILL, HE WAS A VITAL YOUNG MAN. THIS MOST RECENT TREATMENT SEEMS TO HAVE SET IN QUITE NICELY.
ANOTHER TWO DAYS, PERHAPS THREE, AND THAT WILL BE AN END TO IT. UNTIL NEXT TIME, OF COURSE.
THERE WILL ALWAYS BE A NEXT TIME, WON'T THERE?
BUT THEN, I SUPPOSE THERE WILL ALWAYS BE ANOTHER LIKE FREDERICK WAITING. SUPPLY AND DEMAND, YOU MIGHT SAY.
...COME NOW, SQUEAKS, THINK LOGICALLY!
HONESTLY, I HAVE NO IDEA HOW YOU CAN WATCH THAT TRIPE.
WELL, I'M HEADING UP TO BED, MY DEAR, BUT THERE'S NO RUSH. YOU FINISH YOUR DINNER AND JOIN ME WHEN YOU'RE READY.
MRFM

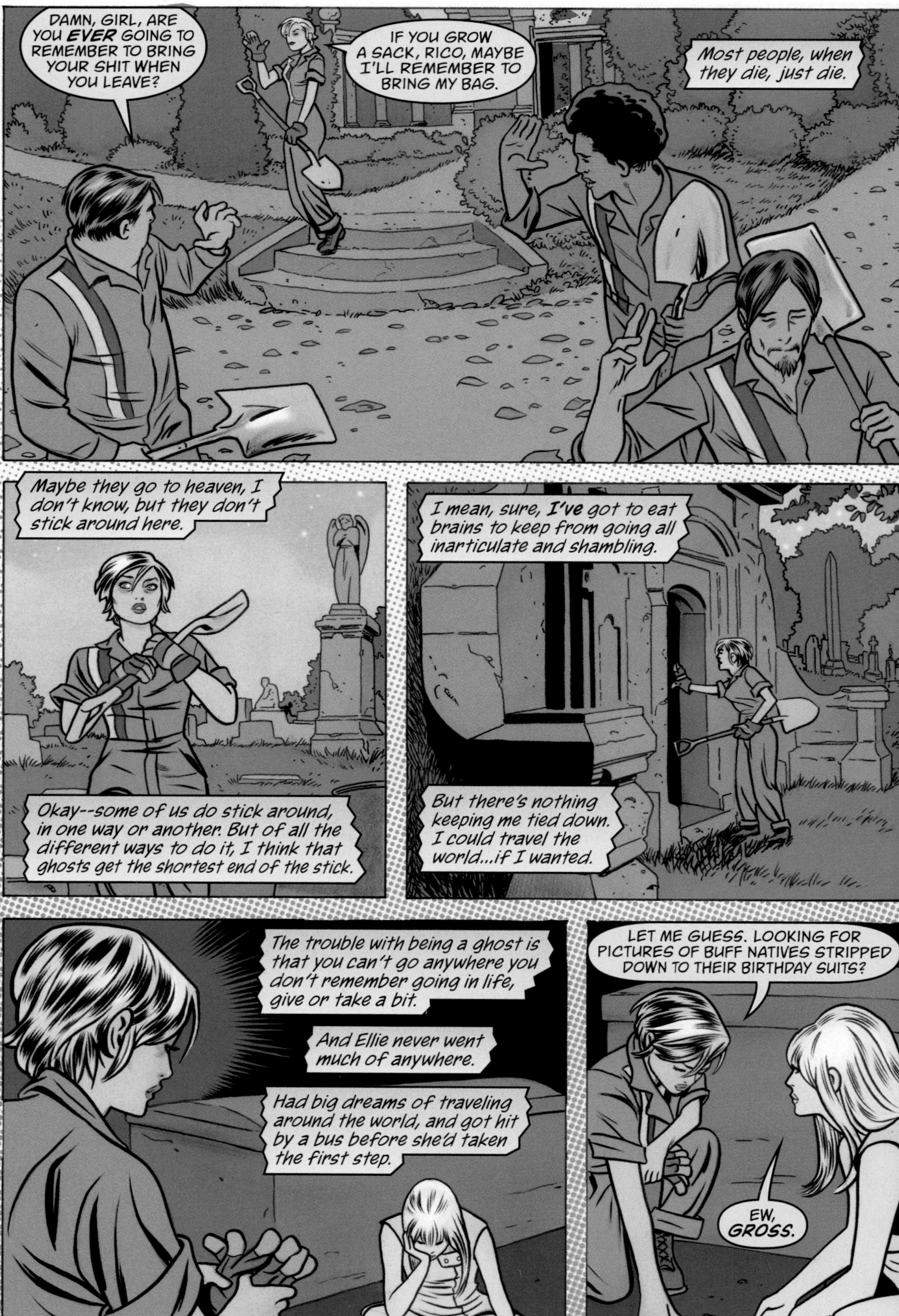
DAMN, GIRL, ARE YOU **EVER** GOING TO REMEMBER TO BRING YOUR SHIT WHEN YOU LEAVE?
IF YOU GROW A SACK, RICO, MAYBE I'LL REMEMBER TO BRING MY BAG.
Most people, when they die, just die.
Maybe they go to heaven, I don't know, but they don't stick around here.
Okay--some of us do stick around, in one way or another. But of all the different ways to do it, I think that ghosts get the shortest end of the stick.
I mean, sure, **I've** got to eat brains to keep from going all inarticulate and shambling.
But there's nothing keeping me tied down. I could travel the world...if I wanted.
The trouble with being a ghost is that you can't go anywhere you don't remember going in life, give or take a bit.
And Ellie never went much of anywhere.
Had big dreams of traveling around the world, and got hit by a bus before she'd taken the first step.
LET ME GUESS. LOOKING FOR PICTURES OF BUFF NATIVES STRIPPED DOWN TO THEIR BIRTHDAY SUITS?
EW, **GROSS.**

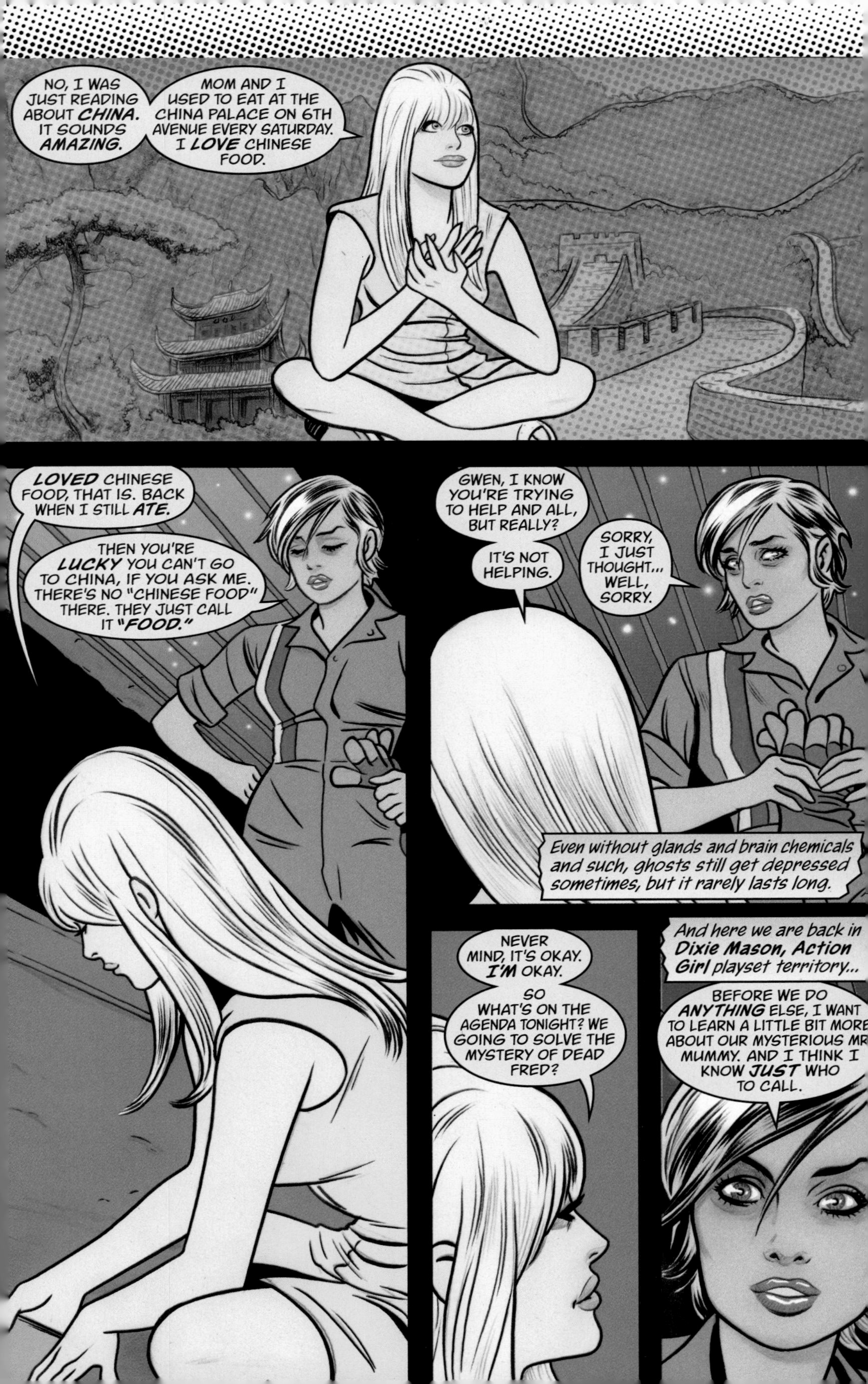
NO, I WAS JUST READING ABOUT CHINA. IT SOUNDS AMAZING.
MOM AND I USED TO EAT AT THE CHINA PALACE ON 6TH AVENUE EVERY SATURDAY. I LOVE CHINESE FOOD.
LOVED CHINESE FOOD, THAT IS. BACK WHEN I STILL ATE.
THEN YOU'RE LUCKY YOU CAN'T GO TO CHINA, IF YOU ASK ME. THERE'S NO "CHINESE FOOD" THERE. THEY JUST CALL IT "FOOD."
GWEN, I KNOW YOU'RE TRYING TO HELP AND ALL, BUT REALLY?
IT'S NOT HELPING.
SORRY, I JUST THOUGHT... WELL, SORRY.
Even without glands and brain chemicals and such, ghosts still get depressed sometimes, but it rarely lasts long.
NEVER MIND, IT'S OKAY. I'M OKAY.
SO WHAT'S ON THE AGENDA TONIGHT? WE GOING TO SOLVE THE MYSTERY OF DEAD FRED?
And here we are back in Dixie Mason, Action Girl playset territory...
BEFORE WE DO ANYTHING ELSE, I WANT TO LEARN A LITTLE BIT MORE ABOUT OUR MYSTERIOUS MR. MUMMY. AND I THINK I KNOW JUST WHO TO CALL.

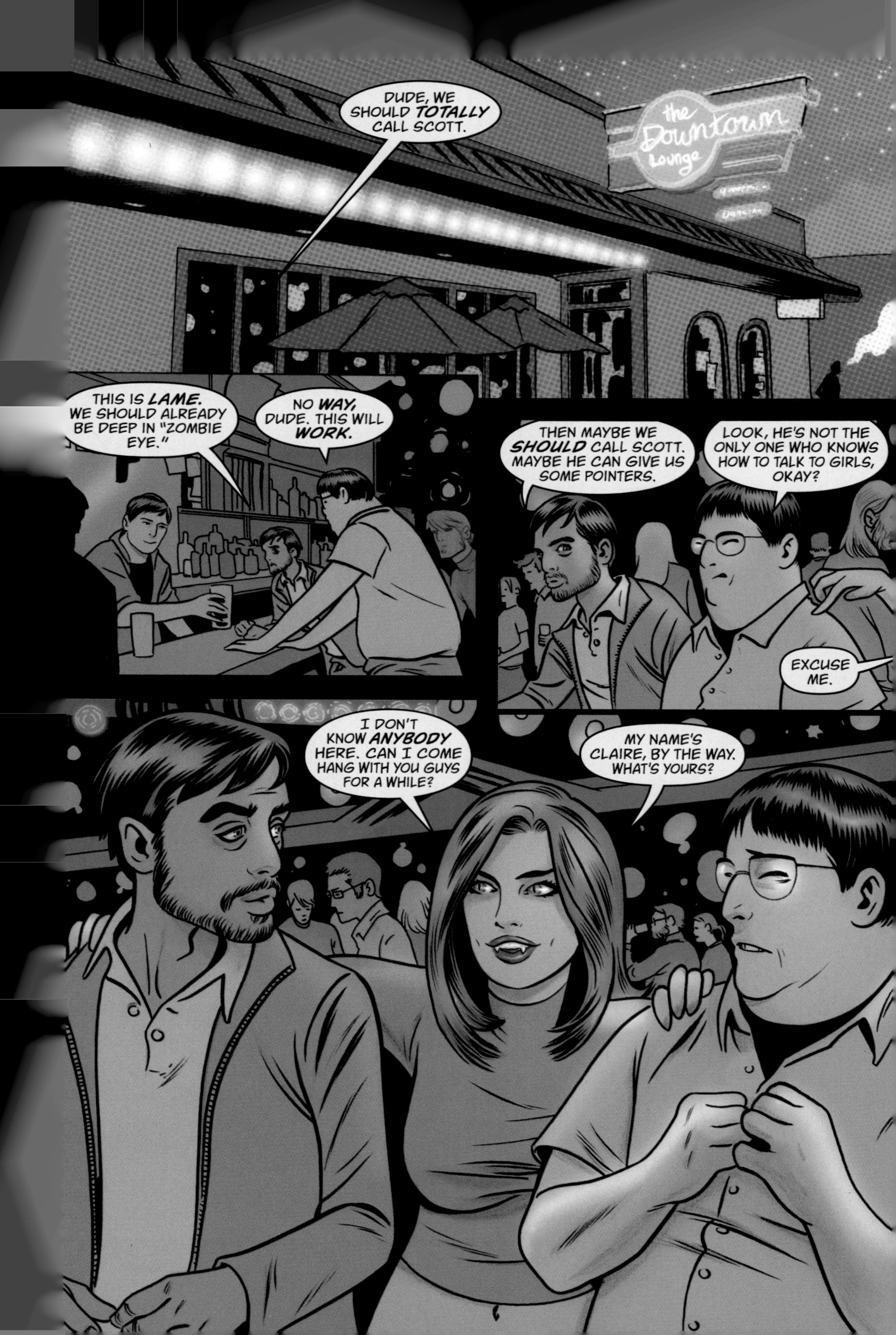
DUDE, WE SHOULD TOTALLY CALL SCOTT.
THIS IS LAME. WE SHOULD ALREADY BE DEEP IN "ZOMBIE EYE."
NO WAY, DUDE. THIS WILL WORK.
THEN MAYBE WE SHOULD CALL SCOTT. MAYBE HE CAN GIVE US SOME POINTERS.
LOOK, HE'S NOT THE ONLY ONE WHO KNOWS HOW TO TALK TO GIRLS, OKAY?
EXCUSE ME.
I DON'T KNOW ANYBODY HERE. CAN I COME HANG WITH YOU GUYS FOR A WHILE?
MY NAME'S CLAIRE, BY THE WAY. WHAT'S YOURS?

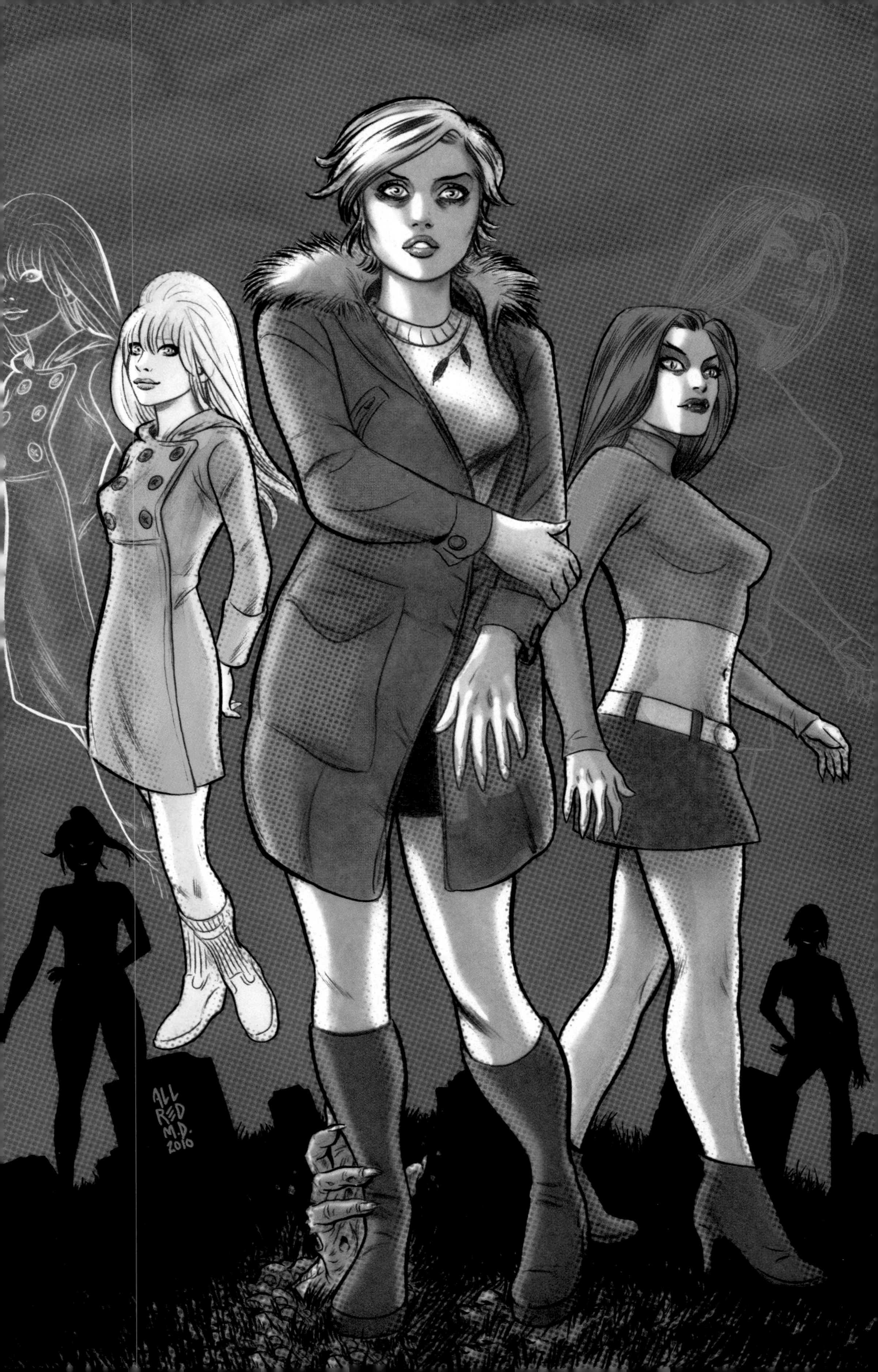
ALL RED M.D. 2010

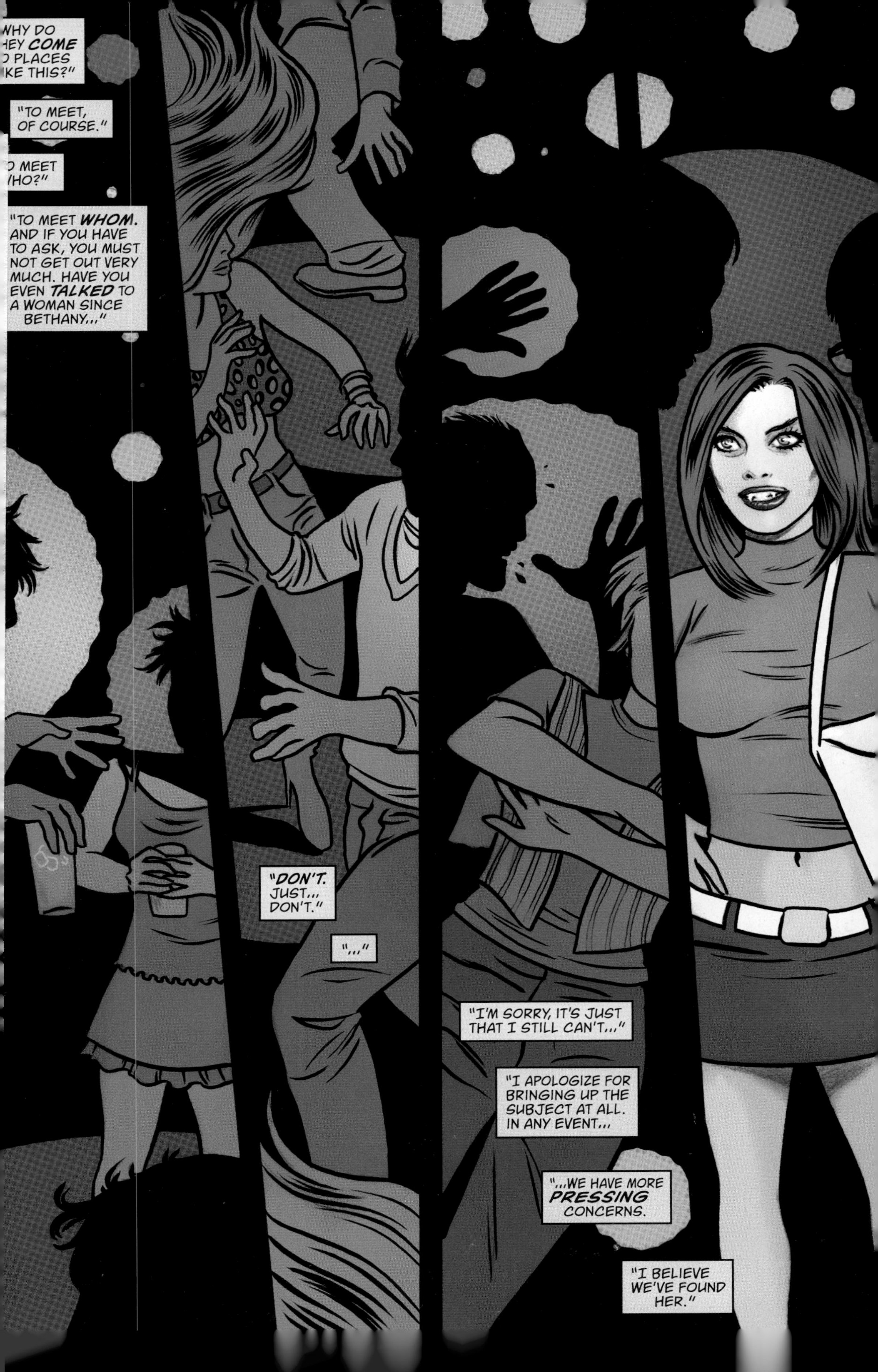

"WHY DO HEY COME O PLACES KE THIS?"
"TO MEET, OF COURSE."
O MEET WHO?"
"TO MEET WHOM. AND IF YOU HAVE TO ASK, YOU MUST NOT GET OUT VERY MUCH. HAVE YOU EVEN TALKED TO A WOMAN SINCE BETHANY..."
"DON'T. JUST... DON'T."
"..."
"I'M SORRY, IT'S JUST THAT I STILL CAN'T..."
"I APOLOGIZE FOR BRINGING UP THE SUBJECT AT ALL. IN ANY EVENT...
"...WE HAVE MORE PRESSING CONCERNS.
"I BELIEVE WE'VE FOUND HER."

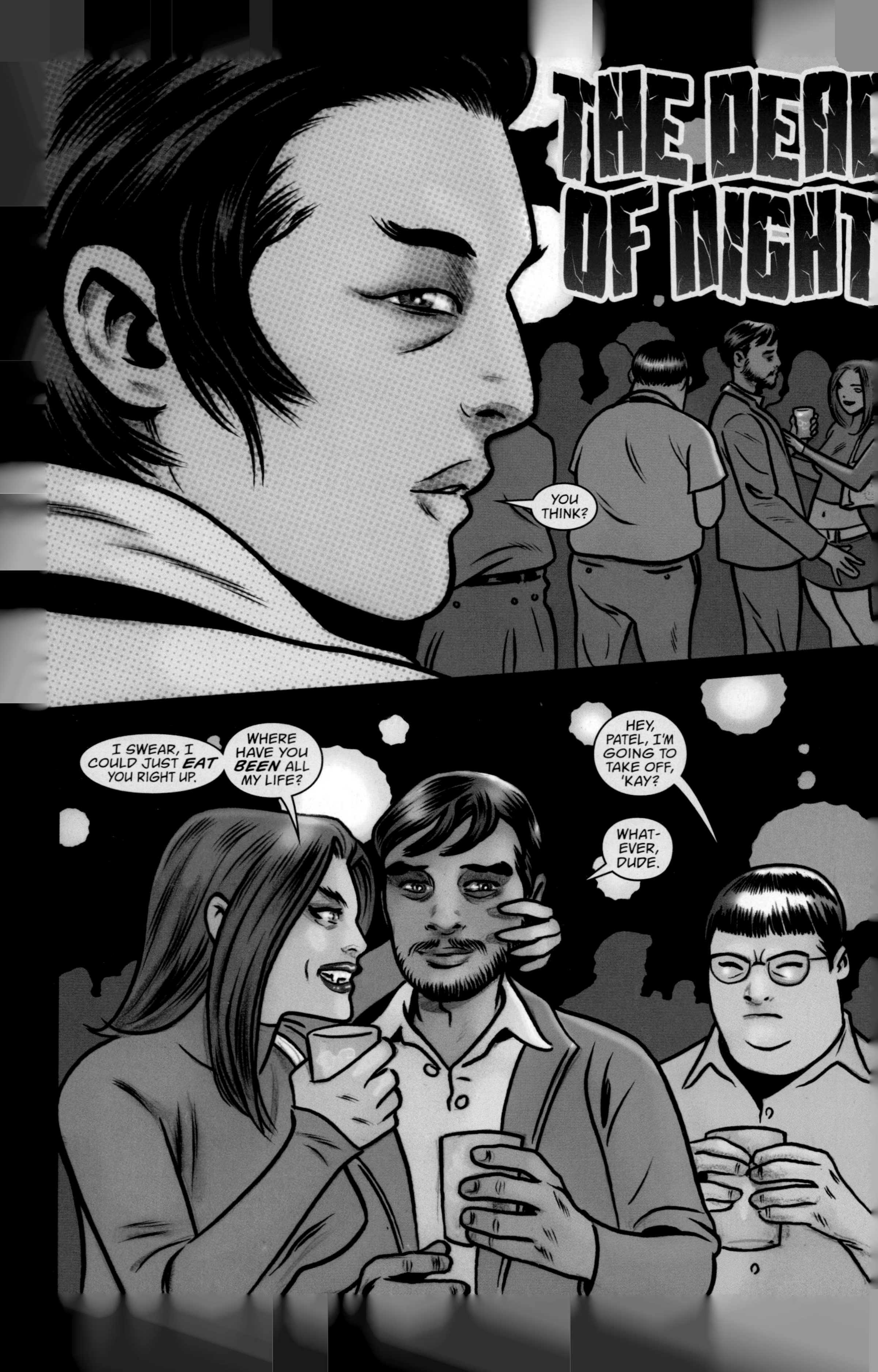
THE DEAD OF NIGHT
YOU THINK?
I SWEAR, I COULD JUST EAT YOU RIGHT UP.
WHERE HAVE YOU BEEN ALL MY LIFE?
HEY, PATEL, I'M GOING TO TAKE OFF, 'KAY?
WHAT-EVER, DUDE.

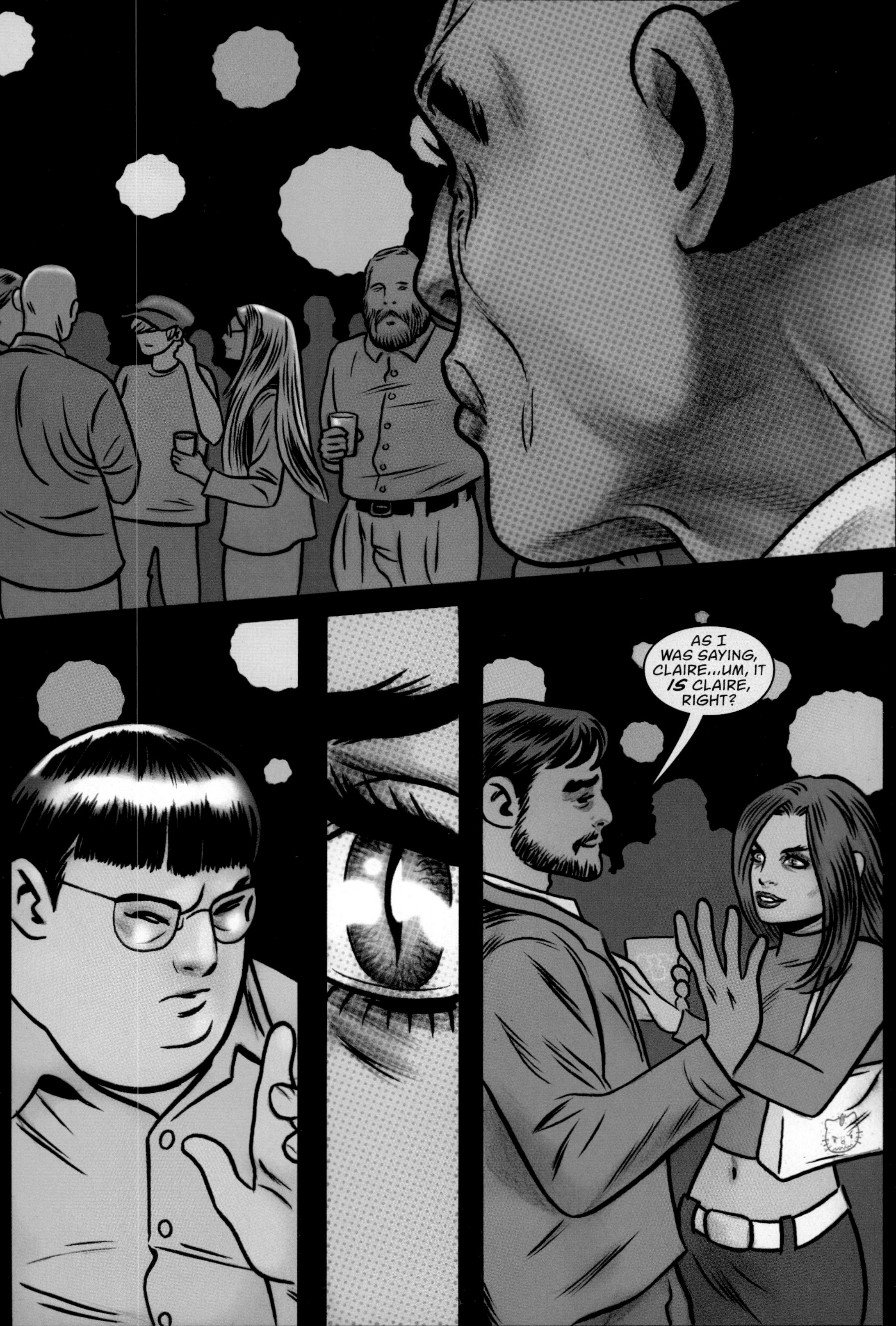
AS I WAS SAYING, CLAIRE...UM, IT IS CLAIRE, RIGHT?

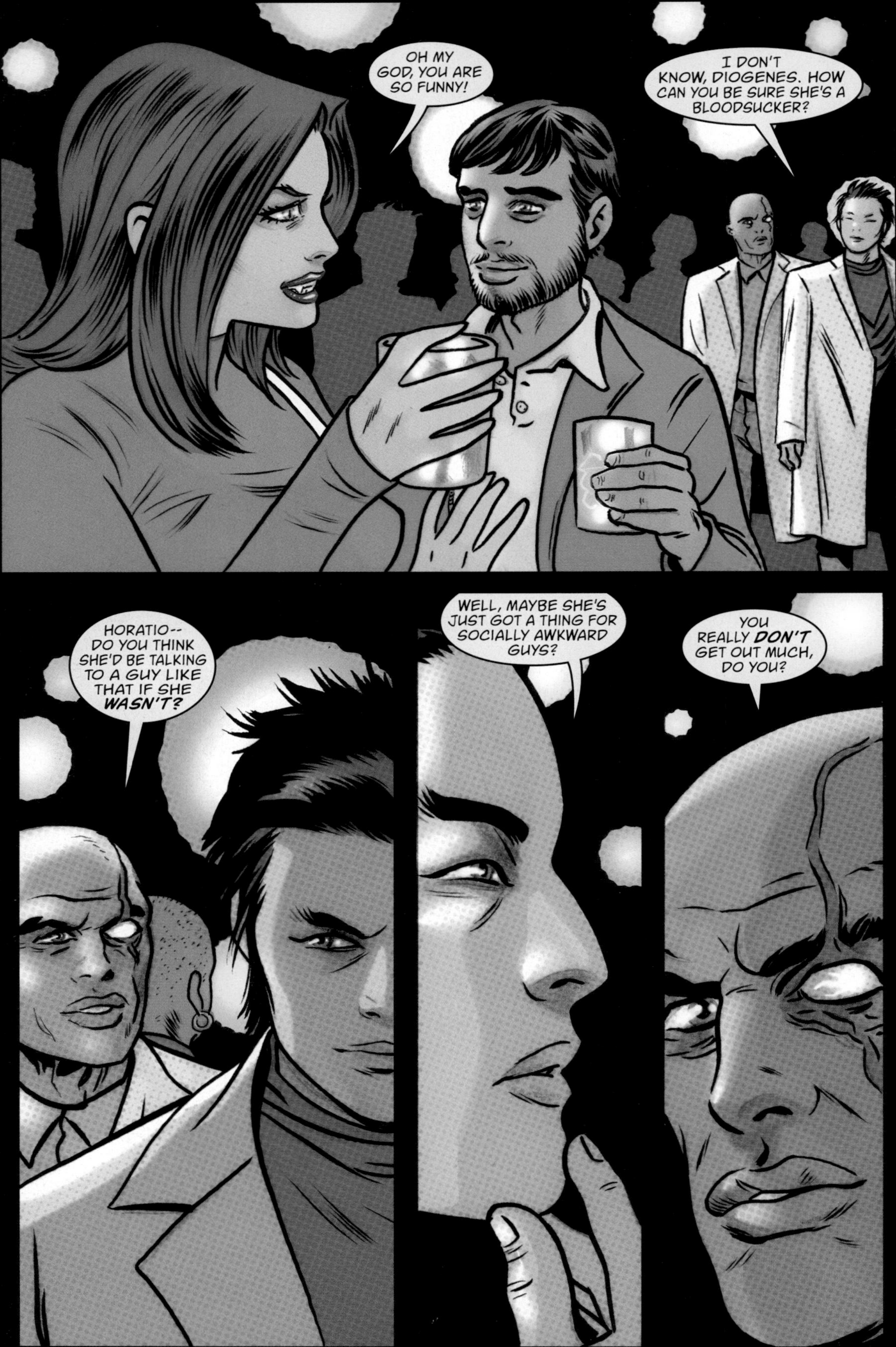
OH MY GOD, YOU ARE SO FUNNY!
I DON'T KNOW, DIOGENES. HOW CAN YOU BE SURE SHE'S A BLOODSUCKER?
HORATIO-- DO YOU THINK SHE'D BE TALKING TO A GUY LIKE THAT IF SHE ***WASN'T?***
WELL, MAYBE SHE'S JUST GOT A THING FOR SOCIALLY AWKWARD GUYS?
YOU REALLY ***DON'T*** GET OUT MUCH, DO YOU?

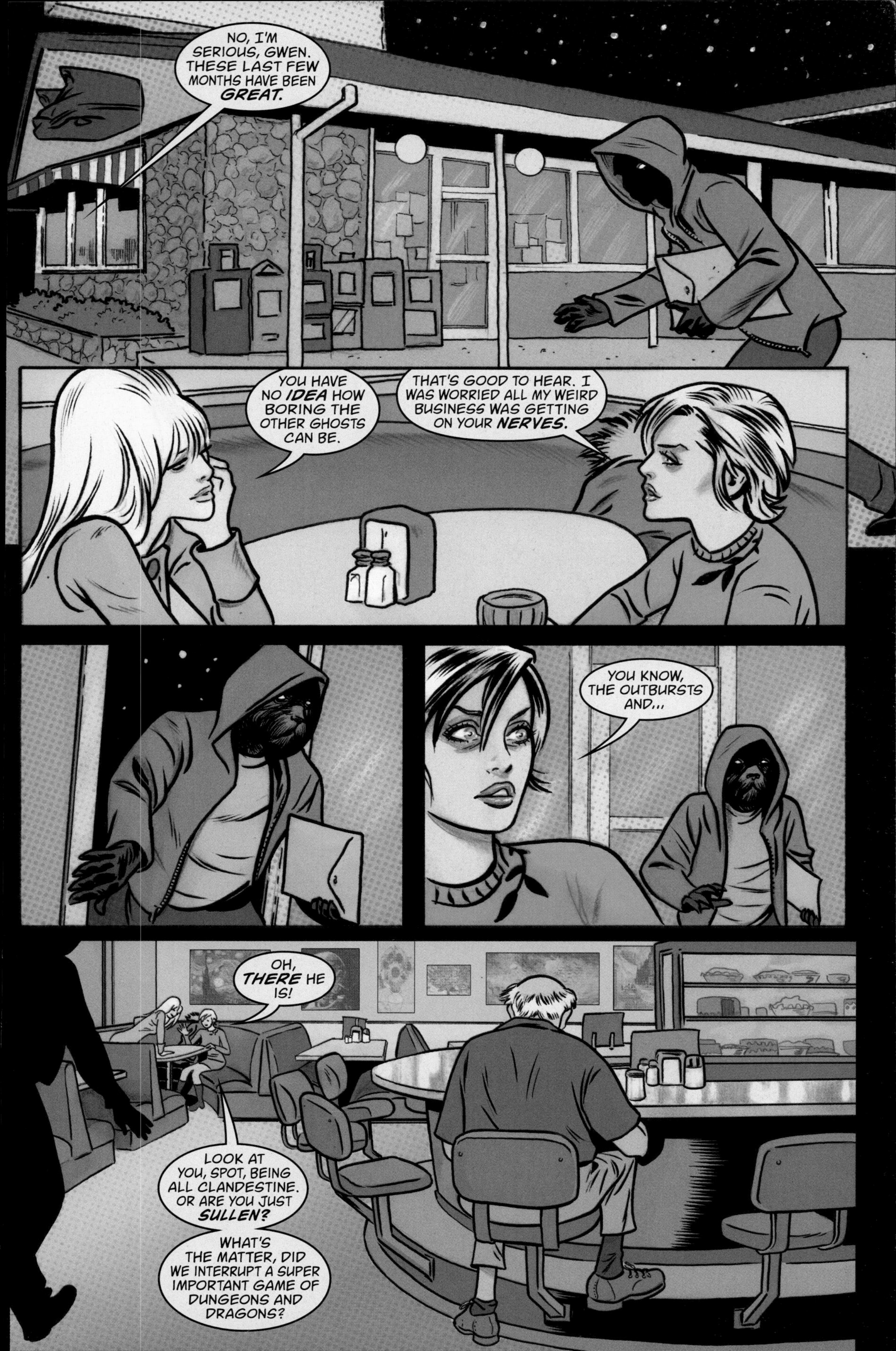

NO, I'M SERIOUS, GWEN. THESE LAST FEW MONTHS HAVE BEEN GREAT.
YOU HAVE NO IDEA HOW BORING THE OTHER GHOSTS CAN BE.
THAT'S GOOD TO HEAR. I WAS WORRIED ALL MY WEIRD BUSINESS WAS GETTING ON YOUR NERVES.
YOU KNOW, THE OUTBURSTS AND...
OH, THERE HE IS!
LOOK AT YOU, SPOT, BEING ALL CLANDESTINE. OR ARE YOU JUST SULLEN?
WHAT'S THE MATTER, DID WE INTERRUPT A SUPER IMPORTANT GAME OF DUNGEONS AND DRAGONS?

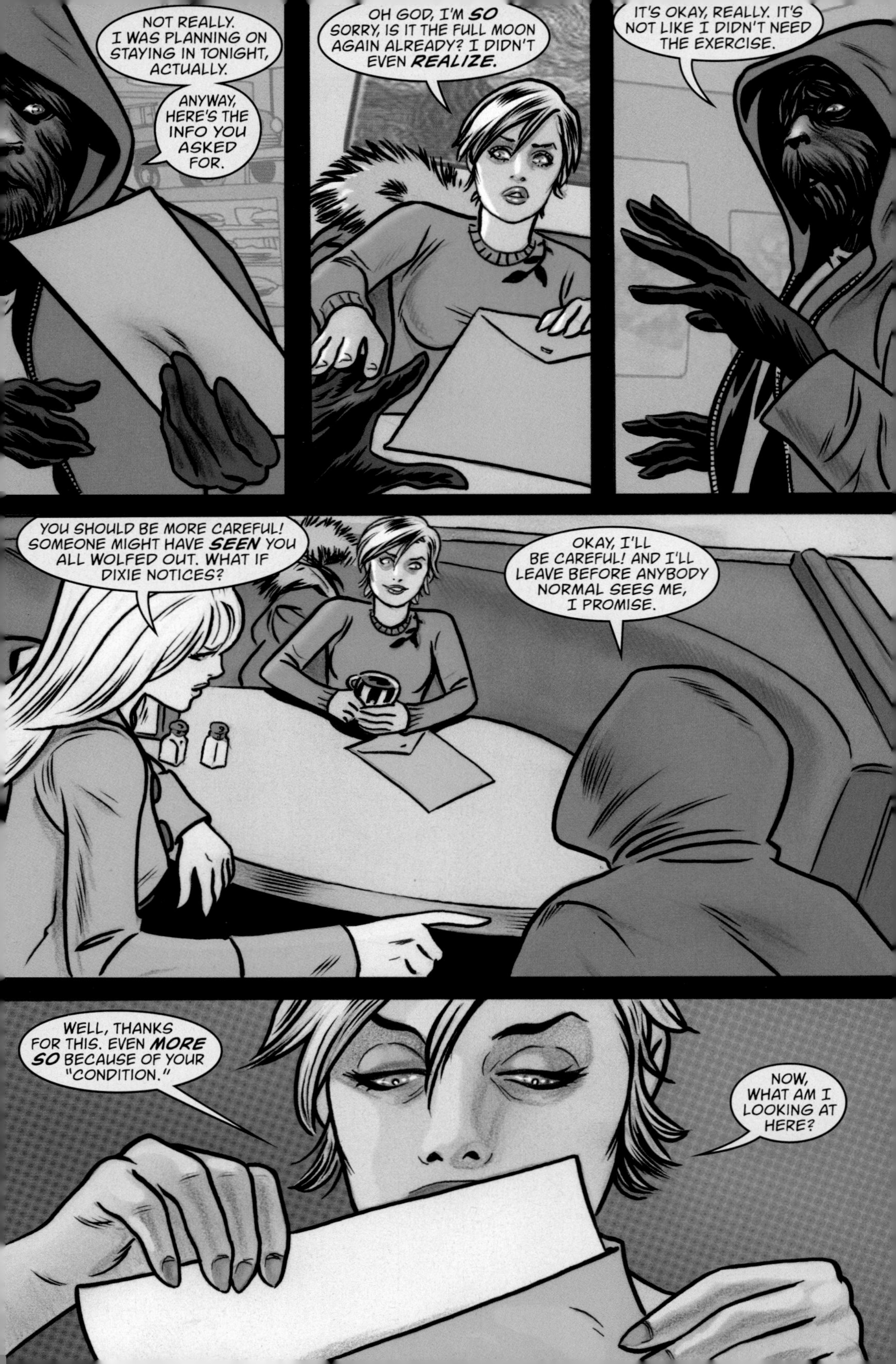
NOT REALLY. I WAS PLANNING ON STAYING IN TONIGHT, ACTUALLY.
ANYWAY, HERE'S THE INFO YOU ASKED FOR.
OH GOD, I'M SO SORRY, IS IT THE FULL MOON AGAIN ALREADY? I DIDN'T EVEN REALIZE.
IT'S OKAY, REALLY. IT'S NOT LIKE I DIDN'T NEED THE EXERCISE.
YOU SHOULD BE MORE CAREFUL! SOMEONE MIGHT HAVE SEEN YOU ALL WOLFED OUT. WHAT IF DIXIE NOTICES?
OKAY, I'LL BE CAREFUL! AND I'LL LEAVE BEFORE ANYBODY NORMAL SEES ME, I PROMISE.
WELL, THANKS FOR THIS. EVEN MORE SO BECAUSE OF YOUR "CONDITION."
NOW, WHAT AM I LOOKING AT HERE?

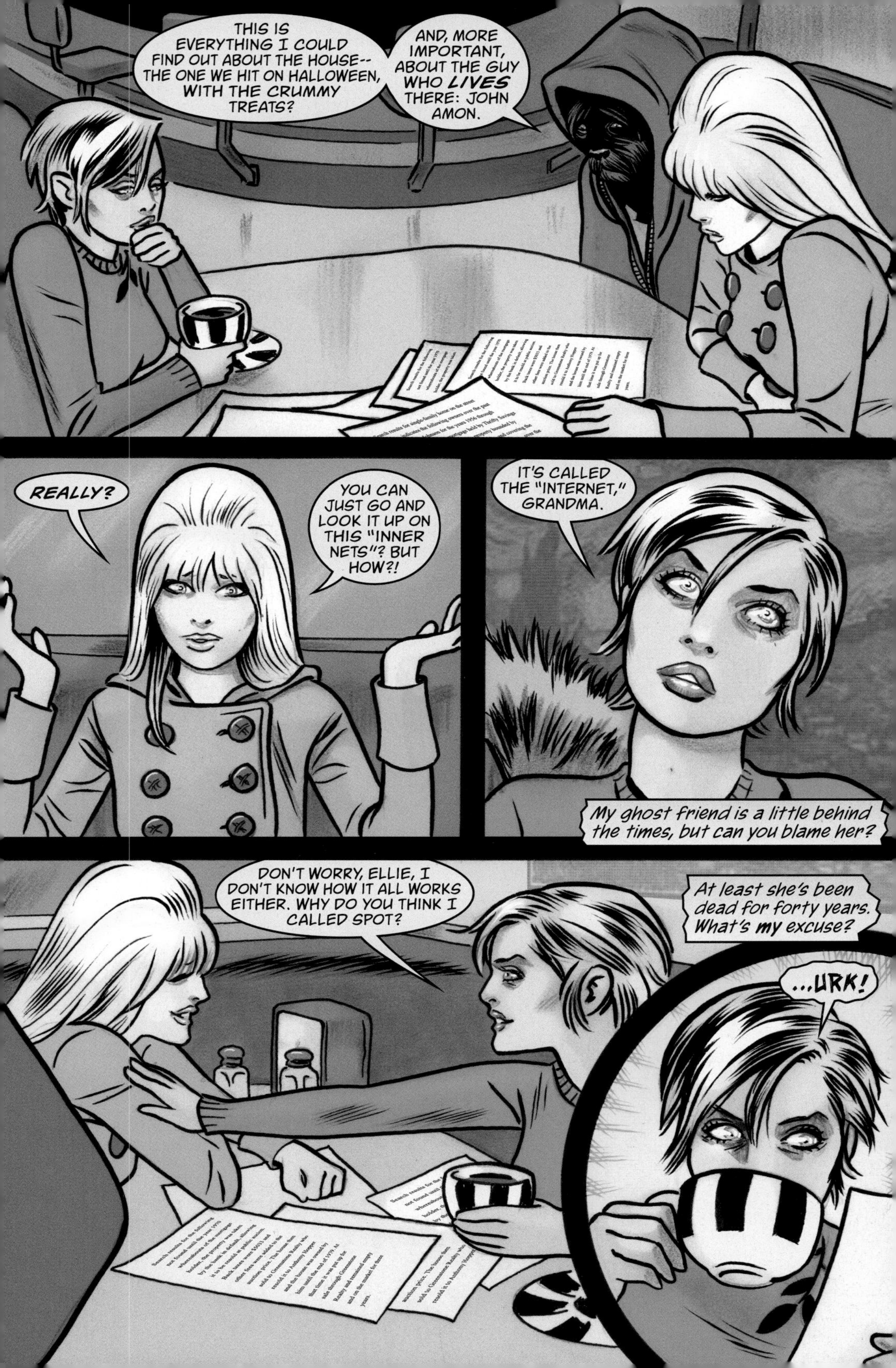
THIS IS EVERYTHING I COULD FIND OUT ABOUT THE HOUSE-- THE ONE WE HIT ON HALLOWEEN, WITH THE CRUMMY TREATS?
AND, MORE IMPORTANT, ABOUT THE GUY WHO LIVES THERE: JOHN AMON.
REALLY?
YOU CAN JUST GO AND LOOK IT UP ON THIS "INNER NETS"? BUT HOW?!
IT'S CALLED THE "INTERNET," GRANDMA.
My ghost friend is a little behind the times, but can you blame her?
DON'T WORRY, ELLIE, I DON'T KNOW HOW IT ALL WORKS EITHER. WHY DO YOU THINK I CALLED SPOT?
At least she's been dead for forty years. What's my excuse?
...URK!

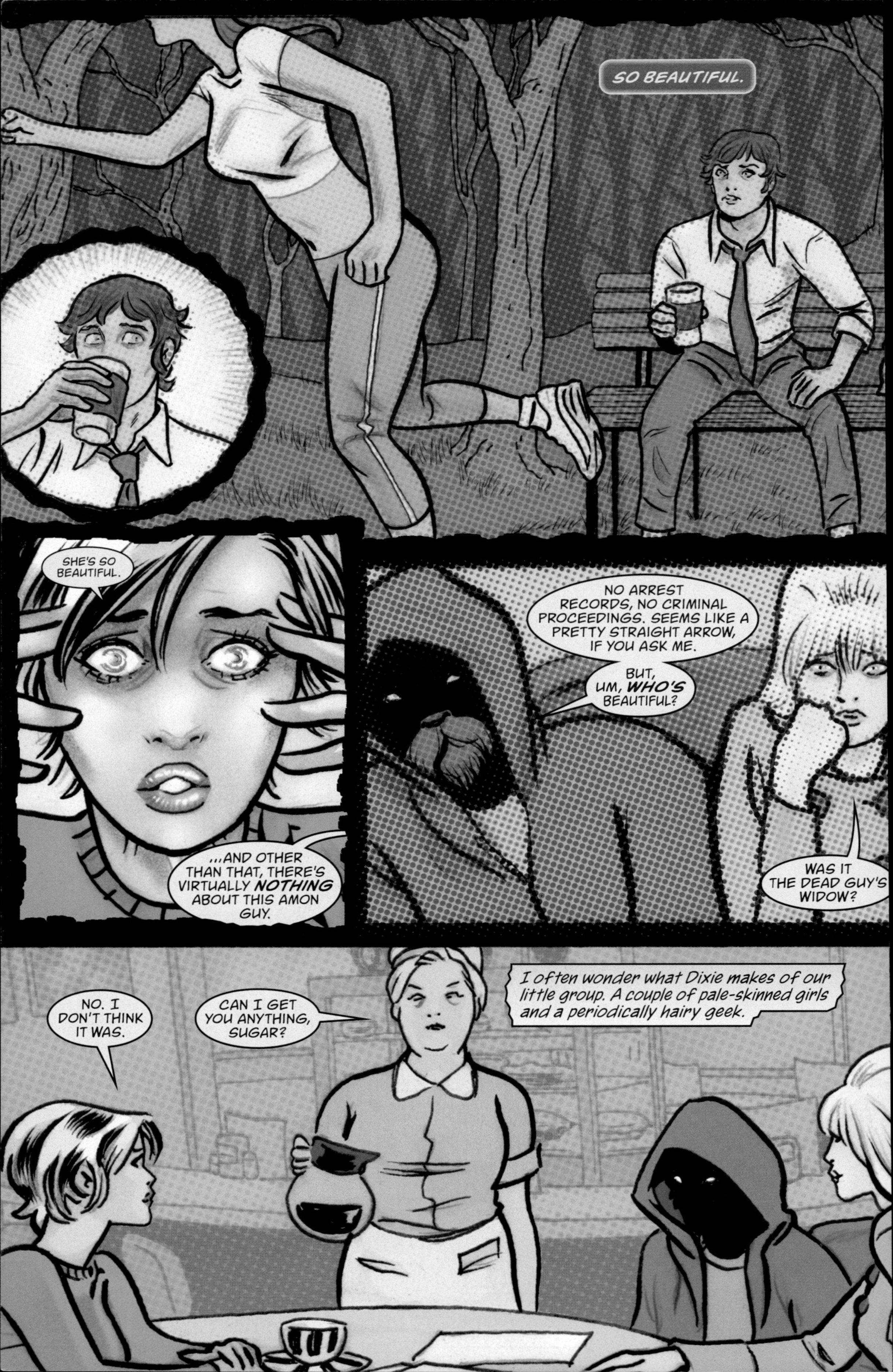
SO BEAUTIFUL.
SHE'S SO BEAUTIFUL.
...AND OTHER THAN THAT, THERE'S VIRTUALLY NOTHING ABOUT THIS AMON GUY.
NO ARREST RECORDS, NO CRIMINAL PROCEEDINGS. SEEMS LIKE A PRETTY STRAIGHT ARROW, IF YOU ASK ME.
BUT, UM, WHO'S BEAUTIFUL?
WAS IT THE DEAD GUY'S WIDOW?
NO. I DON'T THINK IT WAS.
CAN I GET YOU ANYTHING, SUGAR?
I often wonder what Dixie makes of our little group. A couple of pale-skinned girls and a periodically hairy geek.

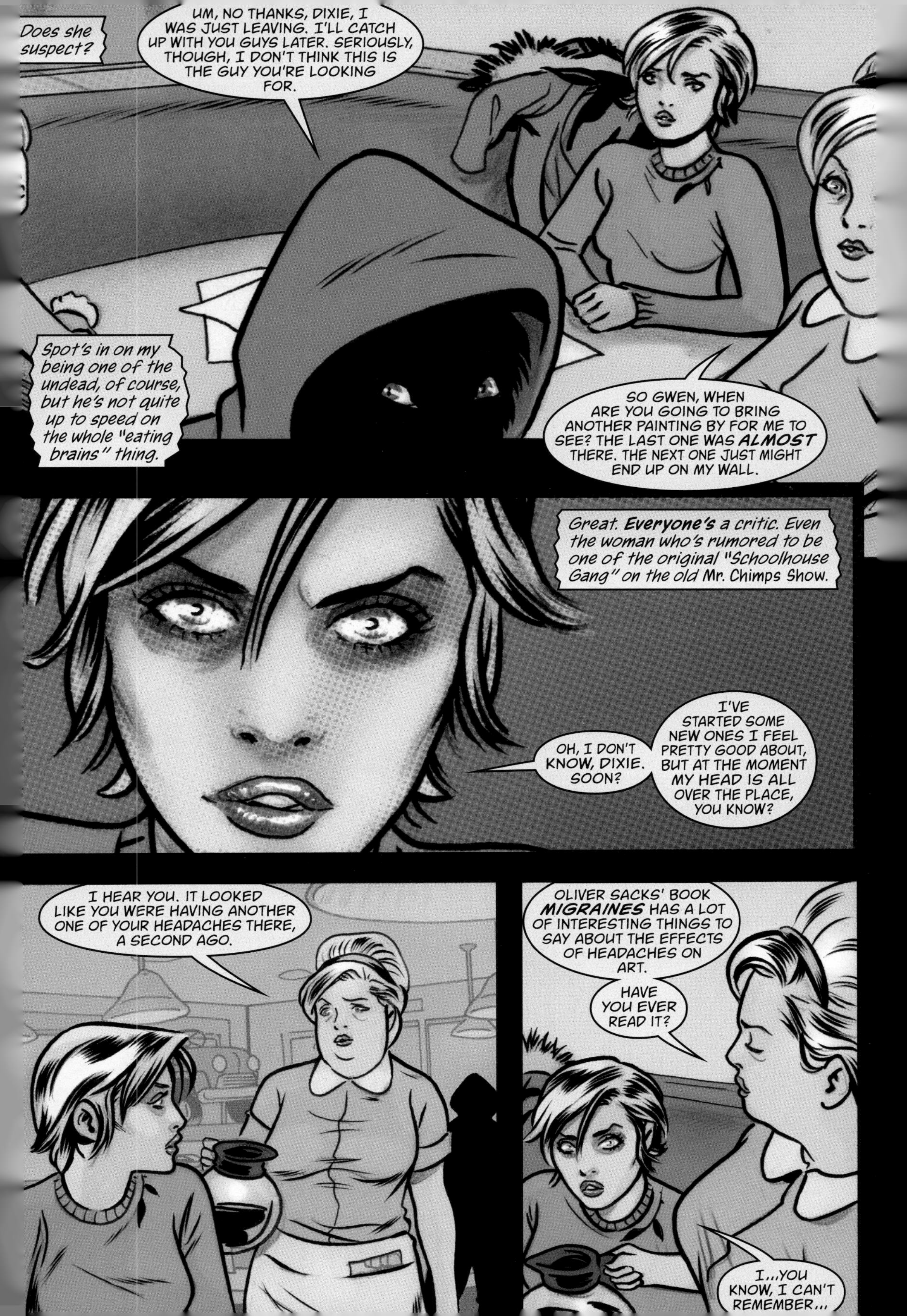
Does she suspect?
UM, NO THANKS, DIXIE, I WAS JUST LEAVING. I'LL CATCH UP WITH YOU GUYS LATER. SERIOUSLY, THOUGH, I DON'T THINK THIS IS THE GUY YOU'RE LOOKING FOR.
Spot's in on my being one of the undead, of course, but he's not quite up to speed on the whole "eating brains" thing.
SO GWEN, WHEN ARE YOU GOING TO BRING ANOTHER PAINTING BY FOR ME TO SEE? THE LAST ONE WAS ALMOST THERE. THE NEXT ONE JUST MIGHT END UP ON MY WALL.
Great. Everyone's a critic. Even the woman who's rumored to be one of the original "Schoolhouse Gang" on the old Mr. Chimps Show.
OH, I DON'T KNOW, DIXIE. SOON?
I'VE STARTED SOME NEW ONES I FEEL PRETTY GOOD ABOUT, BUT AT THE MOMENT MY HEAD IS ALL OVER THE PLACE, YOU KNOW?
I HEAR YOU. IT LOOKED LIKE YOU WERE HAVING ANOTHER ONE OF YOUR HEADACHES THERE, A SECOND AGO.
OLIVER SACKS' BOOK MIGRAINES HAS A LOT OF INTERESTING THINGS TO SAY ABOUT THE EFFECTS OF HEADACHES ON ART.
HAVE YOU EVER READ IT?
I...YOU KNOW, I CAN'T REMEMBER...

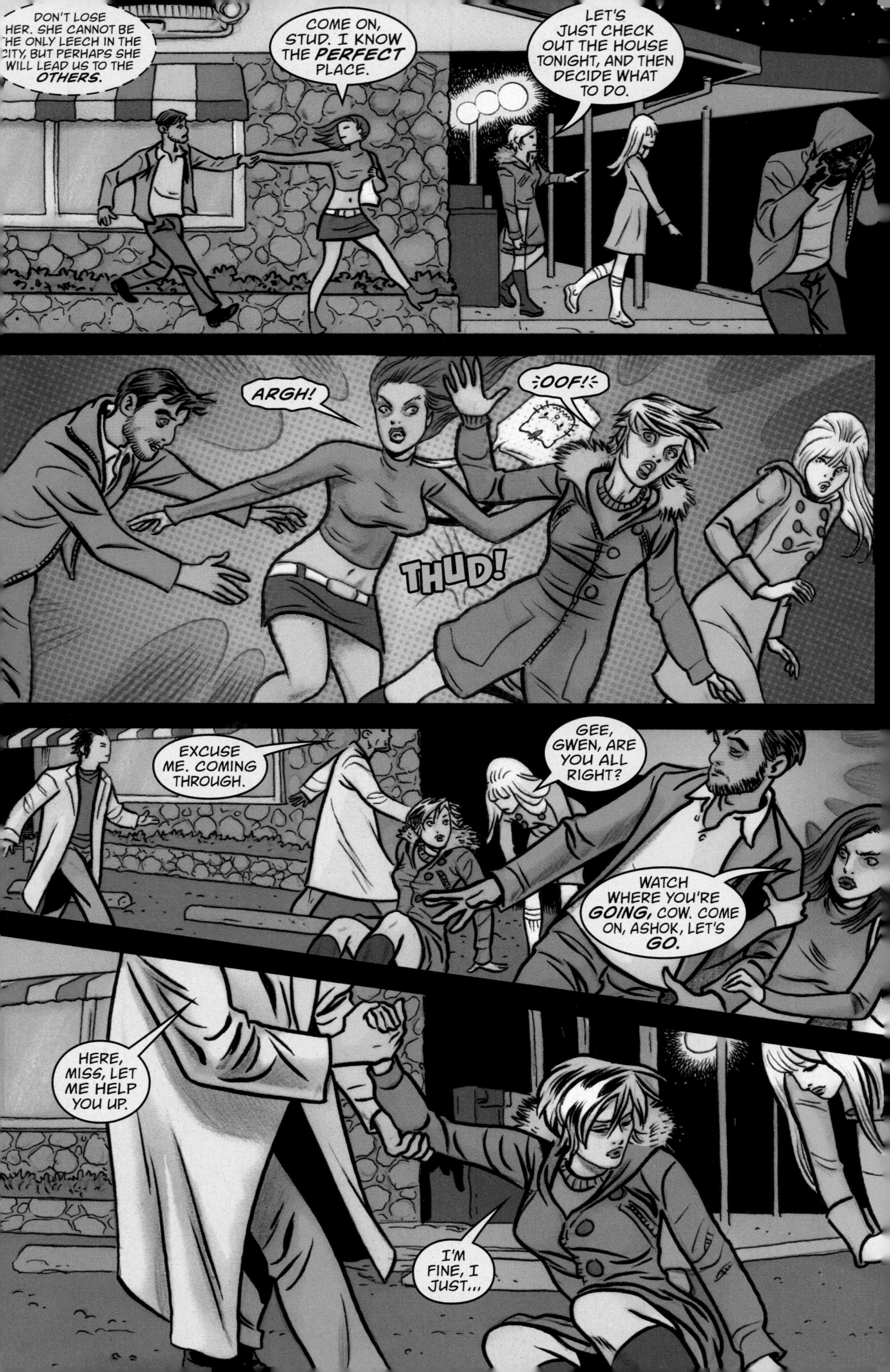
DON'T LOSE HER. SHE CANNOT BE THE ONLY LEECH IN THE CITY, BUT PERHAPS SHE WILL LEAD US TO THE **OTHERS.**
COME ON, STUD. I KNOW THE **PERFECT** PLACE.
LET'S JUST CHECK OUT THE HOUSE TONIGHT, AND THEN DECIDE WHAT TO DO.
ARGH!
OOF!
THUD!
EXCUSE ME. COMING THROUGH.
GEE, GWEN, ARE YOU ALL RIGHT?
WATCH WHERE YOU'RE **GOING,** COW. COME ON, ASHOK, LET'S **GO.**
HERE, MISS, LET ME HELP YOU UP.
I'M FINE, I JUST...

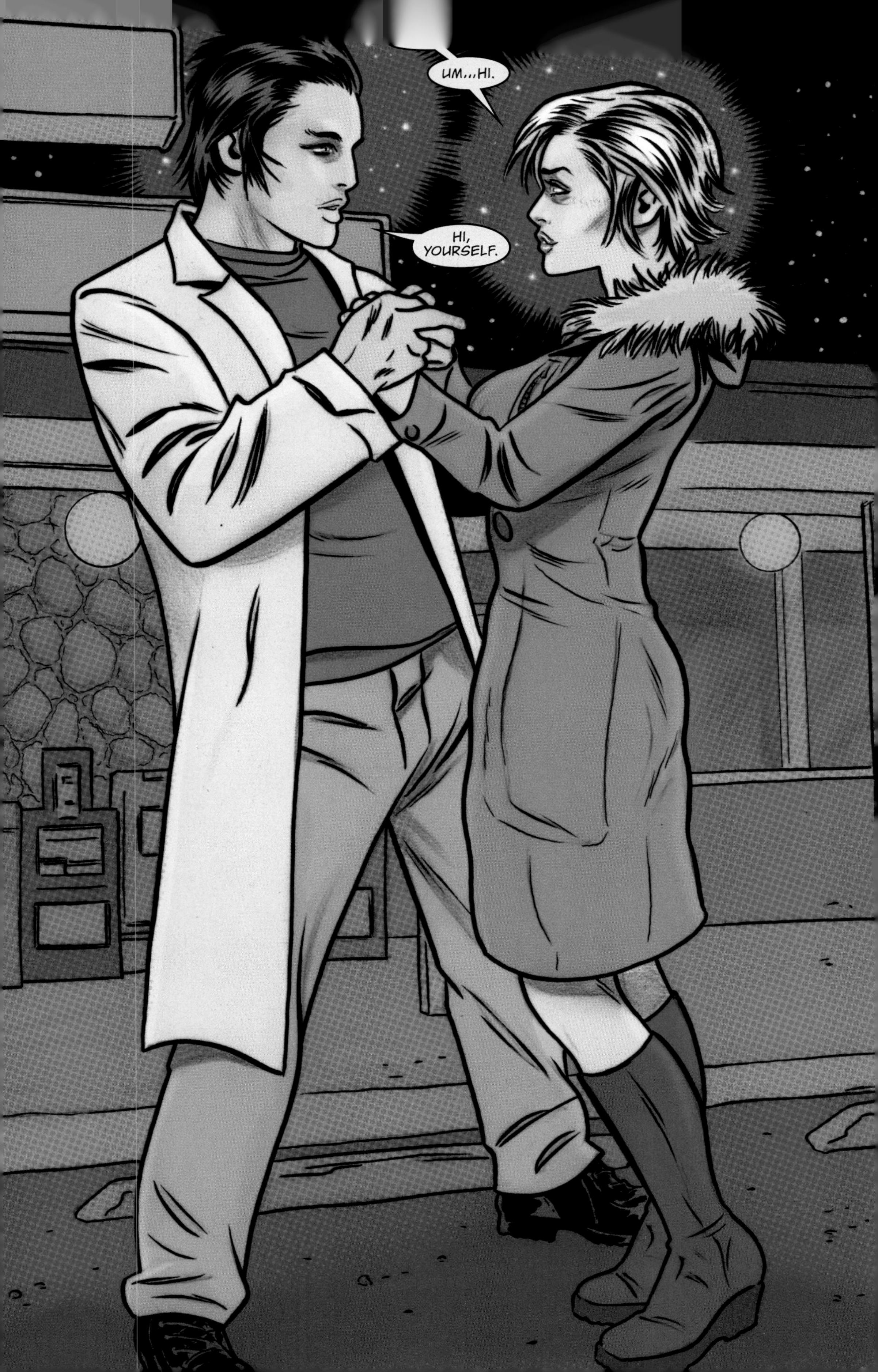
UM...HI.
HI, YOURSELF.

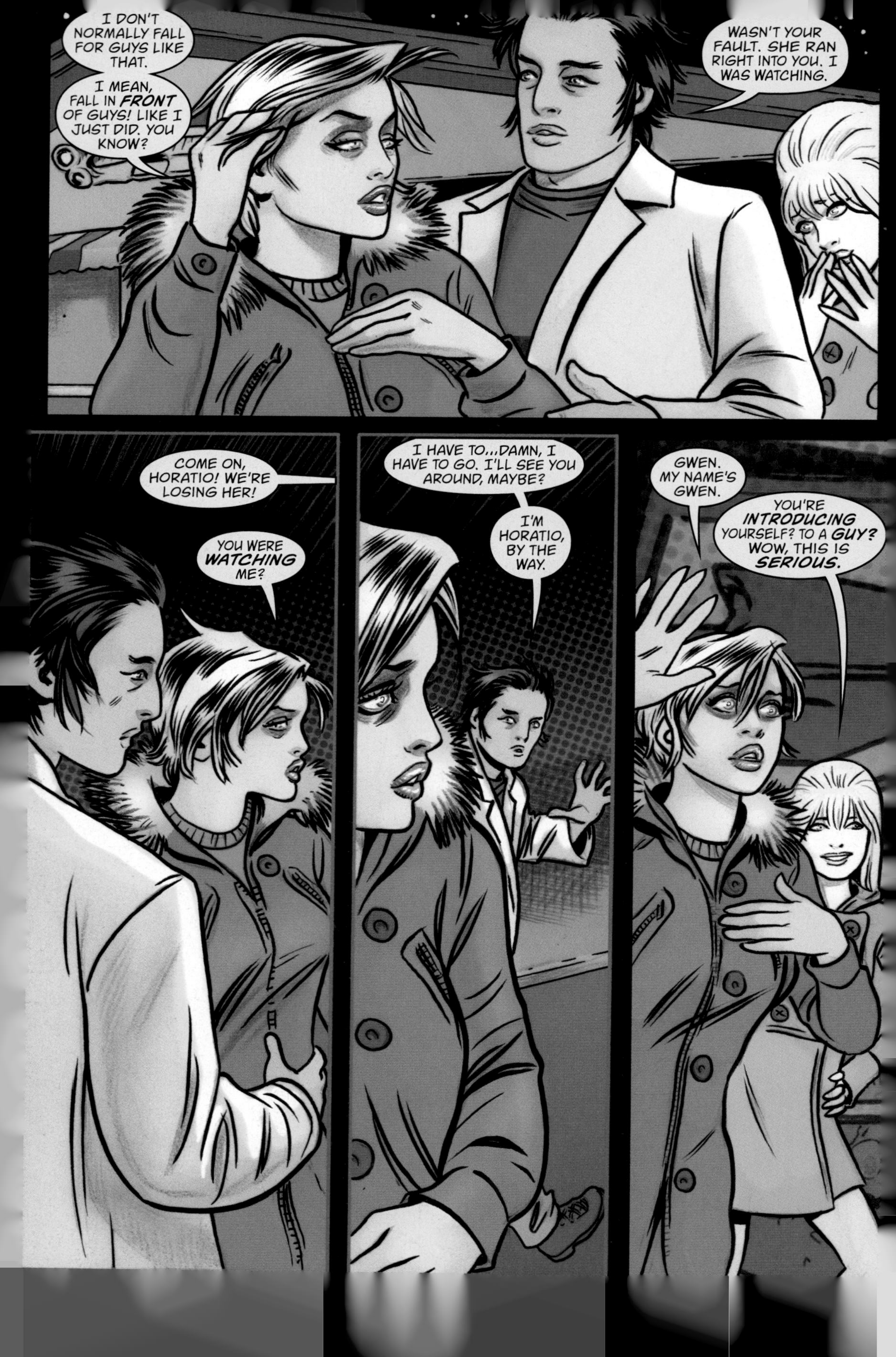

I DON'T NORMALLY FALL FOR GUYS LIKE THAT.
I MEAN, FALL IN *FRONT* OF GUYS! LIKE I JUST DID. YOU KNOW?
WASN'T YOUR FAULT. SHE RAN RIGHT INTO YOU. I WAS WATCHING.
COME ON, HORATIO! WE'RE LOSING HER!
YOU WERE *WATCHING* ME?
I HAVE TO...DAMN, I HAVE TO GO. I'LL SEE YOU AROUND, MAYBE?
I'M HORATIO, BY THE WAY.
GWEN. MY NAME'S GWEN.
YOU'RE *INTRODUCING* YOURSELF? TO A *GUY*? WOW, THIS IS *SERIOUS*.

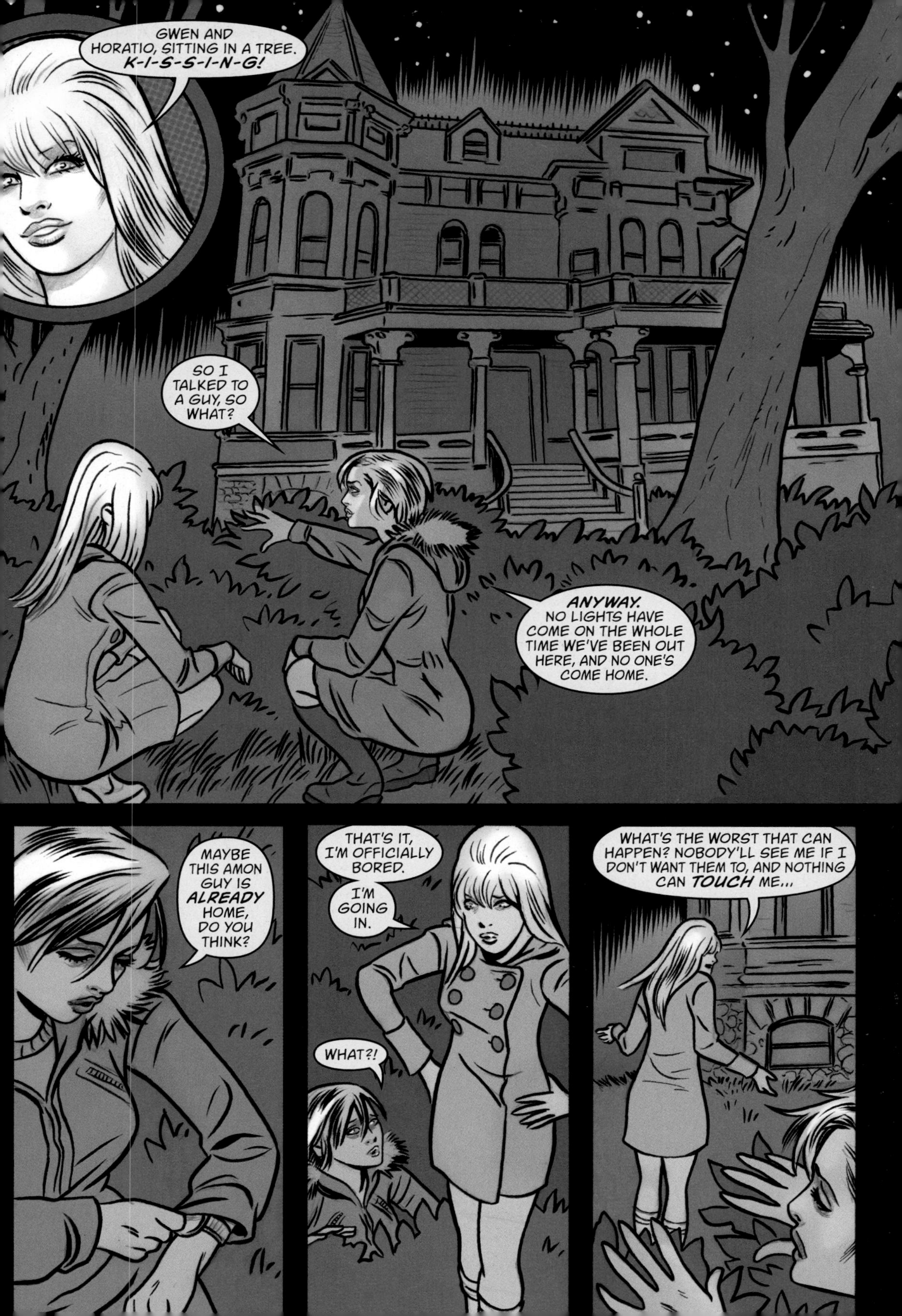
GWEN AND HORATIO, SITTING IN A TREE. K-I-S-S-I-N-G!
SO I TALKED TO A GUY, SO WHAT?
ANYWAY. NO LIGHTS HAVE COME ON THE WHOLE TIME WE'VE BEEN OUT HERE, AND NO ONE'S COME HOME.
MAYBE THIS AMON GUY IS ALREADY HOME, DO YOU THINK?
THAT'S IT, I'M OFFICIALLY BORED.
I'M GOING IN.
WHAT?!
WHAT'S THE WORST THAT CAN HAPPEN? NOBODY'LL SEE ME IF I DON'T WANT THEM TO, AND NOTHING CAN TOUCH ME...

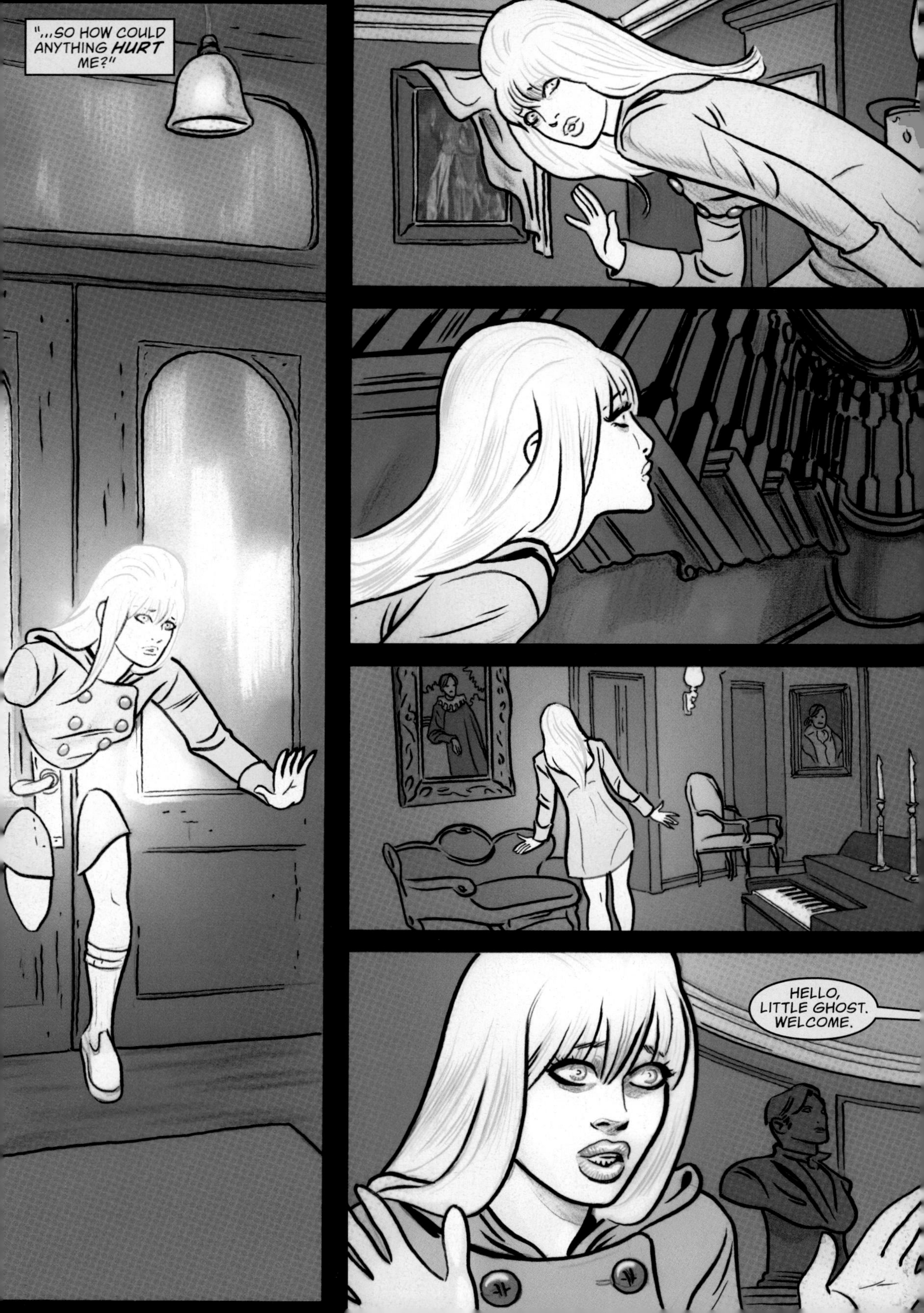
"...SO HOW COULD ANYTHING HURT ME?"
HELLO, LITTLE GHOST. WELCOME.

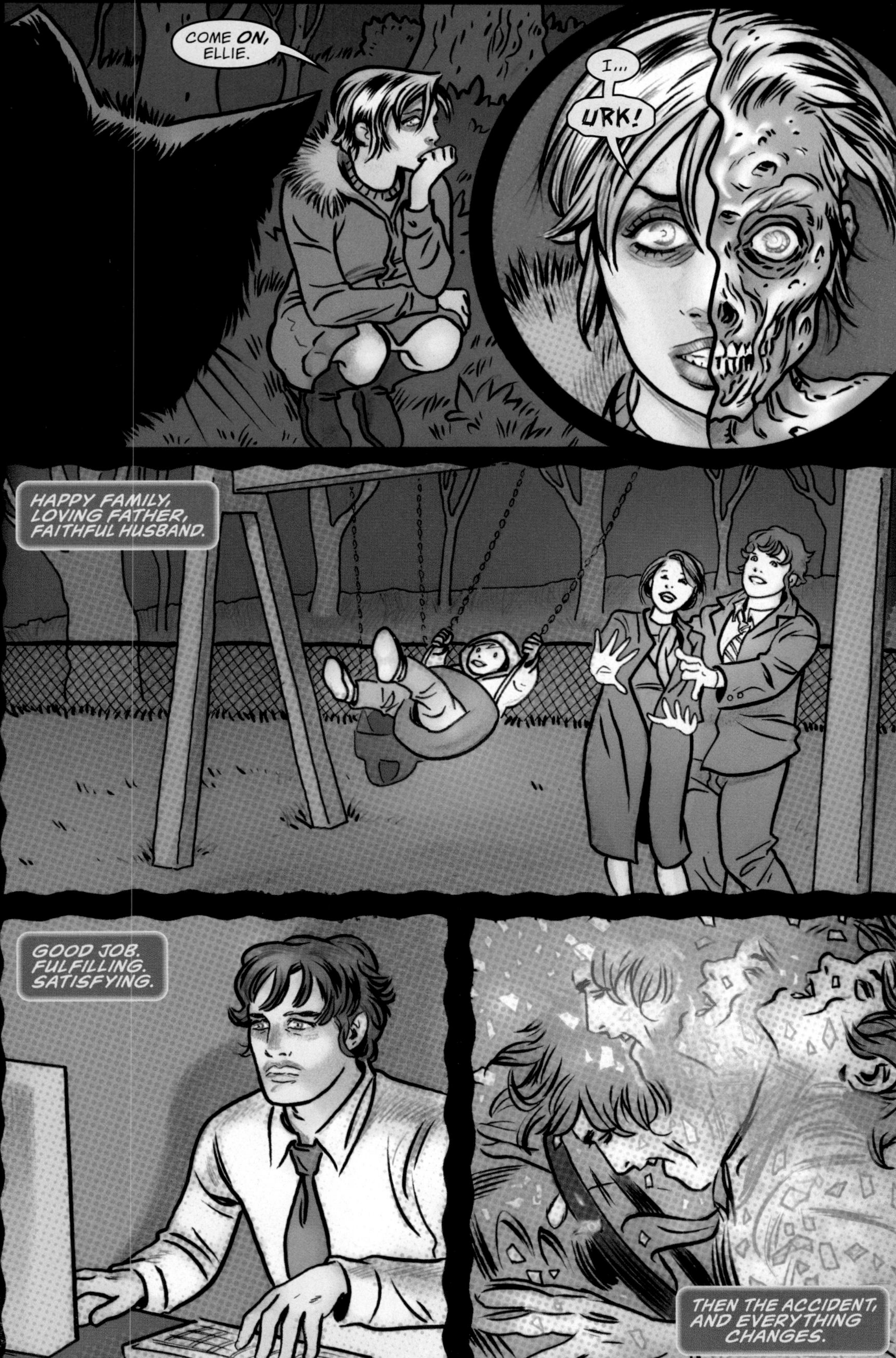
COME ON, ELLIE.
I...
URK!
HAPPY FAMILY, LOVING FATHER, FAITHFUL HUSBAND.
GOOD JOB. FULFILLING. SATISFYING.
THEN THE ACCIDENT, AND EVERYTHING CHANGES.

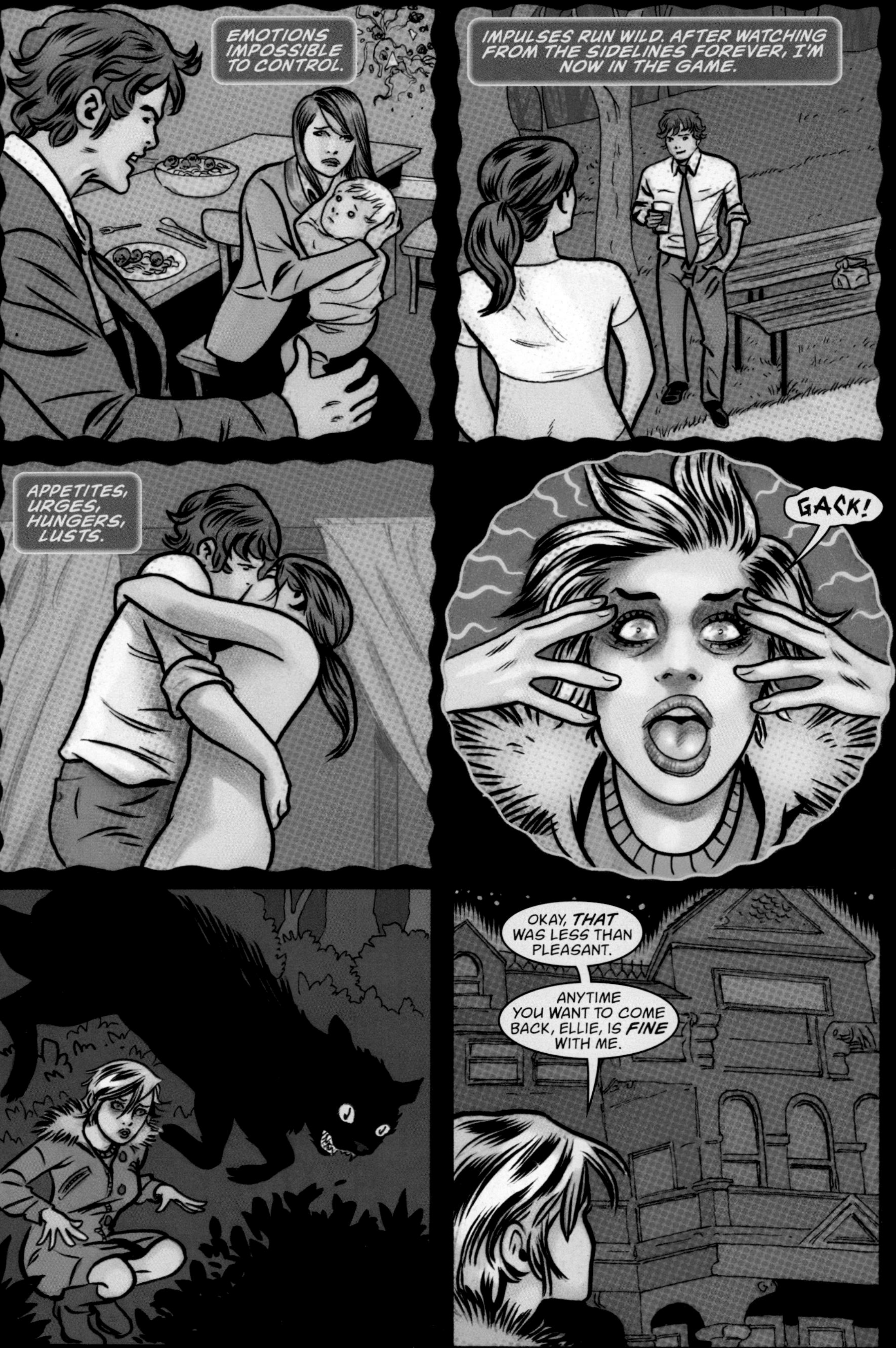
EMOTIONS IMPOSSIBLE TO CONTROL.
IMPULSES RUN WILD. AFTER WATCHING FROM THE SIDELINES FOREVER, I'M NOW IN THE GAME.
APPETITES, URGES, HUNGERS, LUSTS.
GACK!
OKAY, THAT WAS LESS THAN PLEASANT.
ANYTIME YOU WANT TO COME BACK, ELLIE, IS FINE WITH ME.

ALL RIGHT, *FINE.*

IF YOU'RE NOT COMING *OUT,* I'M GOING *IN.*

DON'T GO IN, DANGER, DON'T GO IN, DANGER.

OKAY, FRED, I GET THE PICTURE.

Great. The ghost girl doesn't think to open the latch from the inside.

MMM....

A plus about the whole zom thing? Ex strong an resistant to pain.

SMAS

Not so great? The whole "not healing well" thing.

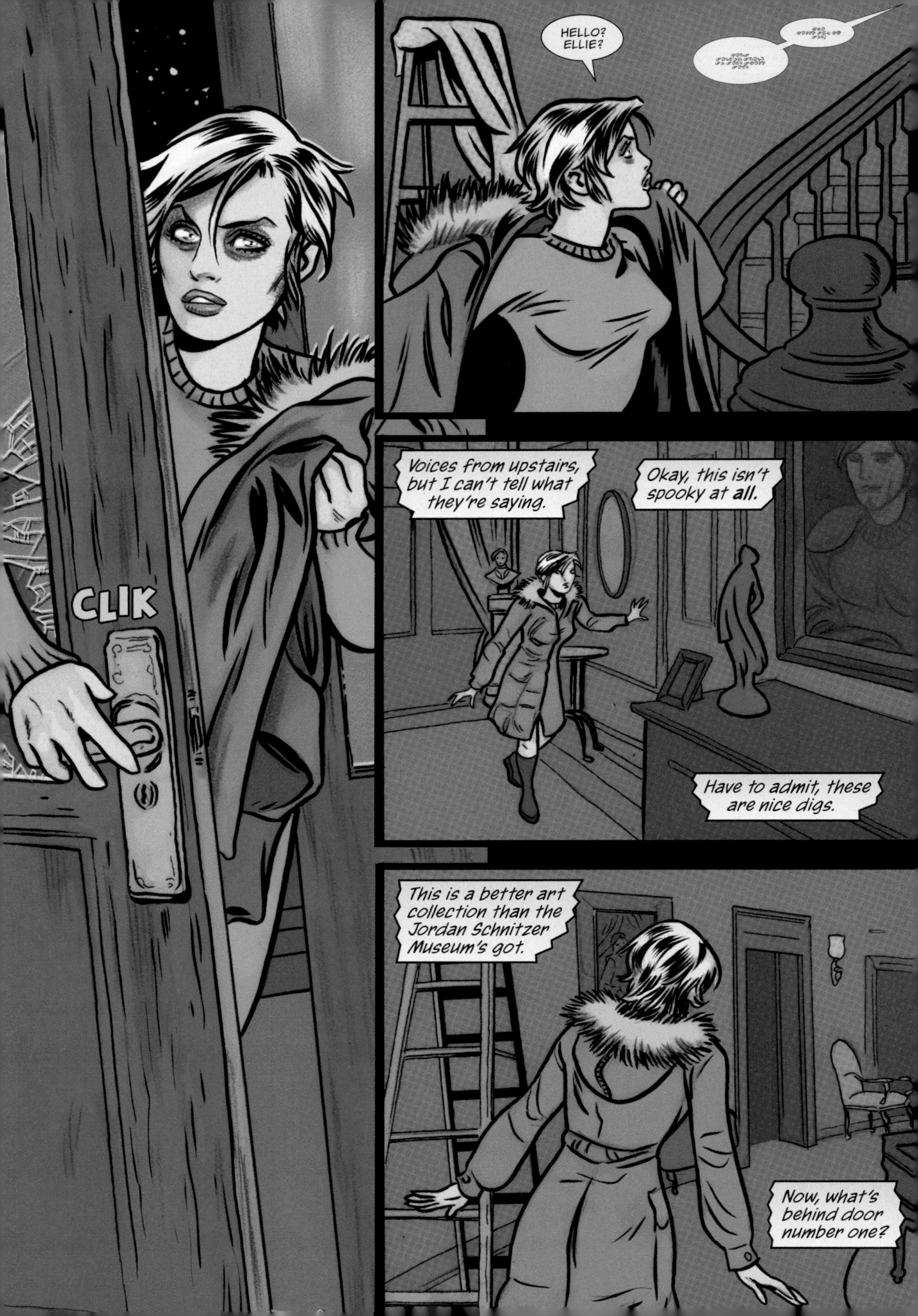
CLIK
HELLO? ELLIE?
Voices from upstairs, but I can't tell what they're saying.
Okay, this isn't spooky at all.
Have to admit, these are nice digs.
This is a better art collection than the Jordan Schnitzer Museum's got.
Now, what's behind door number one?

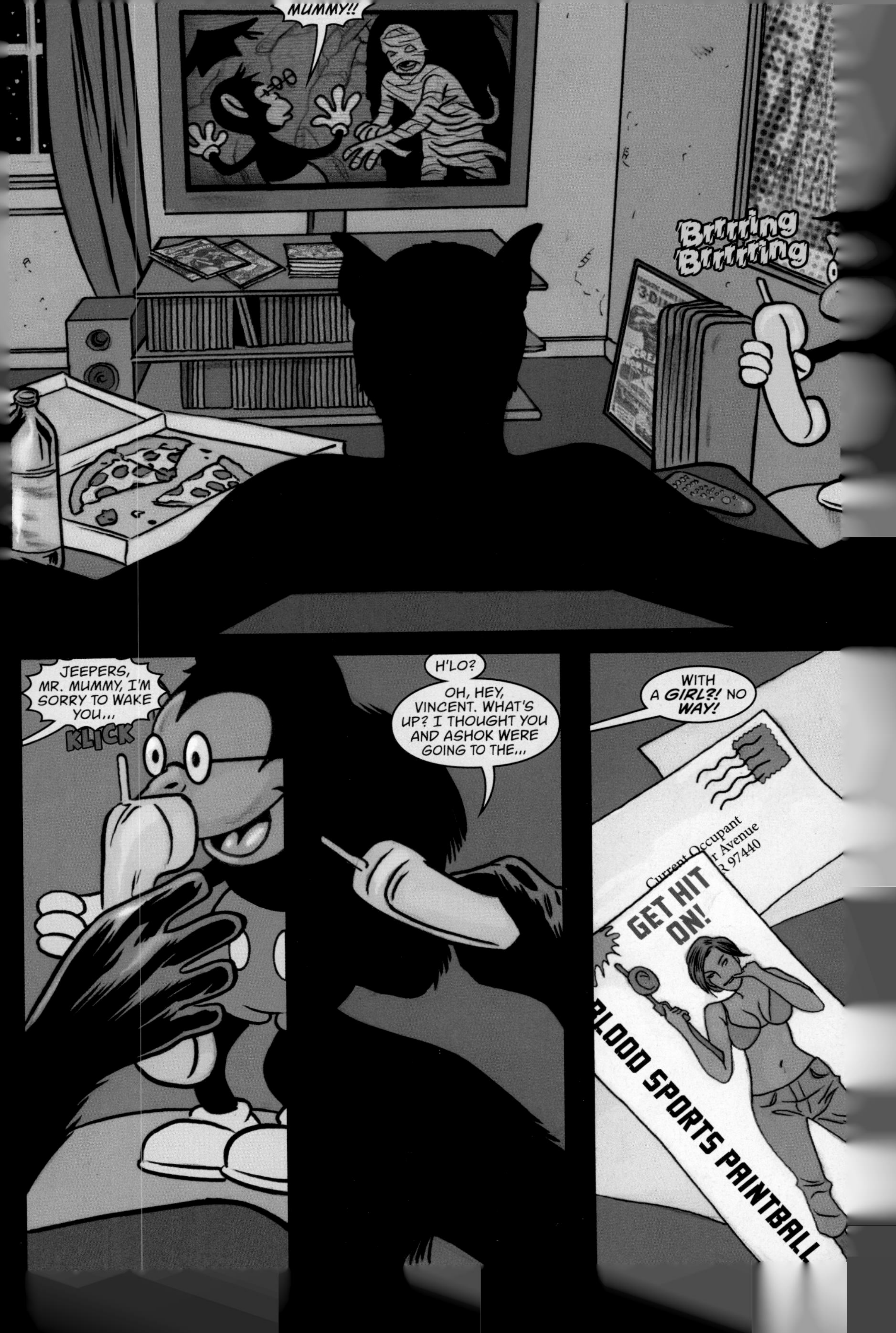
MUMMY!!
BRRRRING BRRRRRING
JEEPERS, MR. MUMMY, I'M SORRY TO WAKE YOU...
KLICK
H'LO?
OH, HEY, VINCENT. WHAT'S UP? I THOUGHT YOU AND ASHOK WERE GOING TO THE...
WITH A GIRL?! NO WAY!
Current Occupant
GET HIT ON!
BLOOD SPORTS PAINTBALL

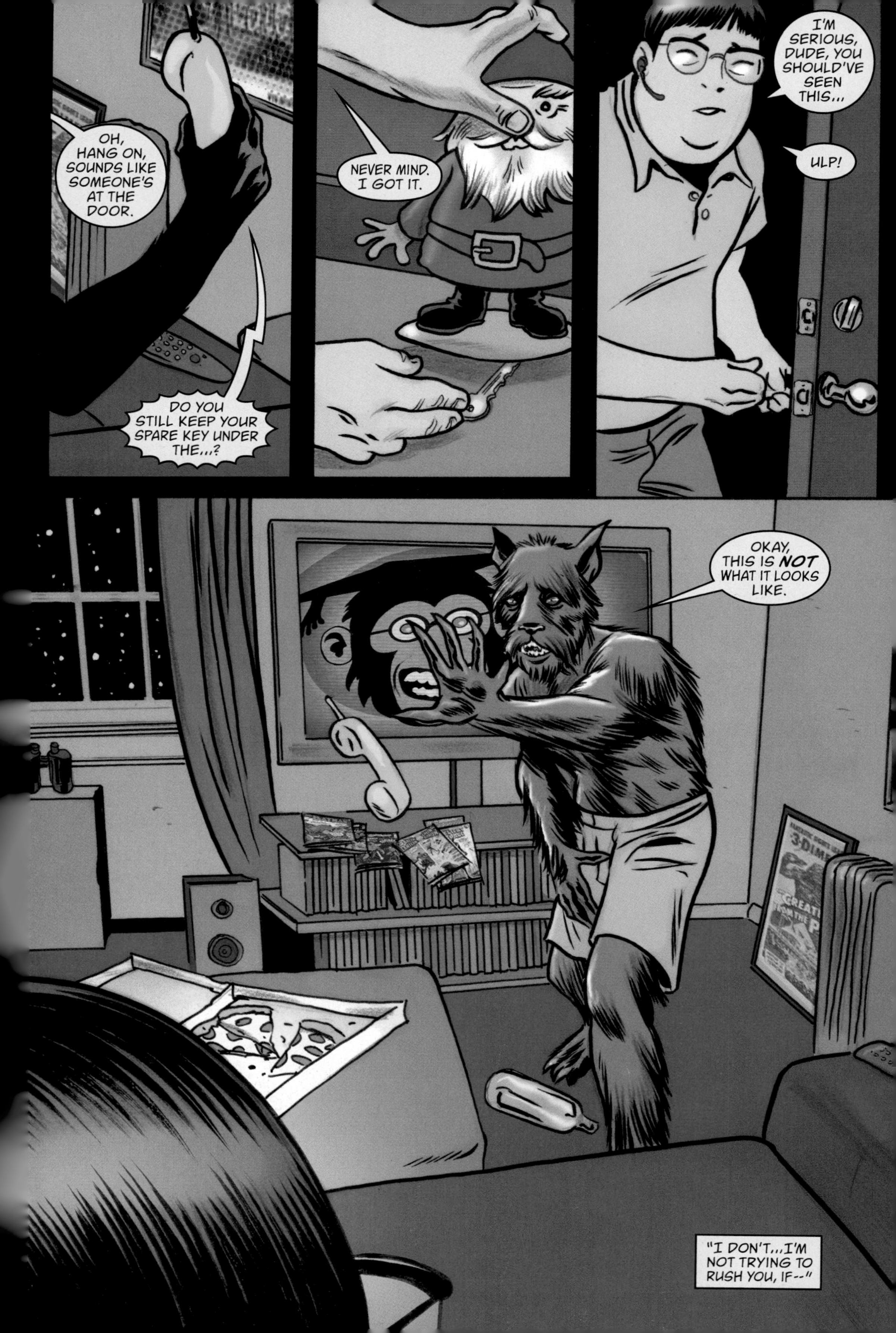
OH, HANG ON, SOUNDS LIKE SOMEONE'S AT THE DOOR.
DO YOU STILL KEEP YOUR SPARE KEY UNDER THE...?
NEVER MIND. I GOT IT.
I'M SERIOUS, DUDE, YOU SHOULD'VE SEEN THIS...
ULP!
OKAY, THIS IS **NOT** WHAT IT LOOKS LIKE.
"I DON'T...I'M NOT TRYING TO RUSH YOU, IF--"

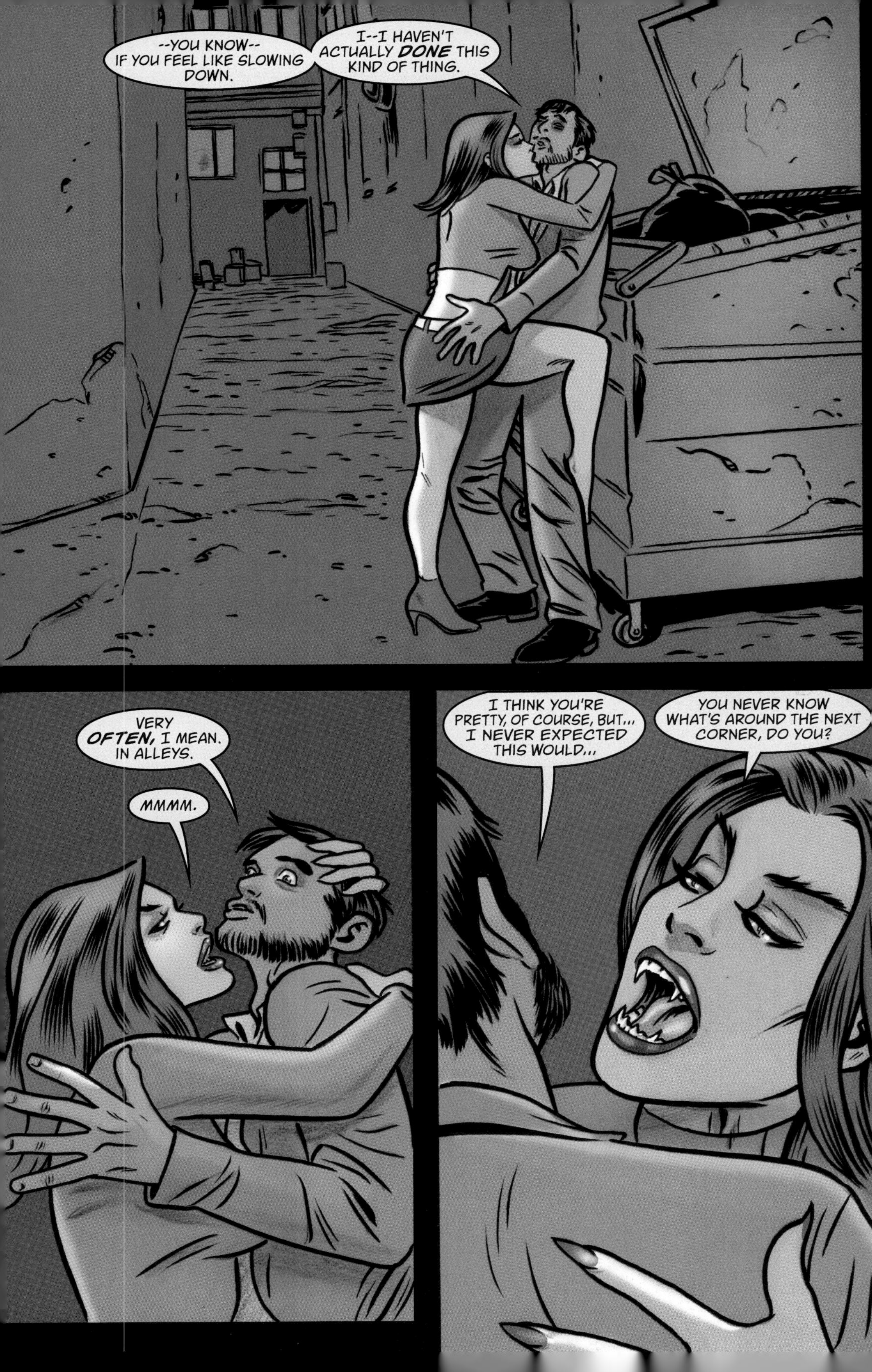
--YOU KNOW-- IF YOU FEEL LIKE SLOWING DOWN.
I--I HAVEN'T ACTUALLY DONE THIS KIND OF THING.
VERY OFTEN, I MEAN. IN ALLEYS.
MMMM.
I THINK YOU'RE PRETTY, OF COURSE, BUT... I NEVER EXPECTED THIS WOULD...
YOU NEVER KNOW WHAT'S AROUND THE NEXT CORNER, DO YOU?

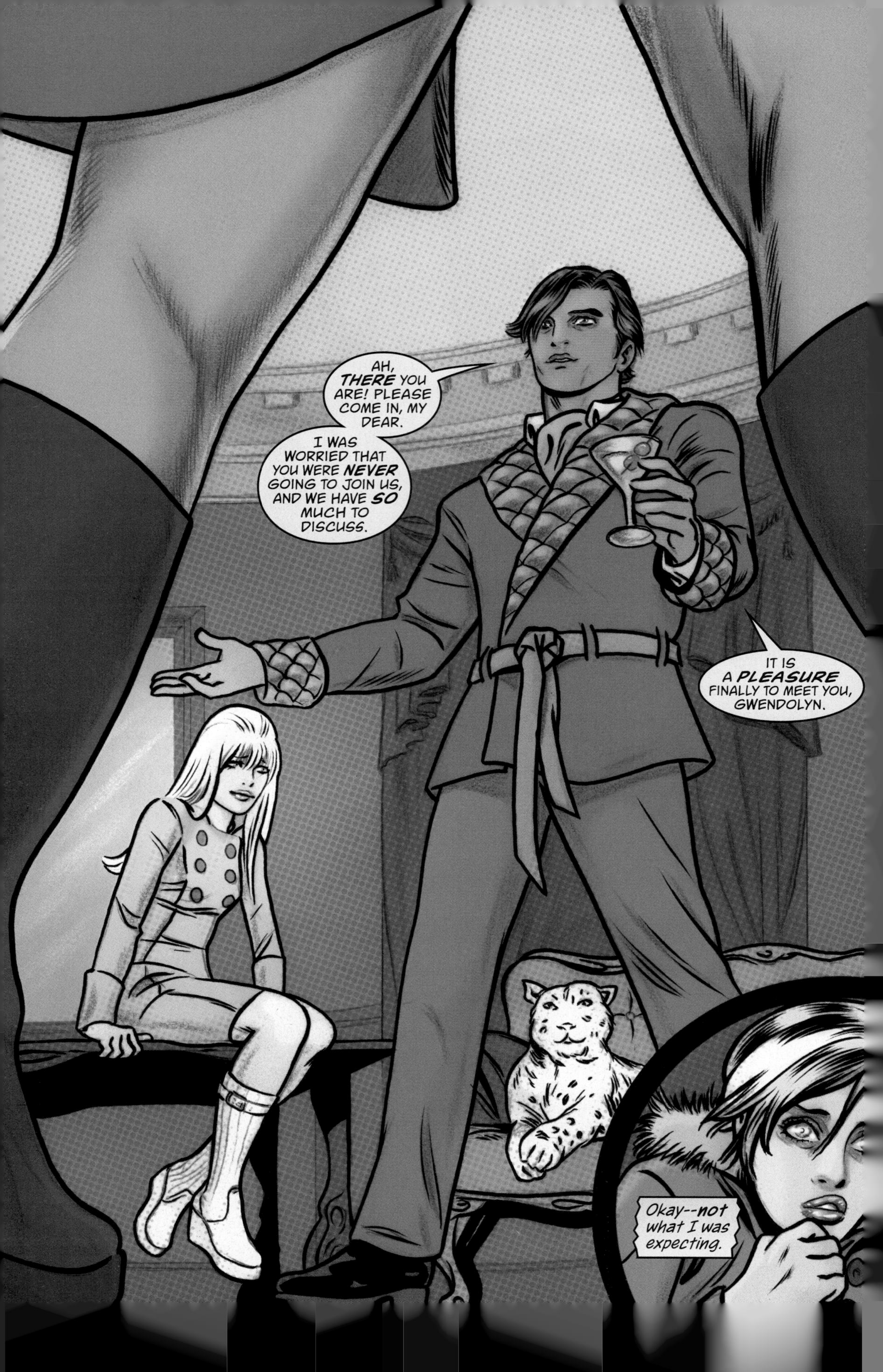
AH, THERE YOU ARE! PLEASE COME IN, MY DEAR.
I WAS WORRIED THAT YOU WERE NEVER GOING TO JOIN US, AND WE HAVE SO MUCH TO DISCUSS.
IT IS A PLEASURE FINALLY TO MEET YOU, GWENDOLYN.
Okay--not what I was expecting.

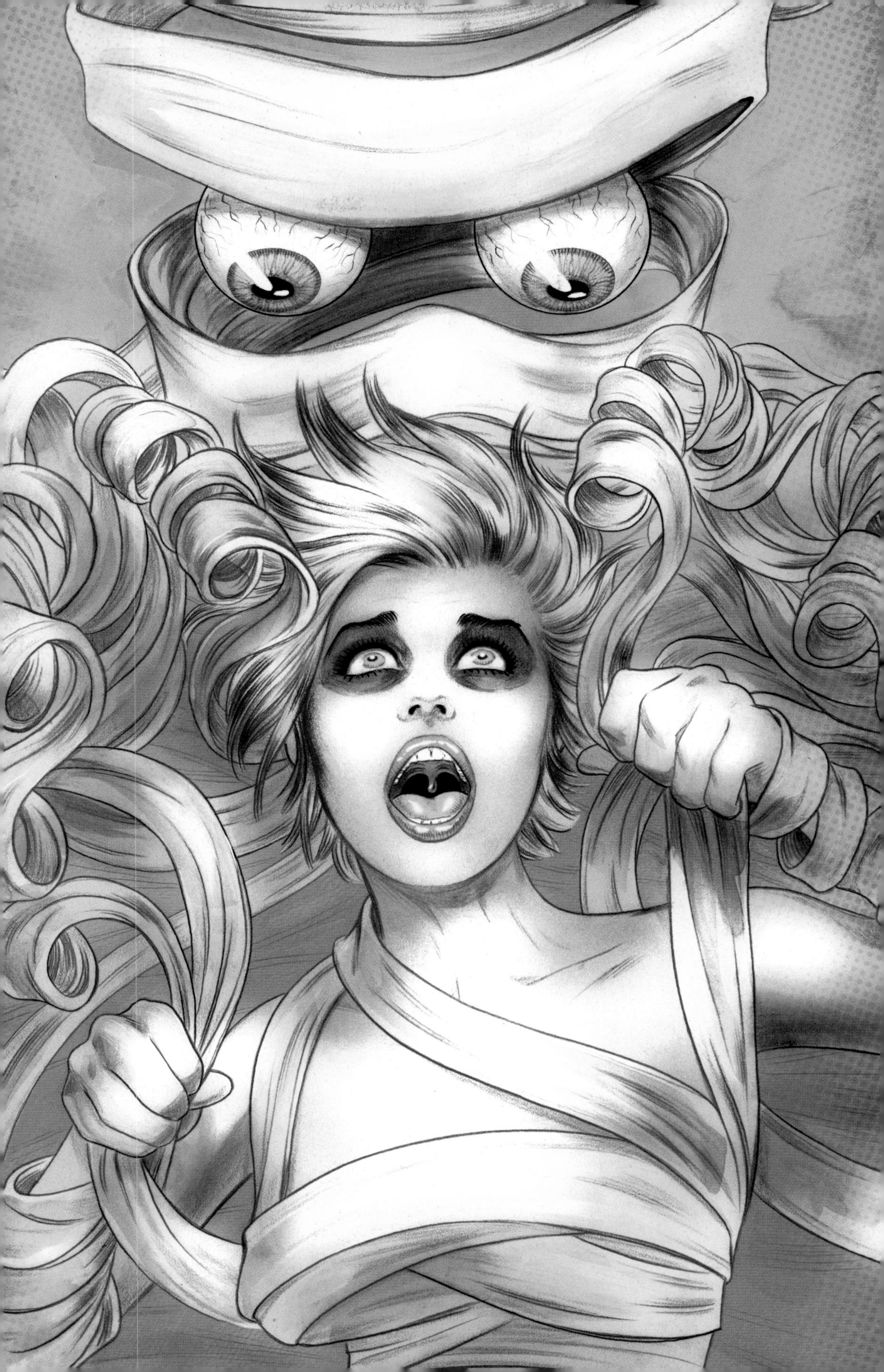

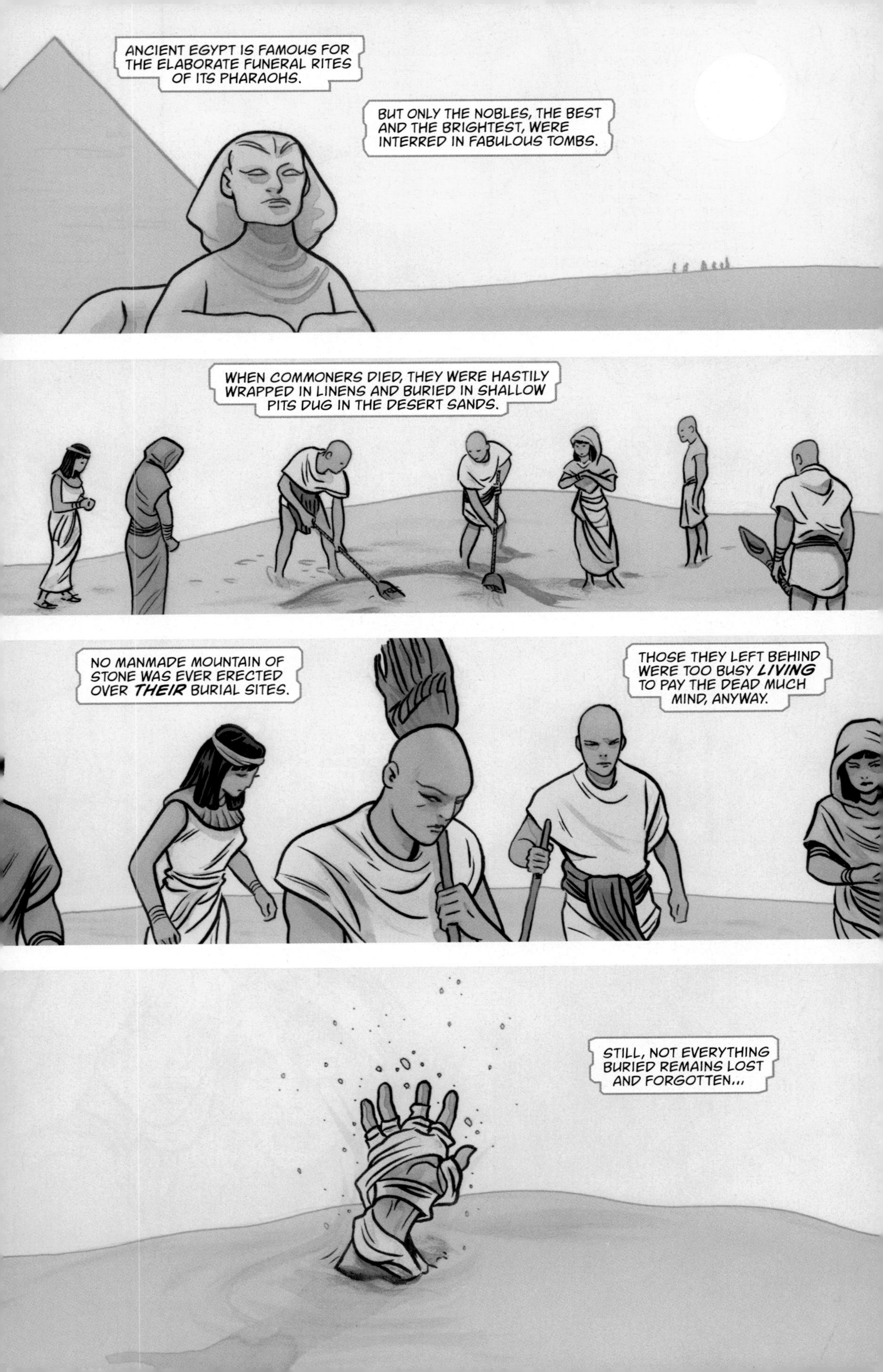
ANCIENT EGYPT IS FAMOUS FOR THE ELABORATE FUNERAL RITES OF ITS PHARAOHS.
BUT ONLY THE NOBLES, THE BEST AND THE BRIGHTEST, WERE INTERRED IN FABULOUS TOMBS.
WHEN COMMONERS DIED, THEY WERE HASTILY WRAPPED IN LINENS AND BURIED IN SHALLOW PITS DUG IN THE DESERT SANDS.
NO MANMADE MOUNTAIN OF STONE WAS EVER ERECTED OVER *THEIR* BURIAL SITES.
THOSE THEY LEFT BEHIND WERE TOO BUSY *LIVING* TO PAY THE DEAD MUCH MIND, ANYWAY.
STILL, NOT EVERYTHING BURIED REMAINS LOST AND FORGOTTEN...

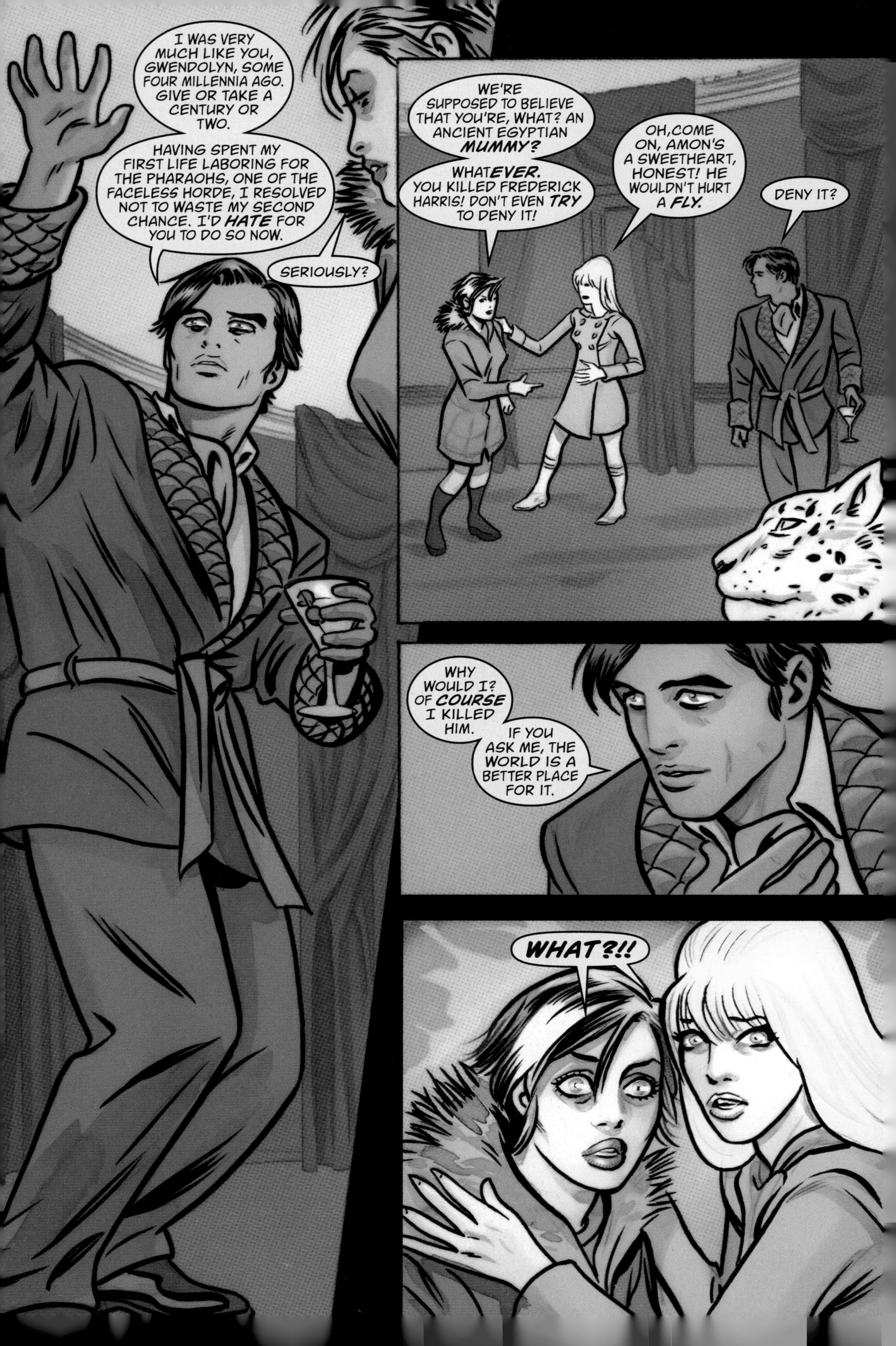

I WAS VERY MUCH LIKE YOU, GWENDOLYN, SOME FOUR MILLENNIA AGO. GIVE OR TAKE A CENTURY OR TWO.
HAVING SPENT MY FIRST LIFE LABORING FOR THE PHARAOHS, ONE OF THE FACELESS HORDE, I RESOLVED NOT TO WASTE MY SECOND CHANCE. I'D HATE FOR YOU TO DO SO NOW.
SERIOUSLY?
WE'RE SUPPOSED TO BELIEVE THAT YOU'RE, WHAT? AN ANCIENT EGYPTIAN MUMMY?
WHATEVER. YOU KILLED FREDERICK HARRIS! DON'T EVEN TRY TO DENY IT!
OH, COME ON, AMON'S A SWEETHEART, HONEST! HE WOULDN'T HURT A FLY.
DENY IT?
WHY WOULD I? OF COURSE I KILLED HIM.
IF YOU ASK ME, THE WORLD IS A BETTER PLACE FOR IT.
WHAT?!!

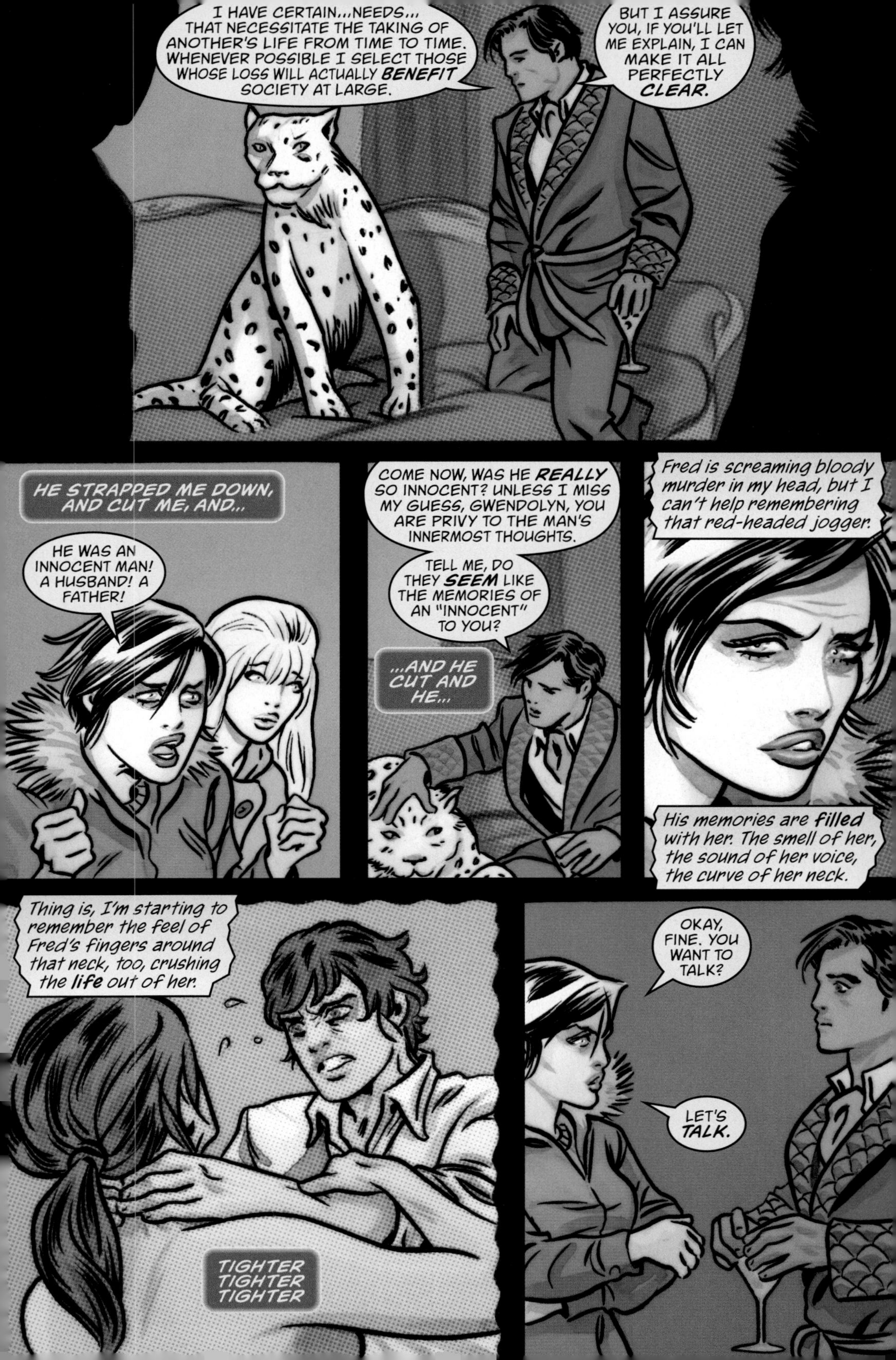
I HAVE CERTAIN...NEEDS... THAT NECESSITATE THE TAKING OF ANOTHER'S LIFE FROM TIME TO TIME. WHENEVER POSSIBLE I SELECT THOSE WHOSE LOSS WILL ACTUALLY BENEFIT SOCIETY AT LARGE.
BUT I ASSURE YOU, IF YOU'LL LET ME EXPLAIN, I CAN MAKE IT ALL PERFECTLY CLEAR.
HE STRAPPED ME DOWN, AND CUT ME, AND...
HE WAS AN INNOCENT MAN! A HUSBAND! A FATHER!
COME NOW, WAS HE REALLY SO INNOCENT? UNLESS I MISS MY GUESS, GWENDOLYN, YOU ARE PRIVY TO THE MAN'S INNERMOST THOUGHTS.
TELL ME, DO THEY SEEM LIKE THE MEMORIES OF AN "INNOCENT" TO YOU?
...AND HE CUT AND HE...
Fred is screaming bloody murder in my head, but I can't help remembering that red-headed jogger.
His memories are filled with her. The smell of her, the sound of her voice, the curve of her neck.
Thing is, I'm starting to remember the feel of Fred's fingers around that neck, too, crushing the life out of her.
TIGHTER TIGHTER TIGHTER
OKAY, FINE. YOU WANT TO TALK?
LET'S TALK.

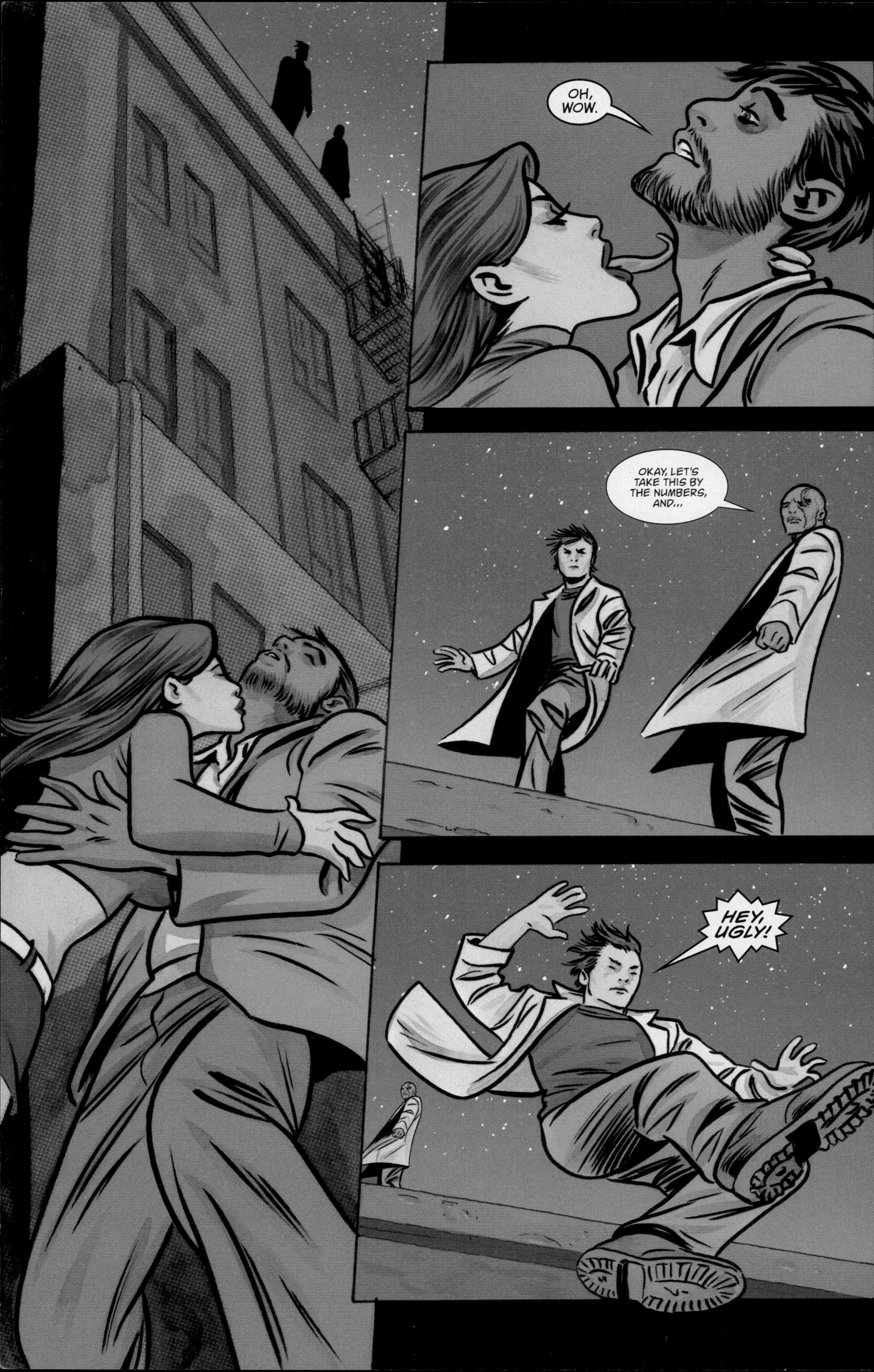
OH, WOW.
OKAY, LET'S TAKE THIS BY THE NUMBERS, AND...
HEY, UGLY!

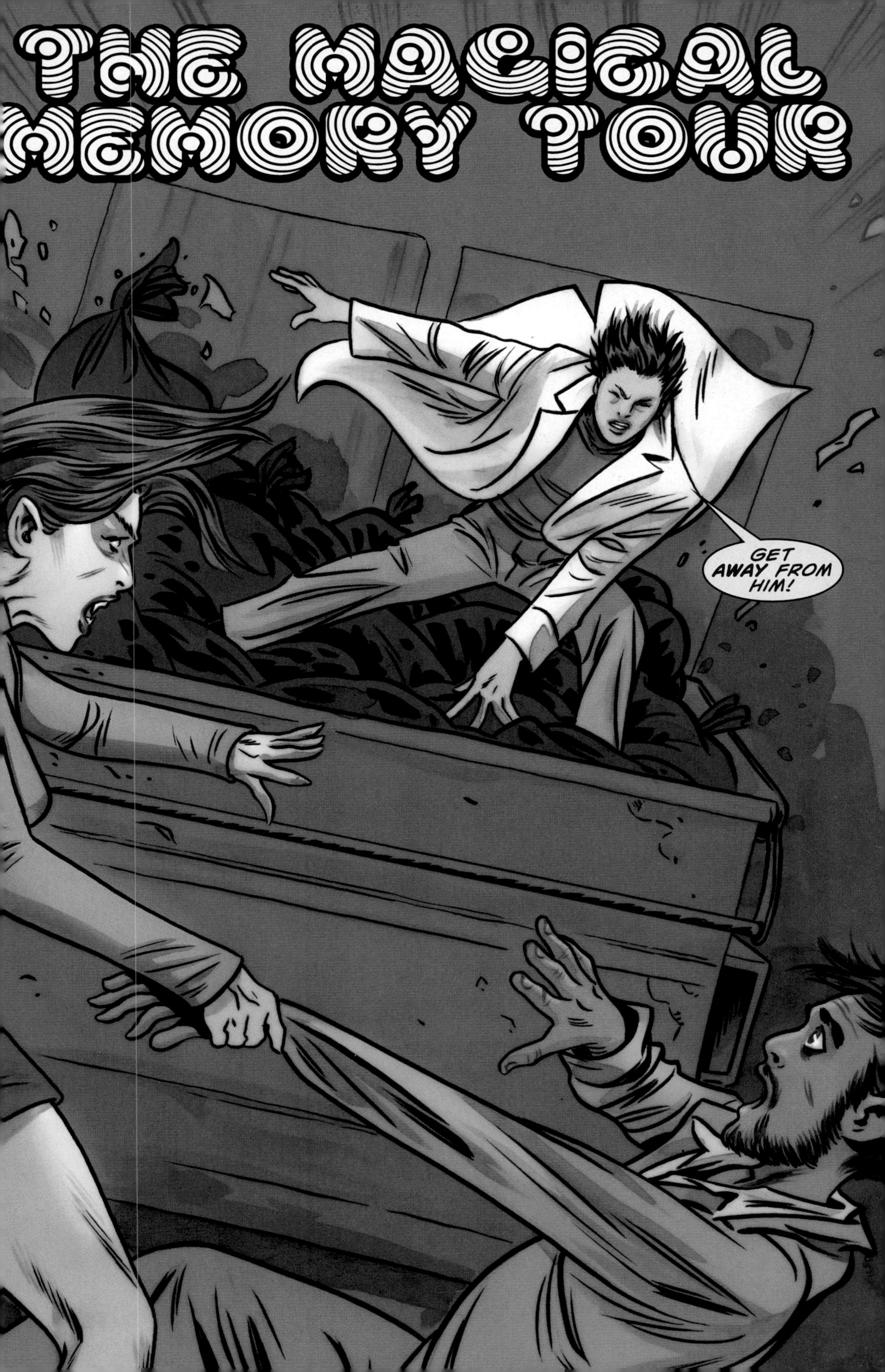
THE MAGICAL MEMORY TOUR
GET AWAY FROM HIM!

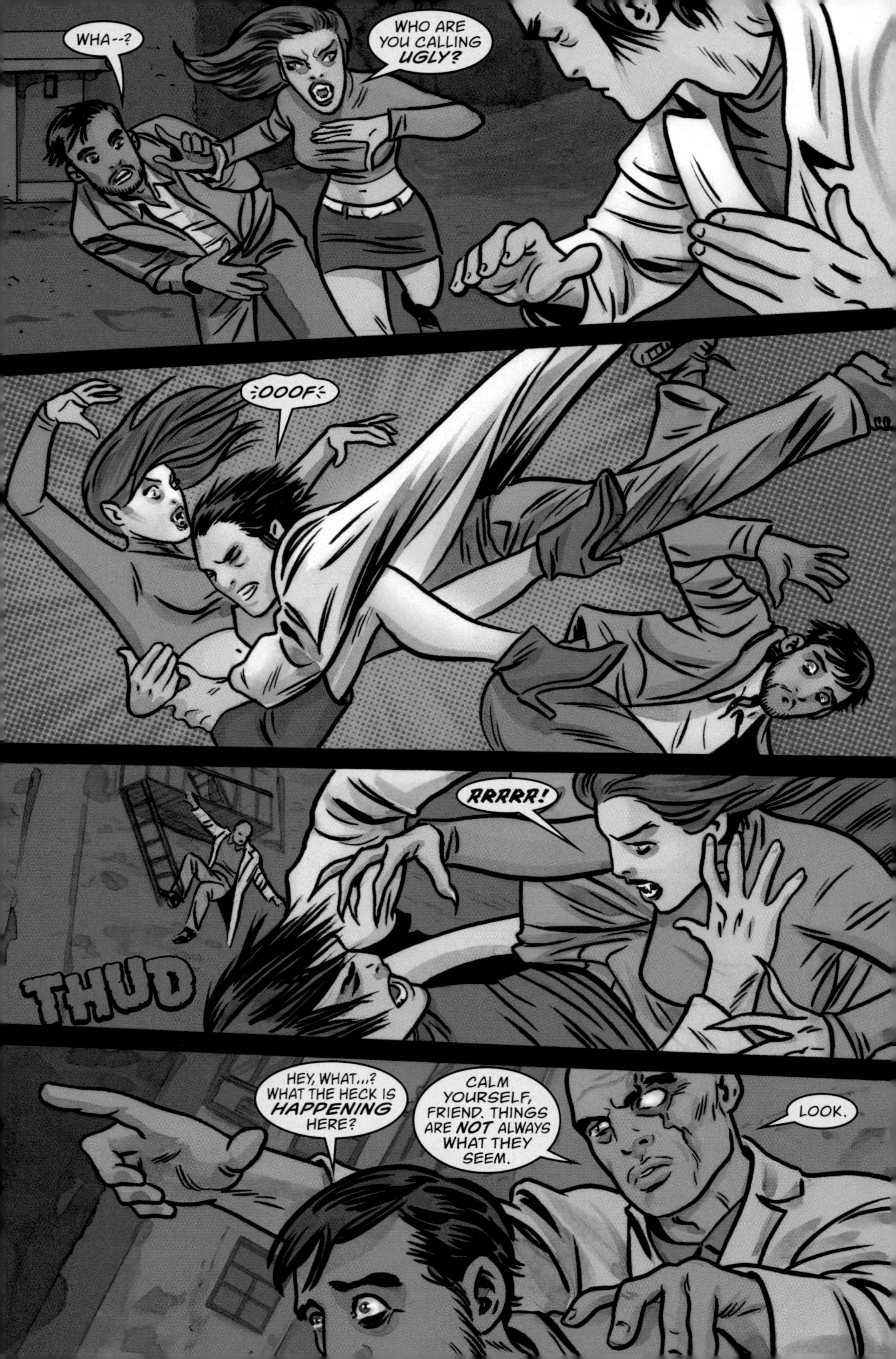
WHA--?
WHO ARE YOU CALLING UGLY?
OOOF
RRRRR!
THUD
HEY, WHAT...? WHAT THE HECK IS HAPPENING HERE?
CALM YOURSELF, FRIEND. THINGS ARE NOT ALWAYS WHAT THEY SEEM.
LOOK.

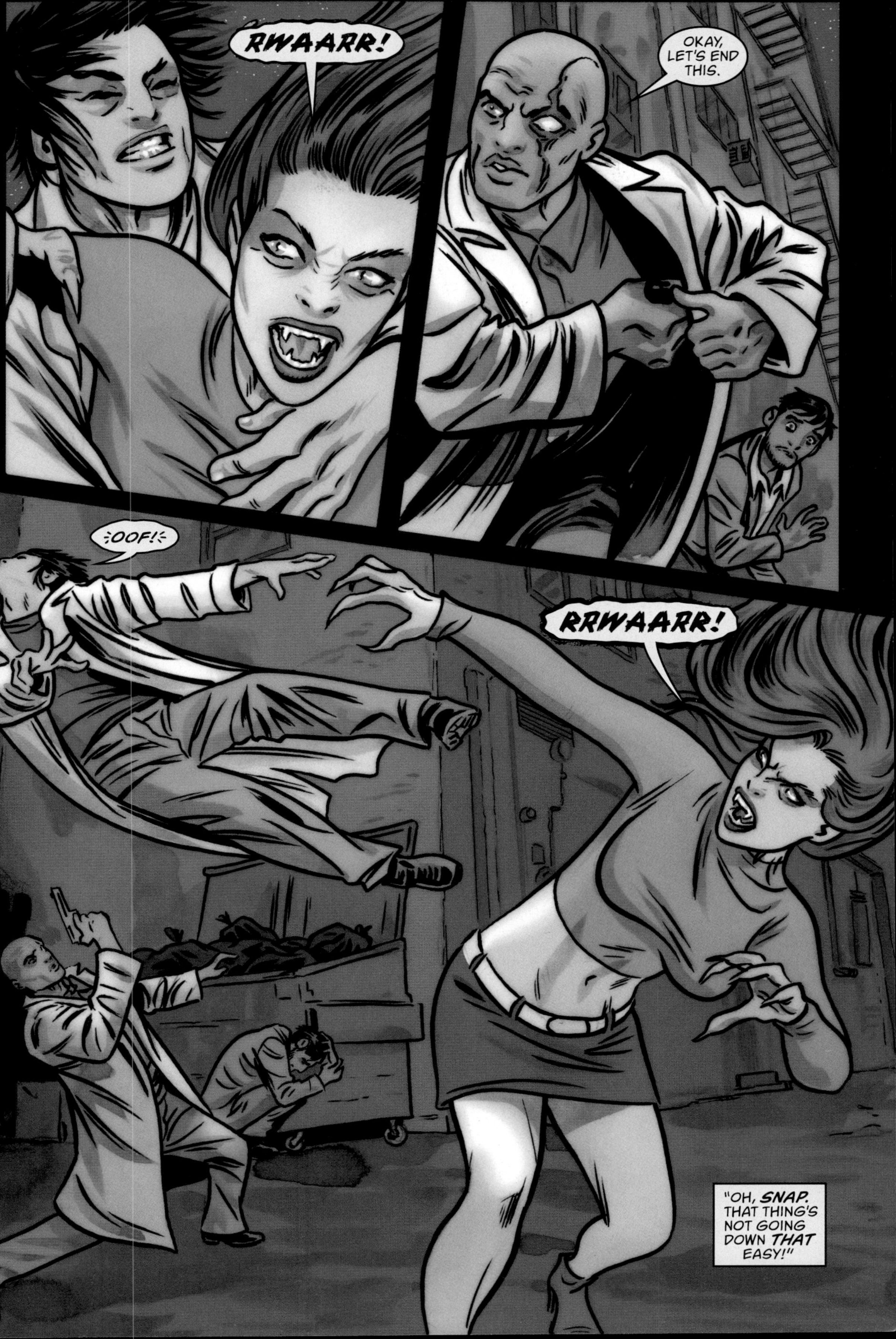
RWAARR!
OKAY, LET'S END THIS.
OOF!
RRWAARR!
"OH, SNAP. THAT THING'S NOT GOING DOWN THAT EASY!"

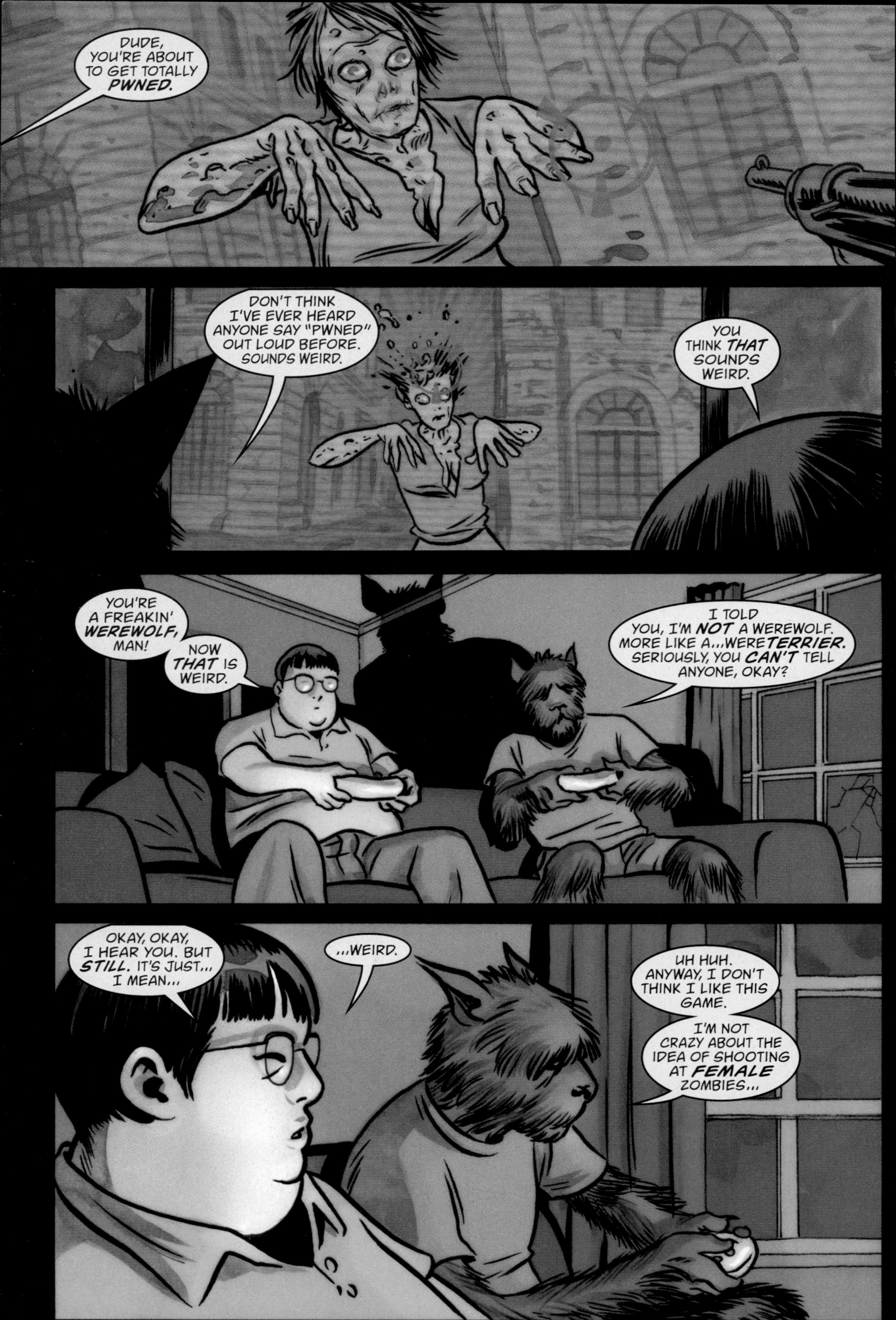
DUDE, YOU'RE ABOUT TO GET TOTALLY PWNED.
DON'T THINK I'VE EVER HEARD ANYONE SAY "PWNED" OUT LOUD BEFORE. SOUNDS WEIRD.
YOU THINK THAT SOUNDS WEIRD.
YOU'RE A FREAKIN' WEREWOLF, MAN!
NOW THAT IS WEIRD.
I TOLD YOU, I'M NOT A WEREWOLF. MORE LIKE A...WERETERRIER. SERIOUSLY, YOU CAN'T TELL ANYONE, OKAY?
OKAY, OKAY, I HEAR YOU. BUT STILL. IT'S JUST... I MEAN...
...WEIRD.
UH HUH. ANYWAY, I DON'T THINK I LIKE THIS GAME.
I'M NOT CRAZY ABOUT THE IDEA OF SHOOTING AT FEMALE ZOMBIES...

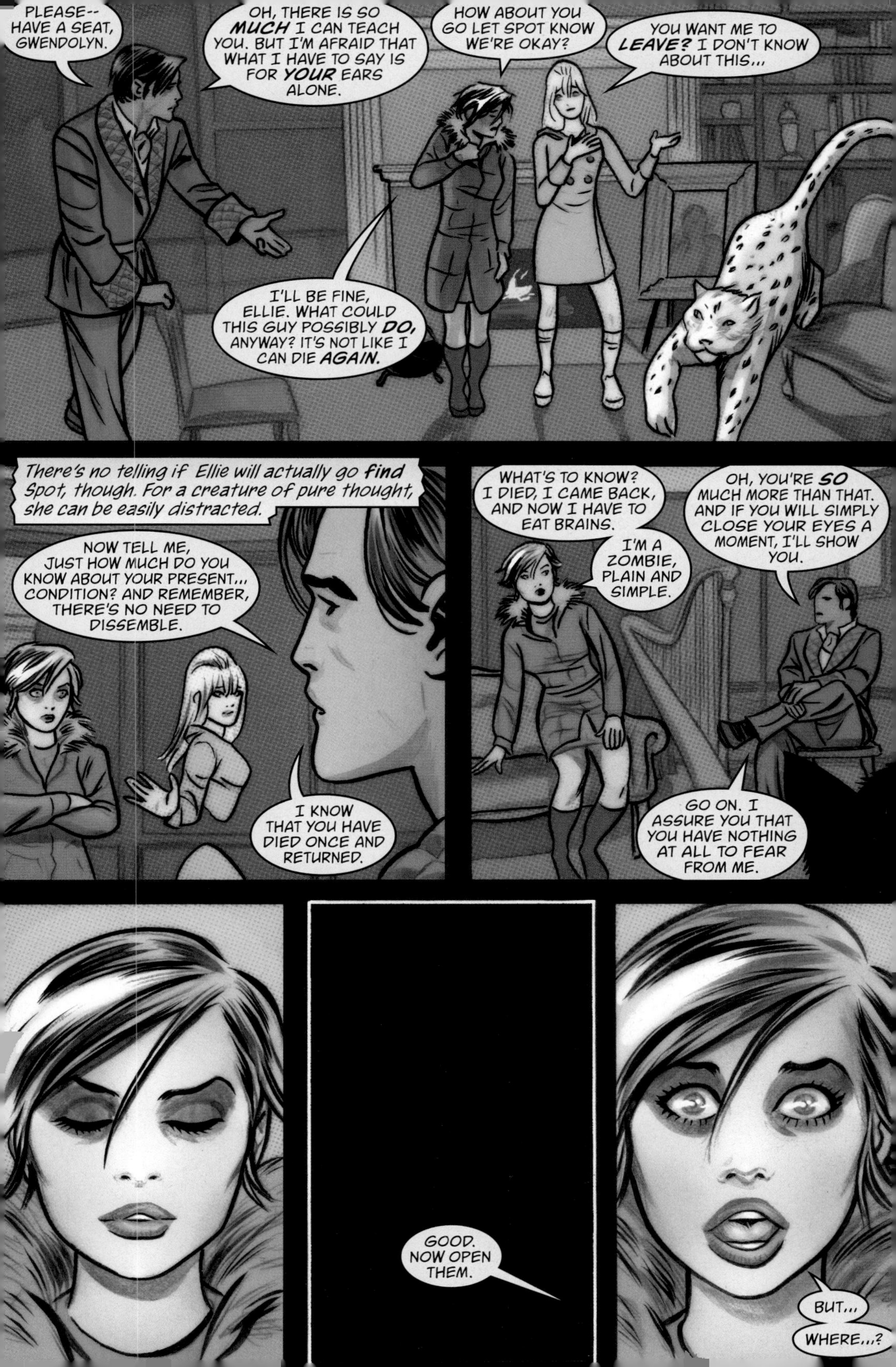
PLEASE-- HAVE A SEAT, GWENDOLYN.
OH, THERE IS SO *MUCH* I CAN TEACH YOU. BUT I'M AFRAID THAT WHAT I HAVE TO SAY IS FOR *YOUR* EARS ALONE.
HOW ABOUT YOU GO LET SPOT KNOW WE'RE OKAY?
YOU WANT ME TO *LEAVE?* I DON'T KNOW ABOUT THIS...
I'LL BE FINE, ELLIE. WHAT COULD THIS GUY POSSIBLY *DO,* ANYWAY? IT'S NOT LIKE I CAN DIE *AGAIN.*
*There's no telling if Ellie will actually go **find** Spot, though. For a creature of pure thought, she can be easily distracted.*
NOW TELL ME, JUST HOW MUCH DO YOU KNOW ABOUT YOUR PRESENT... CONDITION? AND REMEMBER, THERE'S NO NEED TO DISSEMBLE.
I KNOW THAT YOU HAVE DIED ONCE AND RETURNED.
WHAT'S TO KNOW? I DIED, I CAME BACK, AND NOW I HAVE TO EAT BRAINS.
I'M A ZOMBIE, PLAIN AND SIMPLE.
OH, YOU'RE *SO* MUCH MORE THAN THAT. AND IF YOU WILL SIMPLY CLOSE YOUR EYES A MOMENT, I'LL SHOW YOU.
GO ON. I ASSURE YOU THAT YOU HAVE NOTHING AT ALL TO FEAR FROM ME.
GOOD. NOW OPEN THEM.
BUT...
WHERE...?

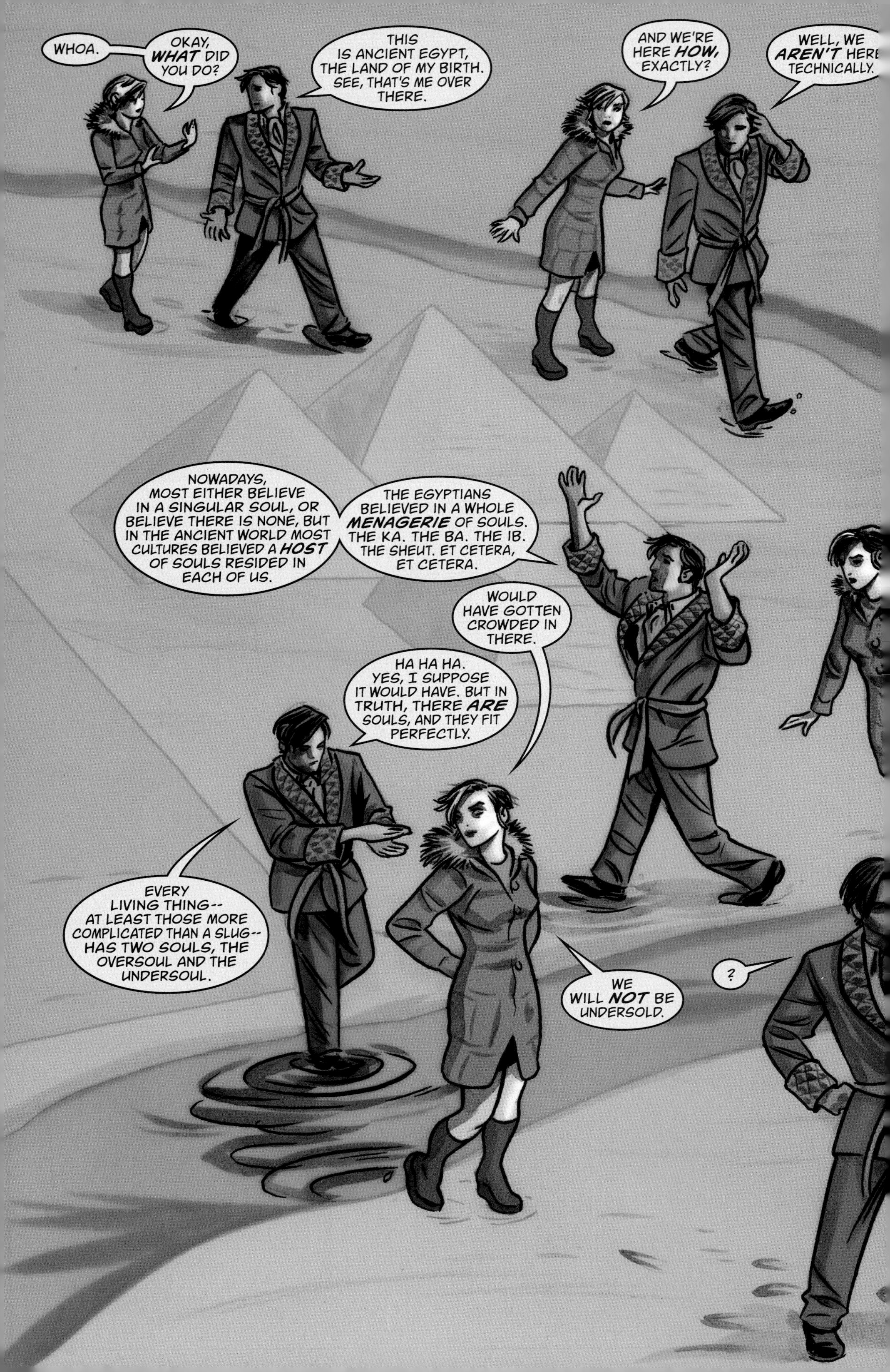
WHOA.
OKAY, WHAT DID YOU DO?
THIS IS ANCIENT EGYPT, THE LAND OF MY BIRTH. SEE, THAT'S ME OVER THERE.
AND WE'RE HERE HOW, EXACTLY?
WELL, WE AREN'T HERE TECHNICALLY.
NOWADAYS, MOST EITHER BELIEVE IN A SINGULAR SOUL, OR BELIEVE THERE IS NONE, BUT IN THE ANCIENT WORLD MOST CULTURES BELIEVED A HOST OF SOULS RESIDED IN EACH OF US.
THE EGYPTIANS BELIEVED IN A WHOLE MENAGERIE OF SOULS. THE KA. THE BA. THE IB. THE SHEUT. ET CETERA, ET CETERA.
WOULD HAVE GOTTEN CROWDED IN THERE.
HA HA HA. YES, I SUPPOSE IT WOULD HAVE. BUT IN TRUTH, THERE ARE SOULS, AND THEY FIT PERFECTLY.
EVERY LIVING THING-- AT LEAST THOSE MORE COMPLICATED THAN A SLUG-- HAS TWO SOULS, THE OVERSOUL AND THE UNDERSOUL.
WE WILL NOT BE UNDERSOLD.
?

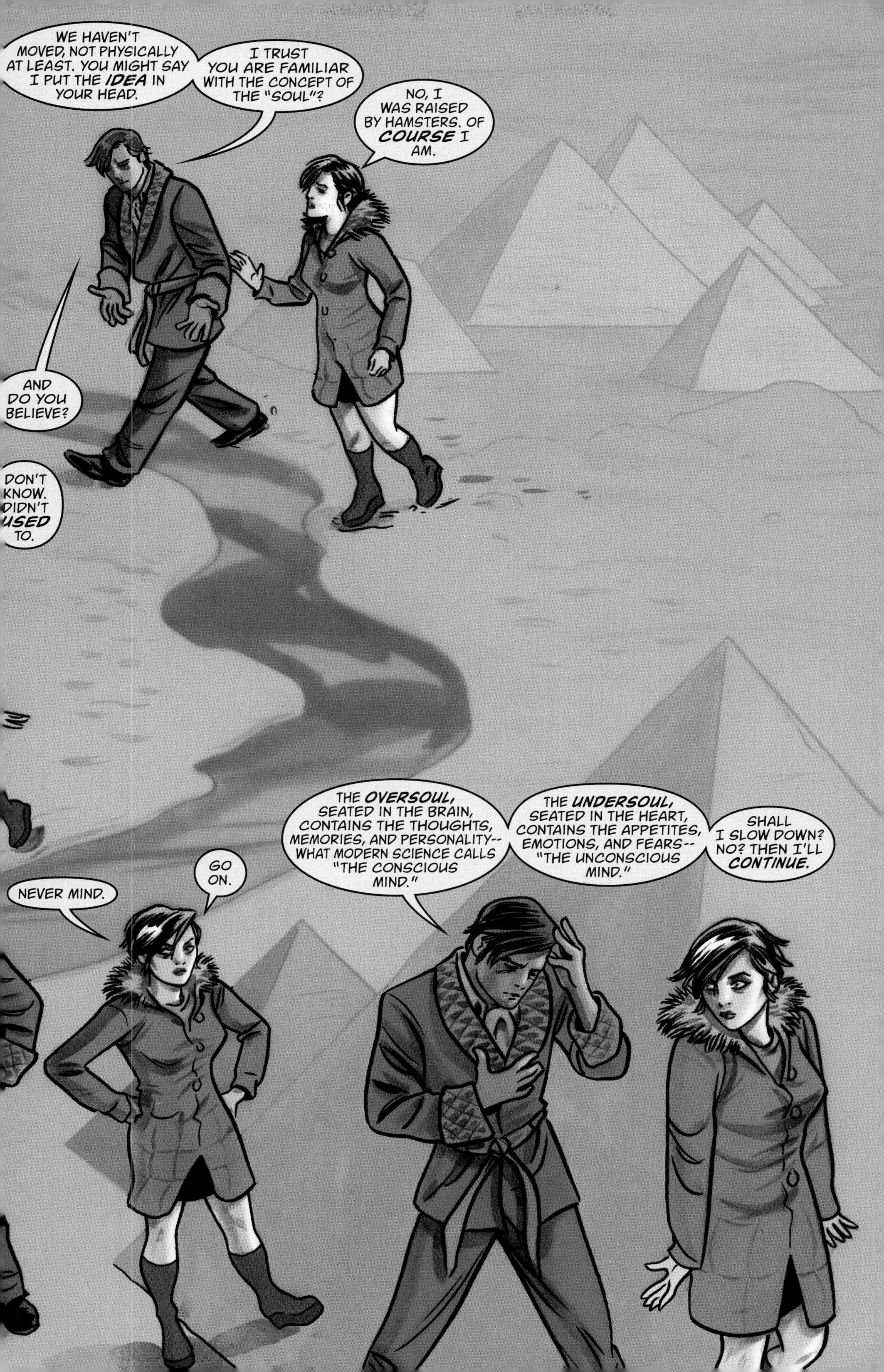
WE HAVEN'T MOVED, NOT PHYSICALLY AT LEAST. YOU MIGHT SAY I PUT THE *IDEA* IN YOUR HEAD.
I TRUST YOU ARE FAMILIAR WITH THE CONCEPT OF THE "SOUL"?
NO, I WAS RAISED BY HAMSTERS. OF *COURSE* I AM.
AND DO YOU BELIEVE?
DON'T KNOW. DIDN'T *USED* TO.
NEVER MIND.
GO ON.
THE *OVERSOUL,* SEATED IN THE BRAIN, CONTAINS THE THOUGHTS, MEMORIES, AND PERSONALITY-- WHAT MODERN SCIENCE CALLS "THE CONSCIOUS MIND."
THE *UNDERSOUL,* SEATED IN THE HEART, CONTAINS THE APPETITES, EMOTIONS, AND FEARS-- "THE UNCONSCIOUS MIND."
SHALL I SLOW DOWN? NO? THEN I'LL *CONTINUE.*

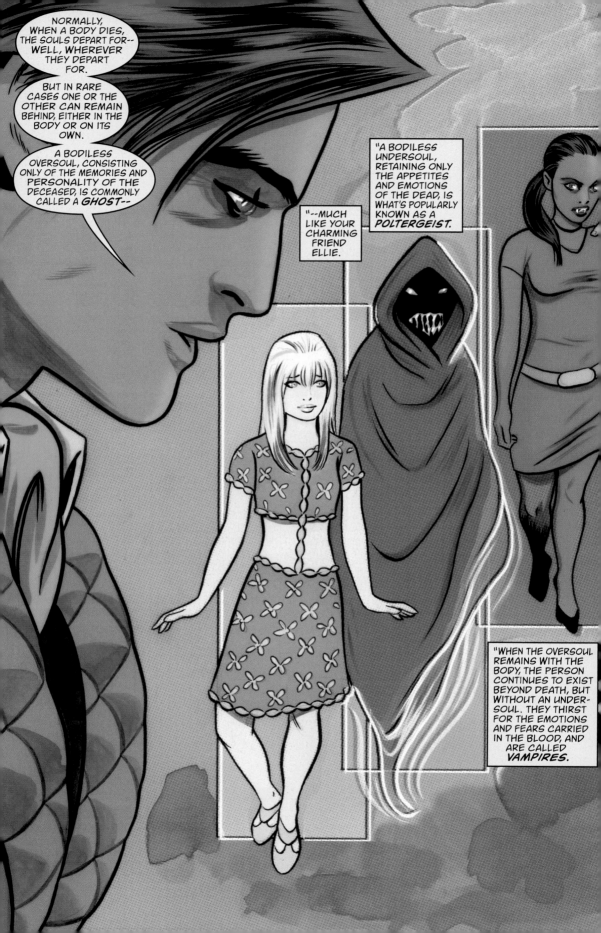

NORMALLY, WHEN A BODY DIES, THE SOULS DEPART FOR-- WELL, WHEREVER THEY DEPART FOR.

BUT IN RARE CASES ONE OR THE OTHER CAN REMAIN BEHIND, EITHER IN THE BODY OR ON ITS OWN.

A BODILESS OVERSOUL, CONSISTING ONLY OF THE MEMORIES AND PERSONALITY OF THE DECEASED, IS COMMONLY CALLED A *GHOST*--

"--MUCH LIKE YOUR CHARMING FRIEND ELLIE.

"A BODILESS UNDERSOUL, RETAINING ONLY THE APPETITES AND EMOTIONS OF THE DEAD, IS WHAT'S POPULARLY KNOWN AS A *POLTERGEIST.*

"WHEN THE OVERSOUL REMAINS WITH THE BODY, THE PERSON CONTINUES TO EXIST BEYOND DEATH, BUT WITHOUT AN UNDER-SOUL. THEY THIRST FOR THE EMOTIONS AND FEARS CARRIED IN THE BLOOD, AND ARE CALLED *VAMPIRES.*

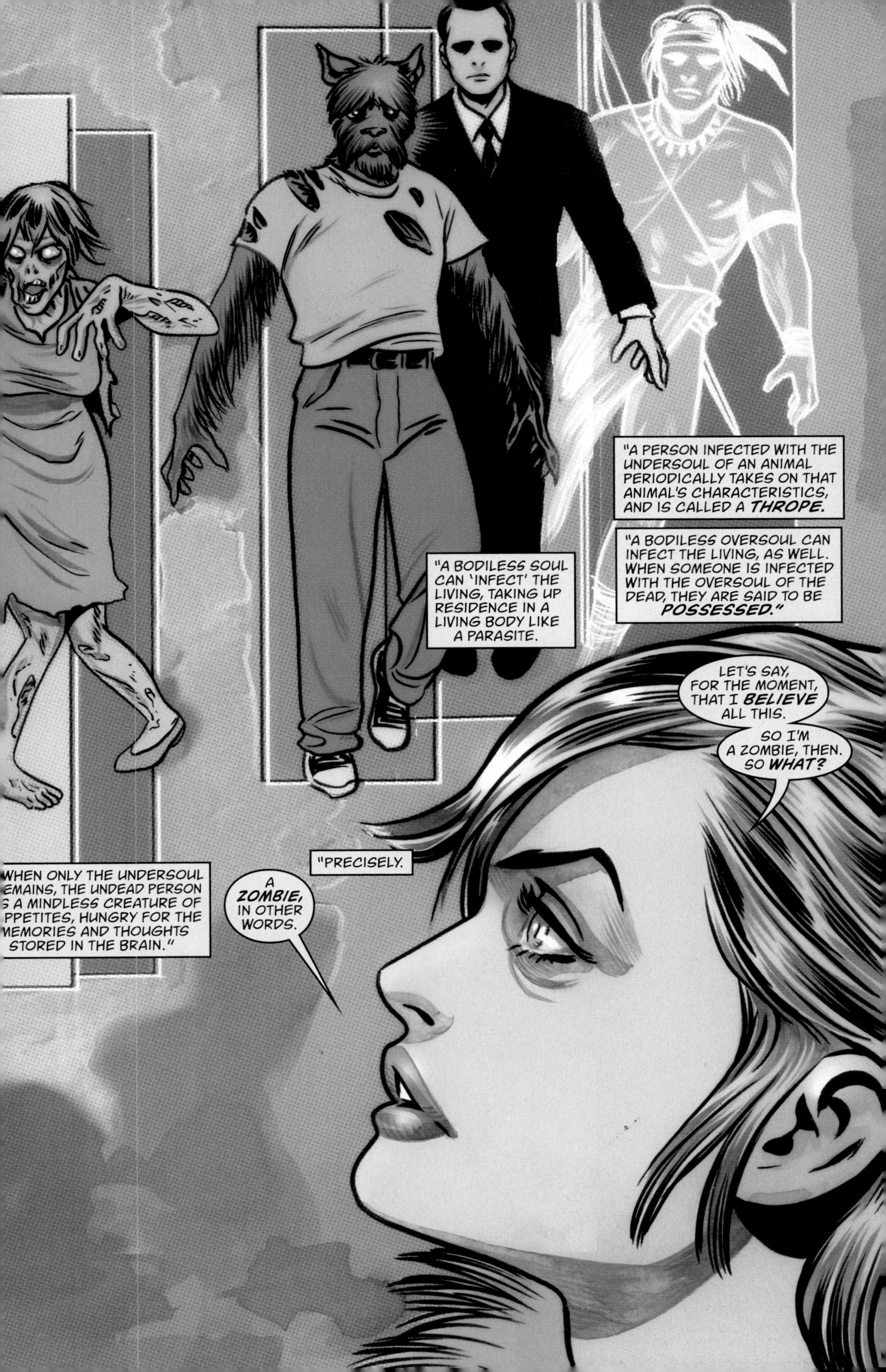
"A PERSON INFECTED WITH THE UNDERSOUL OF AN ANIMAL PERIODICALLY TAKES ON THAT ANIMAL'S CHARACTERISTICS, AND IS CALLED A THROPE.
"A BODILESS SOUL CAN 'INFECT' THE LIVING, TAKING UP RESIDENCE IN A LIVING BODY LIKE A PARASITE.
"A BODILESS OVERSOUL CAN INFECT THE LIVING, AS WELL. WHEN SOMEONE IS INFECTED WITH THE OVERSOUL OF THE DEAD, THEY ARE SAID TO BE POSSESSED."
LET'S SAY, FOR THE MOMENT, THAT I BELIEVE ALL THIS.
SO I'M A ZOMBIE, THEN. SO WHAT?
WHEN ONLY THE UNDERSOUL EMAINS, THE UNDEAD PERSON S A MINDLESS CREATURE OF PPETITES, HUNGRY FOR THE MEMORIES AND THOUGHTS STORED IN THE BRAIN."
A ZOMBIE, IN OTHER WORDS.
"PRECISELY.

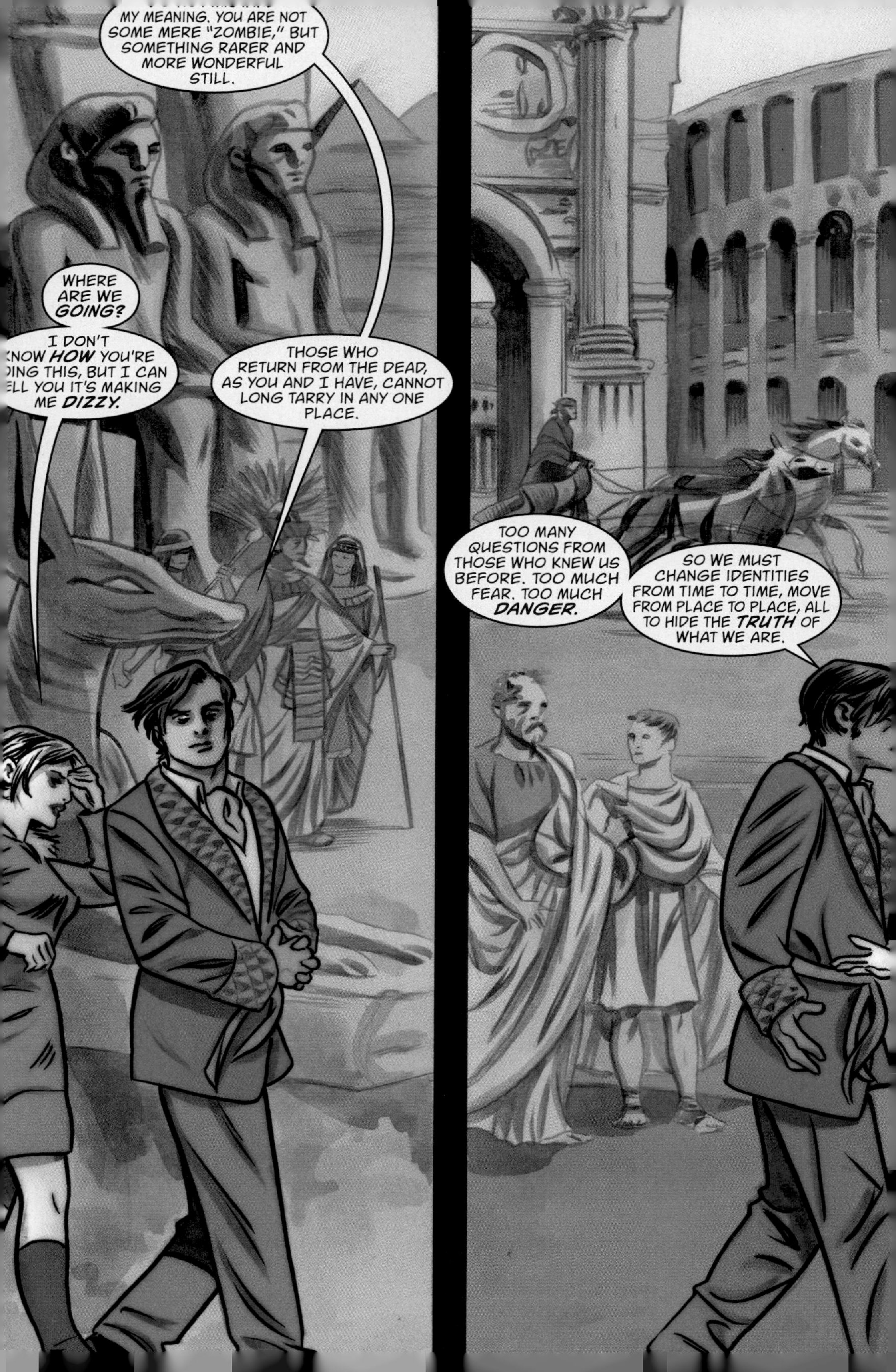
MY MEANING. YOU ARE NOT SOME MERE "ZOMBIE," BUT SOMETHING RARER AND MORE WONDERFUL STILL.
WHERE ARE WE *GOING?*
I DON'T NOW **HOW** YOU'RE OING THIS, BUT I CAN ELL YOU IT'S MAKING ME ***DIZZY.***
THOSE WHO RETURN FROM THE DEAD, AS YOU AND I HAVE, CANNOT LONG TARRY IN ANY ONE PLACE.
TOO MANY QUESTIONS FROM THOSE WHO KNEW US BEFORE. TOO MUCH FEAR. TOO MUCH ***DANGER.***
SO WE MUST CHANGE IDENTITIES FROM TIME TO TIME, MOVE FROM PLACE TO PLACE, ALL TO HIDE THE ***TRUTH*** OF WHAT WE ARE.

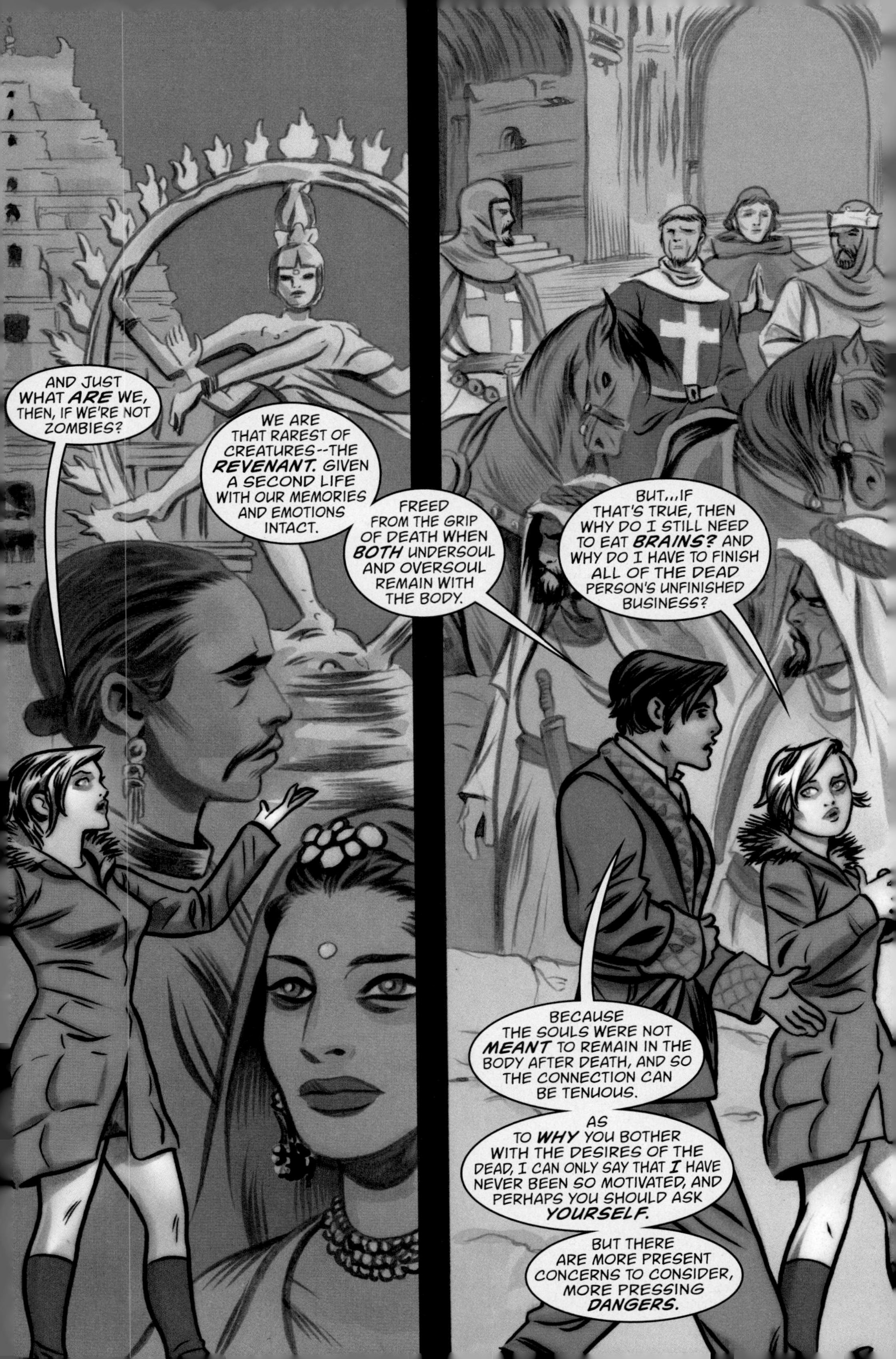
AND JUST WHAT ARE WE, THEN, IF WE'RE NOT ZOMBIES?
WE ARE THAT RAREST OF CREATURES--THE REVENANT. GIVEN A SECOND LIFE WITH OUR MEMORIES AND EMOTIONS INTACT.
FREED FROM THE GRIP OF DEATH WHEN BOTH UNDERSOUL AND OVERSOUL REMAIN WITH THE BODY.
BUT...IF THAT'S TRUE, THEN WHY DO I STILL NEED TO EAT BRAINS? AND WHY DO I HAVE TO FINISH ALL OF THE DEAD PERSON'S UNFINISHED BUSINESS?
BECAUSE THE SOULS WERE NOT MEANT TO REMAIN IN THE BODY AFTER DEATH, AND SO THE CONNECTION CAN BE TENUOUS.
AS TO WHY YOU BOTHER WITH THE DESIRES OF THE DEAD, I CAN ONLY SAY THAT I HAVE NEVER BEEN SO MOTIVATED, AND PERHAPS YOU SHOULD ASK YOURSELF.
BUT THERE ARE MORE PRESENT CONCERNS TO CONSIDER, MORE PRESSING DANGERS.

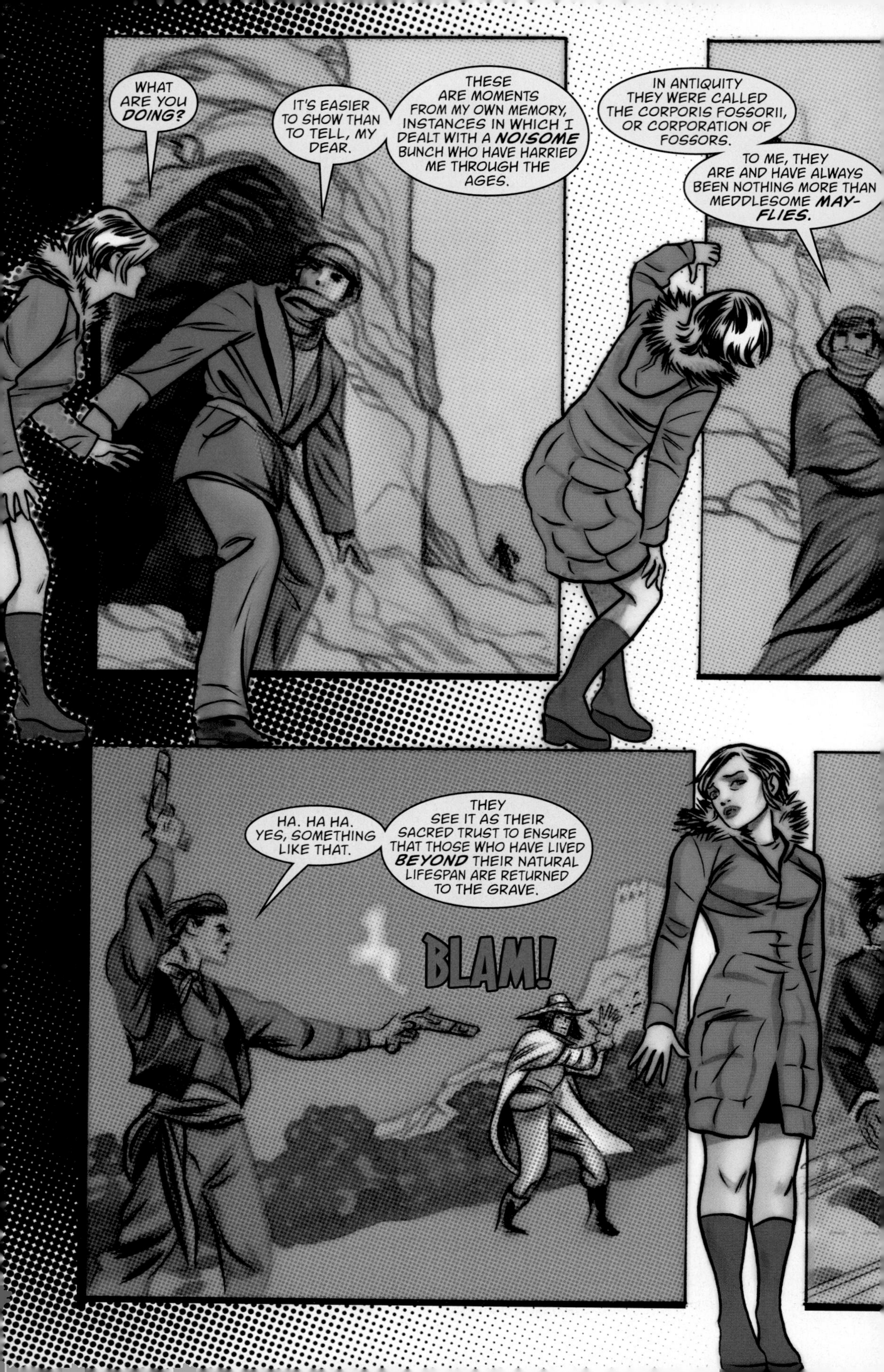
WHAT ARE YOU DOING?
IT'S EASIER TO SHOW THAN TO TELL, MY DEAR.
THESE ARE MOMENTS FROM MY OWN MEMORY, INSTANCES IN WHICH I DEALT WITH A NOISOME BUNCH WHO HAVE HARRIED ME THROUGH THE AGES.
IN ANTIQUITY THEY WERE CALLED THE CORPORIS FOSSORII, OR CORPORATION OF FOSSORS.
TO ME, THEY ARE AND HAVE ALWAYS BEEN NOTHING MORE THAN MEDDLESOME MAY-FLIES.
HA. HA HA. YES, SOMETHING LIKE THAT.
THEY SEE IT AS THEIR SACRED TRUST TO ENSURE THAT THOSE WHO HAVE LIVED BEYOND THEIR NATURAL LIFESPAN ARE RETURNED TO THE GRAVE.
BLAM!

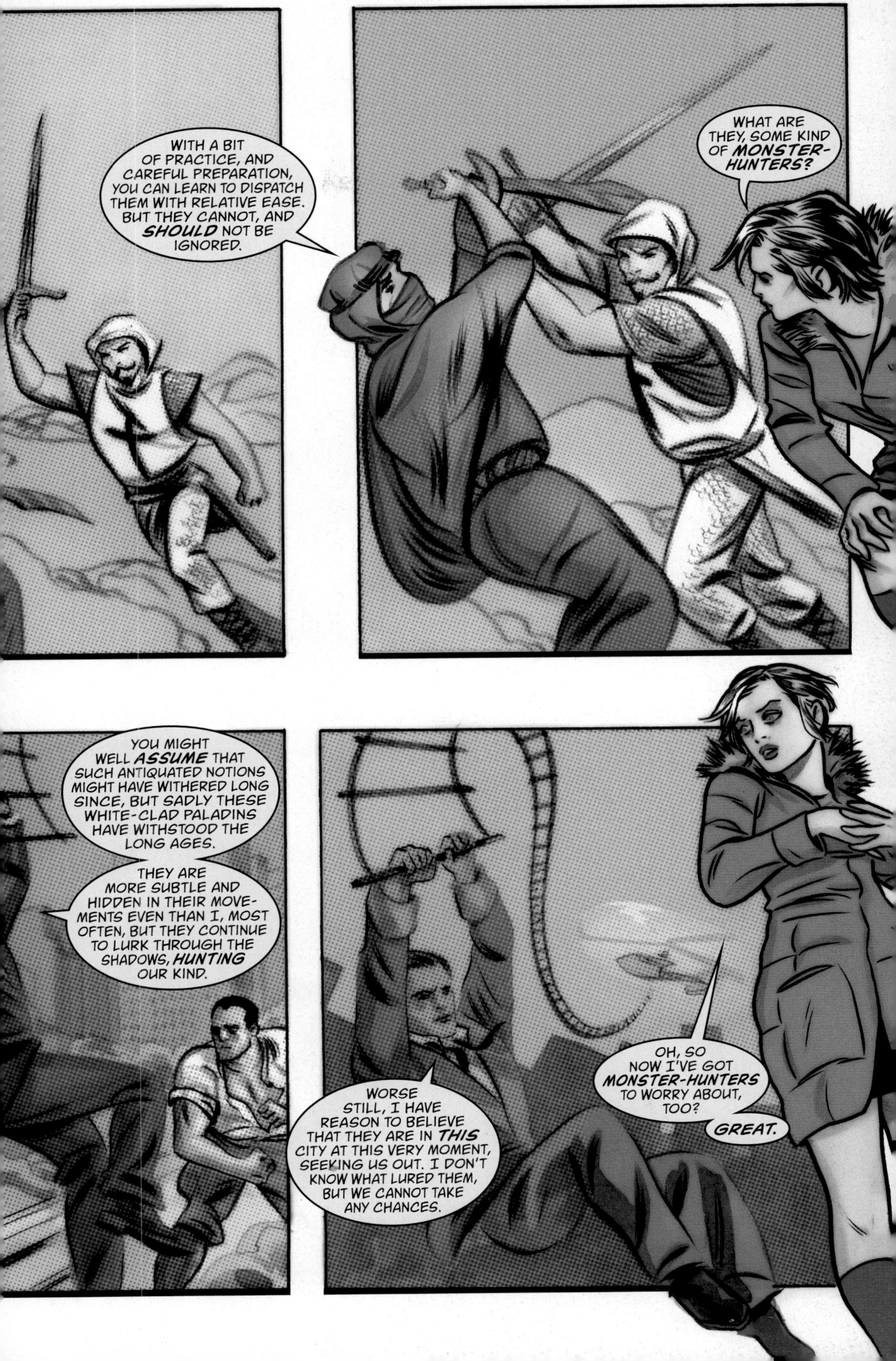
WITH A BIT OF PRACTICE, AND CAREFUL PREPARATION, YOU CAN LEARN TO DISPATCH THEM WITH RELATIVE EASE. BUT THEY CANNOT, AND SHOULD NOT BE IGNORED.
WHAT ARE THEY, SOME KIND OF MONSTER-HUNTERS?
YOU MIGHT WELL ASSUME THAT SUCH ANTIQUATED NOTIONS MIGHT HAVE WITHERED LONG SINCE, BUT SADLY THESE WHITE-CLAD PALADINS HAVE WITHSTOOD THE LONG AGES.
THEY ARE MORE SUBTLE AND HIDDEN IN THEIR MOVEMENTS EVEN THAN I, MOST OFTEN, BUT THEY CONTINUE TO LURK THROUGH THE SHADOWS, HUNTING OUR KIND.
WORSE STILL, I HAVE REASON TO BELIEVE THAT THEY ARE IN THIS CITY AT THIS VERY MOMENT, SEEKING US OUT. I DON'T KNOW WHAT LURED THEM, BUT WE CANNOT TAKE ANY CHANCES.
OH, SO NOW I'VE GOT MONSTER-HUNTERS TO WORRY ABOUT, TOO?
GREAT.

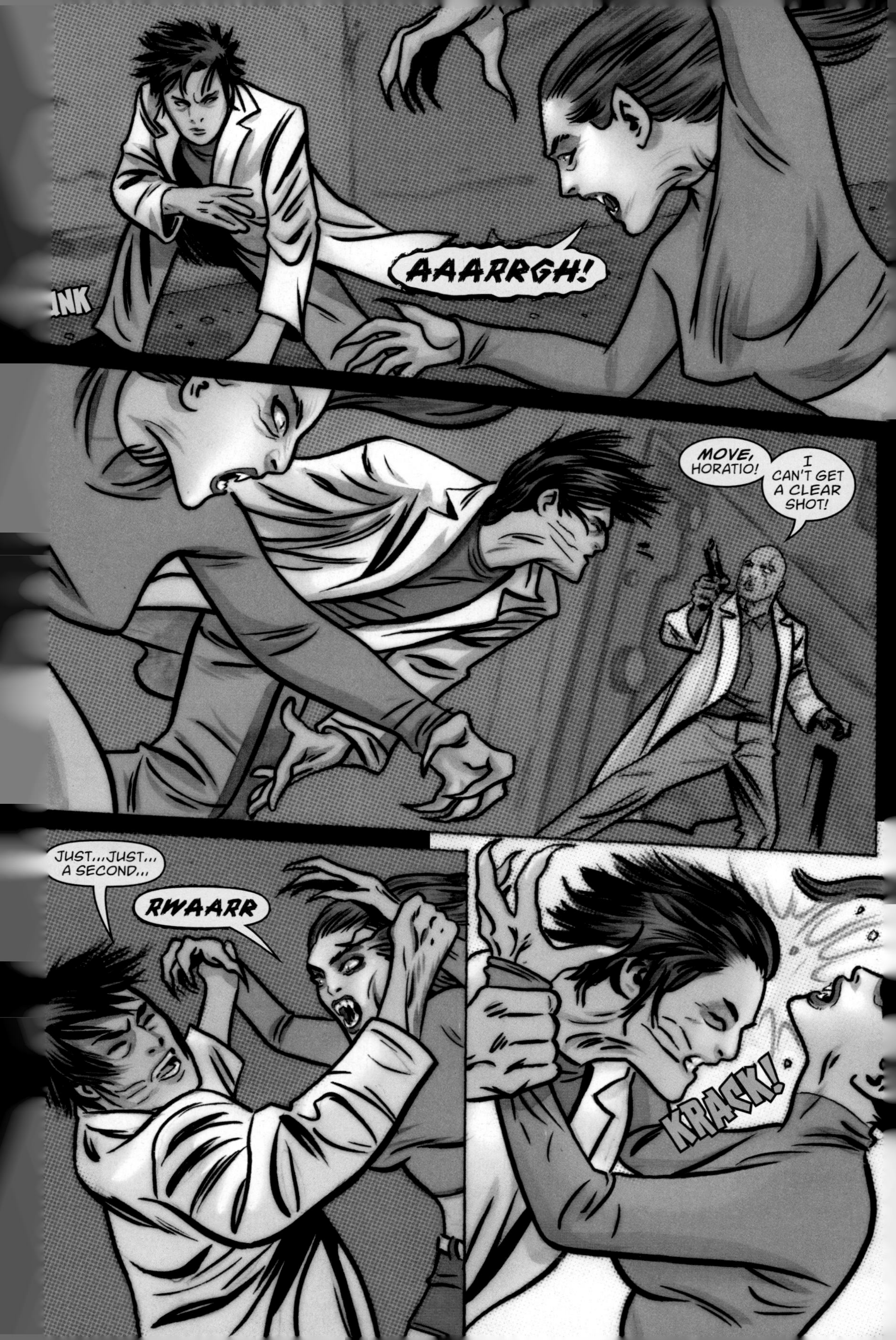

AAARRGH!
MOVE, HORATIO!
I CAN'T GET A CLEAR SHOT!
JUST...JUST... A SECOND...
RWAARR
KRACK!

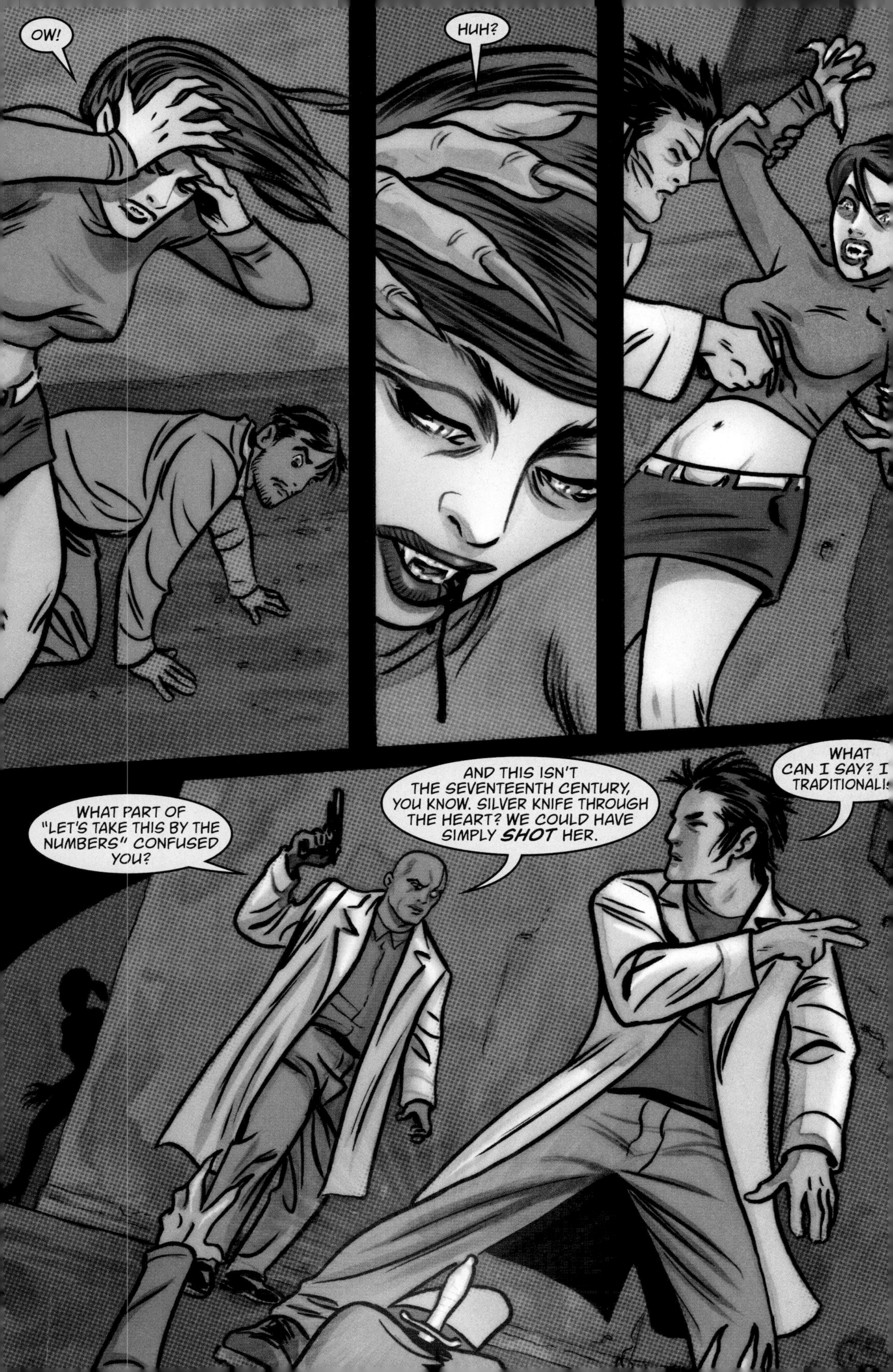
OW!
HUH?
WHAT PART OF "LET'S TAKE THIS BY THE NUMBERS" CONFUSED YOU?
AND THIS ISN'T THE SEVENTEENTH CENTURY, YOU KNOW. SILVER KNIFE THROUGH THE HEART? WE COULD HAVE SIMPLY SHOT HER.
WHAT CAN I SAY? I TRADITIONALI

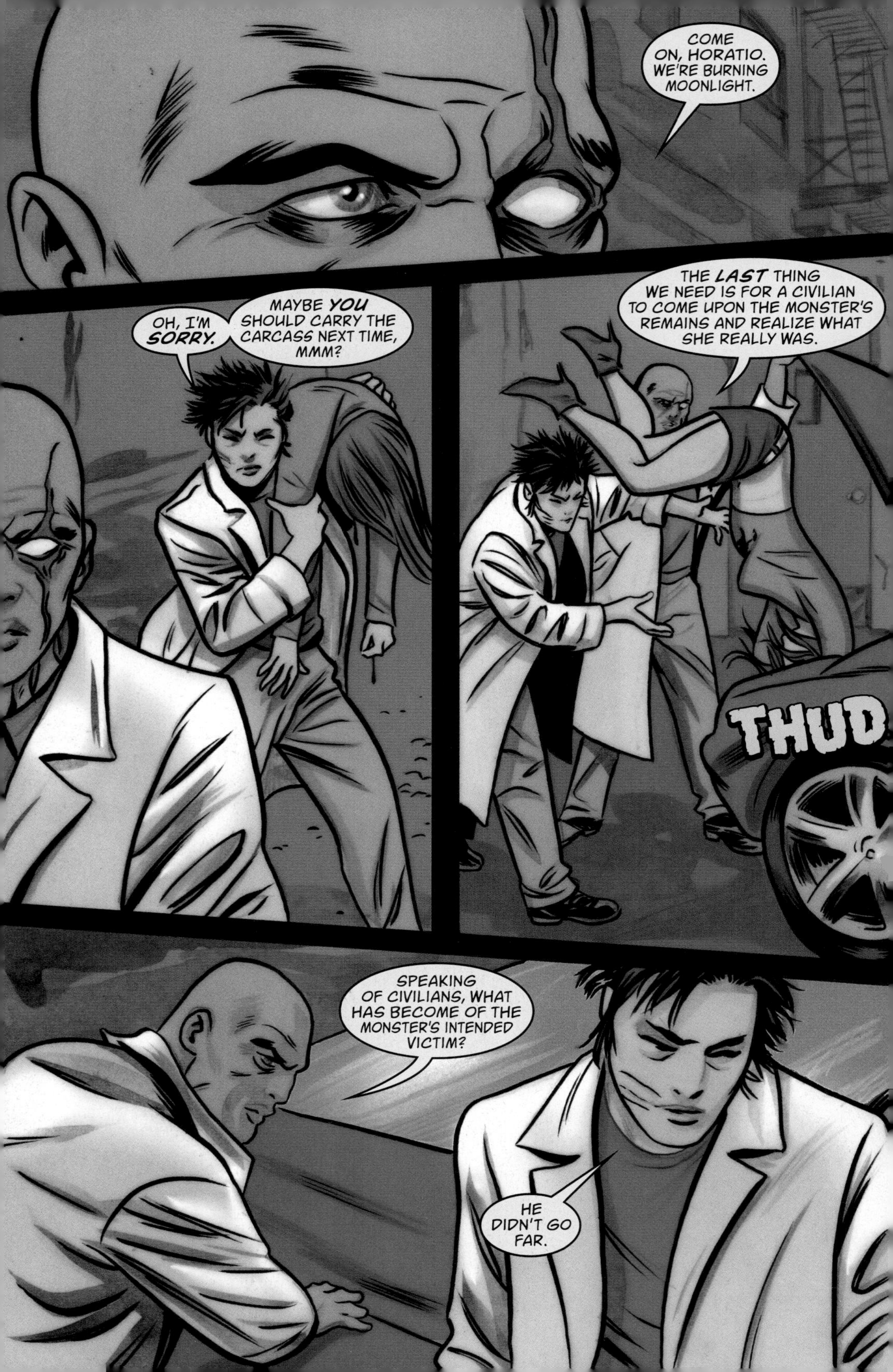
COME ON, HORATIO. WE'RE BURNING MOONLIGHT.
OH, I'M *SORRY.*
MAYBE *YOU* SHOULD CARRY THE CARCASS NEXT TIME, MMM?
THE *LAST* THING WE NEED IS FOR A CIVILIAN TO COME UPON THE MONSTER'S REMAINS AND REALIZE WHAT SHE REALLY WAS.
THUD
SPEAKING OF CIVILIANS, WHAT HAS BECOME OF THE MONSTER'S INTENDED VICTIM?
HE DIDN'T GO FAR.

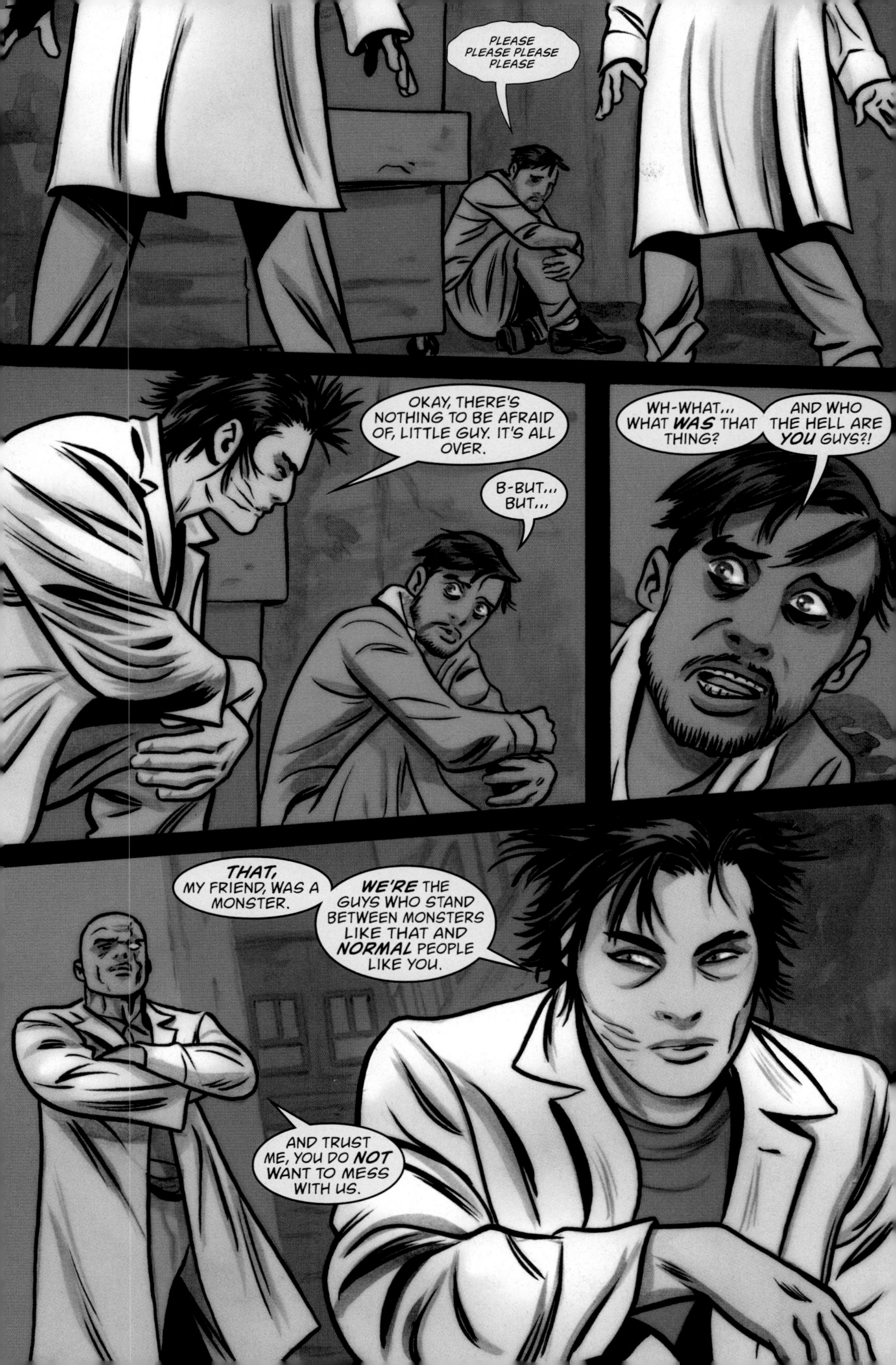
PLEASE
PLEASE PLEASE
PLEASE
OKAY, THERE'S NOTHING TO BE AFRAID OF, LITTLE GUY. IT'S ALL OVER.
B-BUT... BUT...
WH-WHAT... WHAT WAS THAT THING?
AND WHO THE HELL ARE YOU GUYS?!
THAT, MY FRIEND, WAS A MONSTER.
WE'RE THE GUYS WHO STAND BETWEEN MONSTERS LIKE THAT AND NORMAL PEOPLE LIKE YOU.
AND TRUST ME, YOU DO NOT WANT TO MESS WITH US.

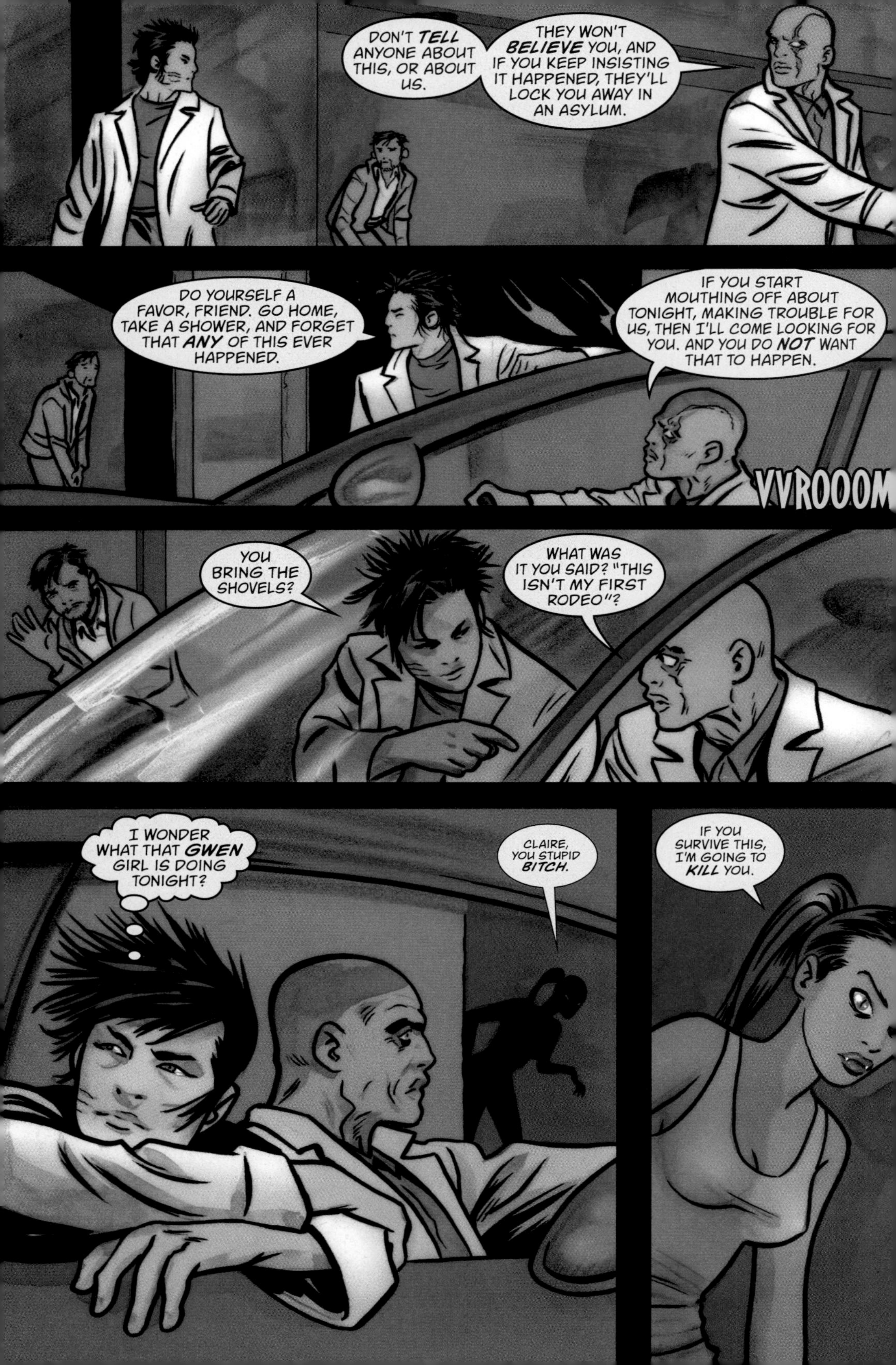
DON'T TELL ANYONE ABOUT THIS, OR ABOUT US.
THEY WON'T BELIEVE YOU, AND IF YOU KEEP INSISTING IT HAPPENED, THEY'LL LOCK YOU AWAY IN AN ASYLUM.
DO YOURSELF A FAVOR, FRIEND. GO HOME, TAKE A SHOWER, AND FORGET THAT ANY OF THIS EVER HAPPENED.
IF YOU START MOUTHING OFF ABOUT TONIGHT, MAKING TROUBLE FOR US, THEN I'LL COME LOOKING FOR YOU. AND YOU DO NOT WANT THAT TO HAPPEN.
VVROOOM
YOU BRING THE SHOVELS?
WHAT WAS IT YOU SAID? "THIS ISN'T MY FIRST RODEO"?
I WONDER WHAT THAT GWEN GIRL IS DOING TONIGHT?
CLAIRE, YOU STUPID BITCH.
IF YOU SURVIVE THIS, I'M GOING TO KILL YOU.

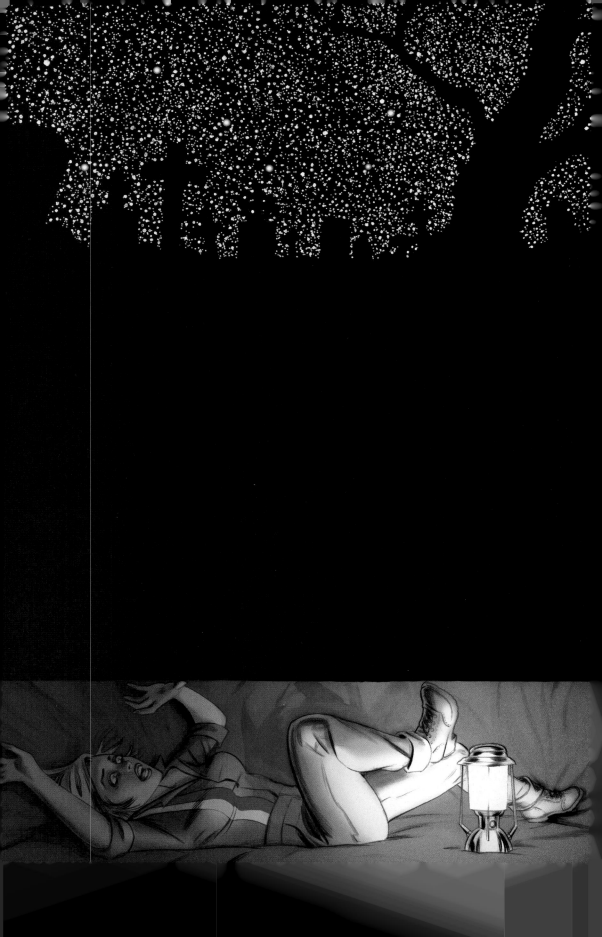

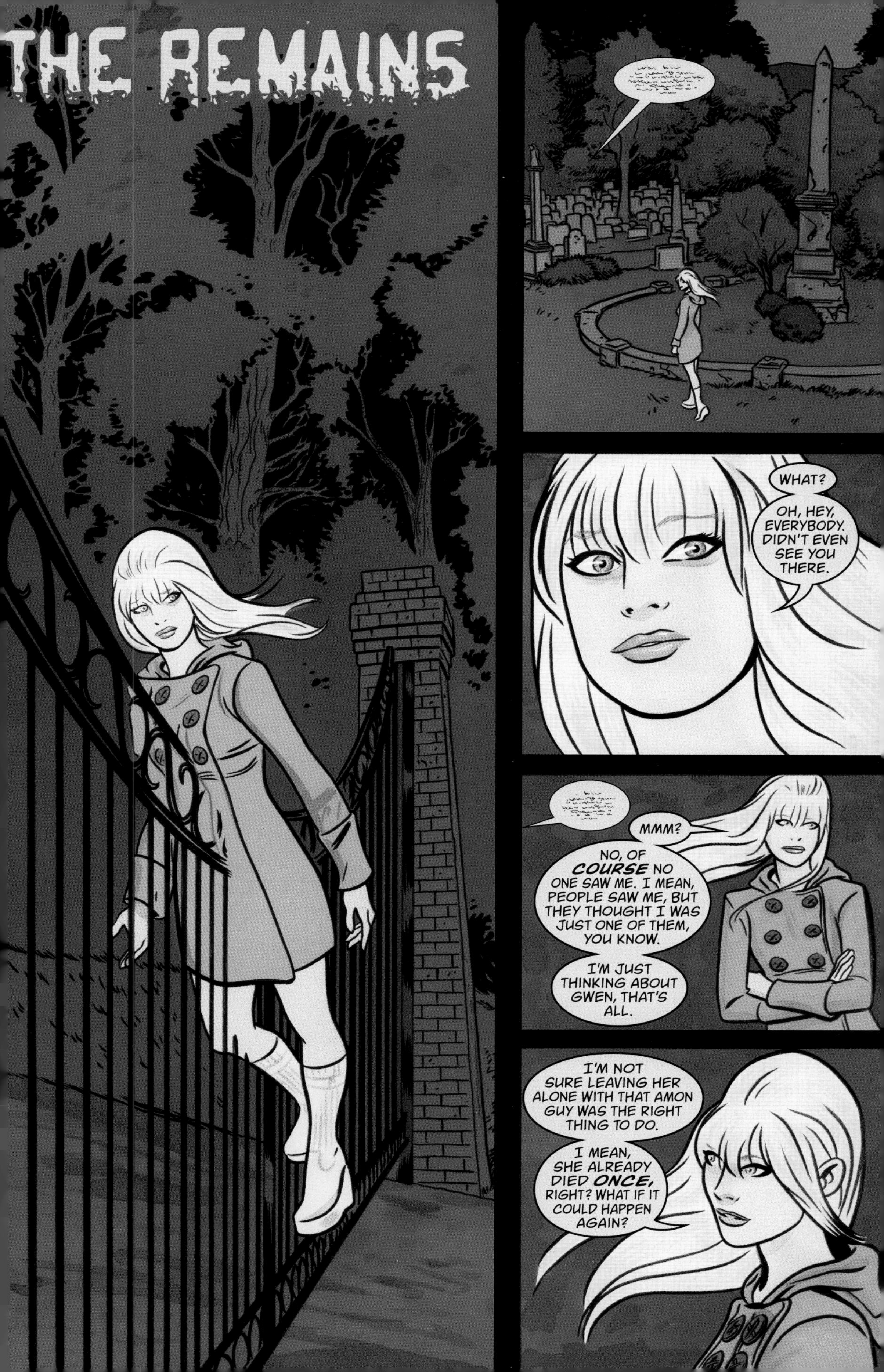
THE REMAINS
WHAT?
OH, HEY, EVERYBODY. DIDN'T EVEN SEE YOU THERE.
MMM?
NO, OF COURSE NO ONE SAW ME. I MEAN, PEOPLE SAW ME, BUT THEY THOUGHT I WAS JUST ONE OF THEM, YOU KNOW.
I'M JUST THINKING ABOUT GWEN, THAT'S ALL.
I'M NOT SURE LEAVING HER ALONE WITH THAT AMON GUY WAS THE RIGHT THING TO DO.
I MEAN, SHE ALREADY DIED ONCE, RIGHT? WHAT IF IT COULD HAPPEN AGAIN?

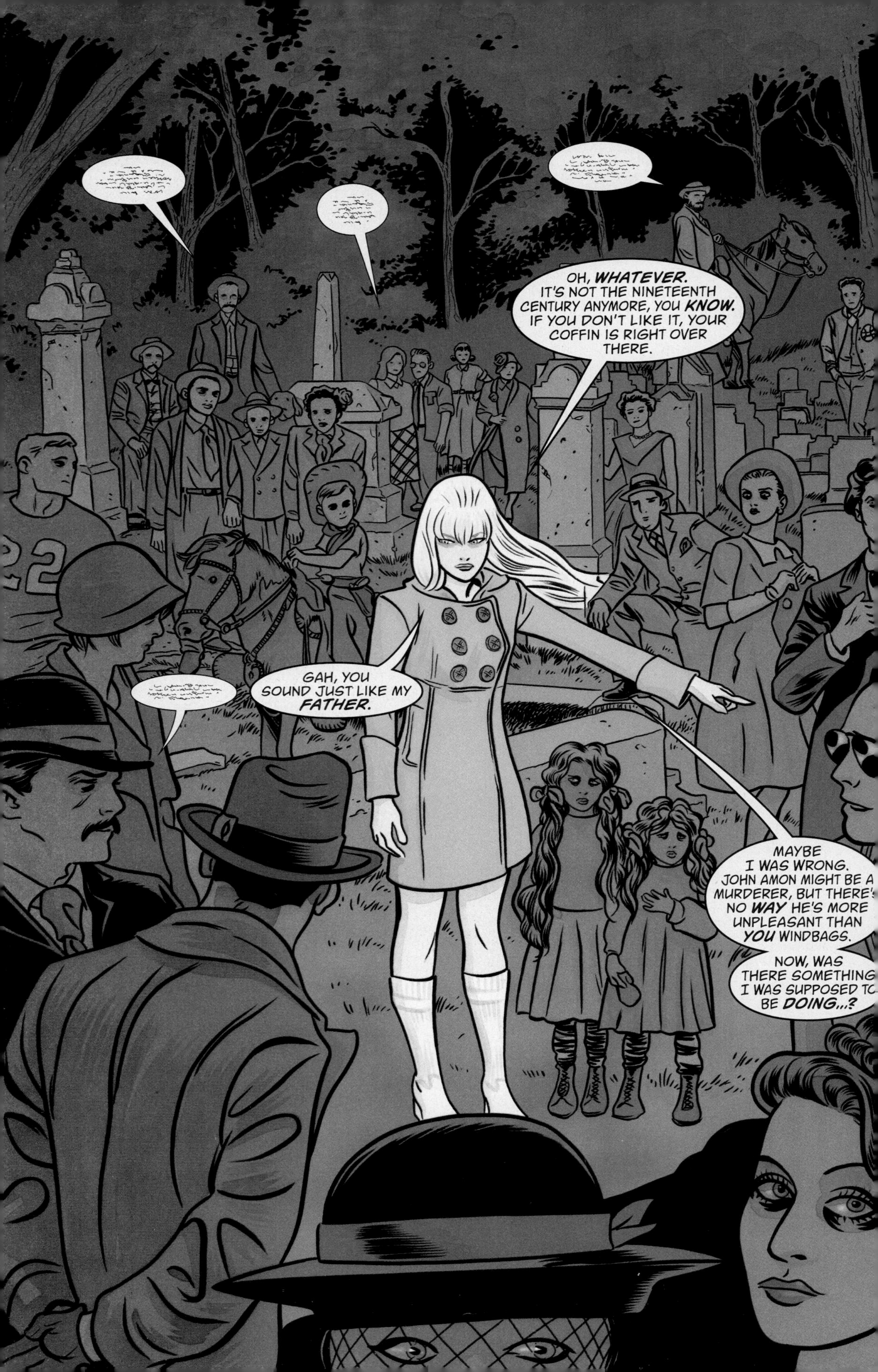
OH, *WHATEVER.* IT'S NOT THE NINETEENTH CENTURY ANYMORE, YOU *KNOW.* IF YOU DON'T LIKE IT, YOUR COFFIN IS RIGHT OVER THERE.
GAH, YOU SOUND JUST LIKE MY *FATHER.*
MAYBE I WAS WRONG. JOHN AMON MIGHT BE A MURDERER, BUT THERE'S NO *WAY* HE'S MORE UNPLEASANT THAN *YOU* WINDBAGS.
NOW, WAS THERE SOMETHING I WAS SUPPOSED TO BE *DOING...?*

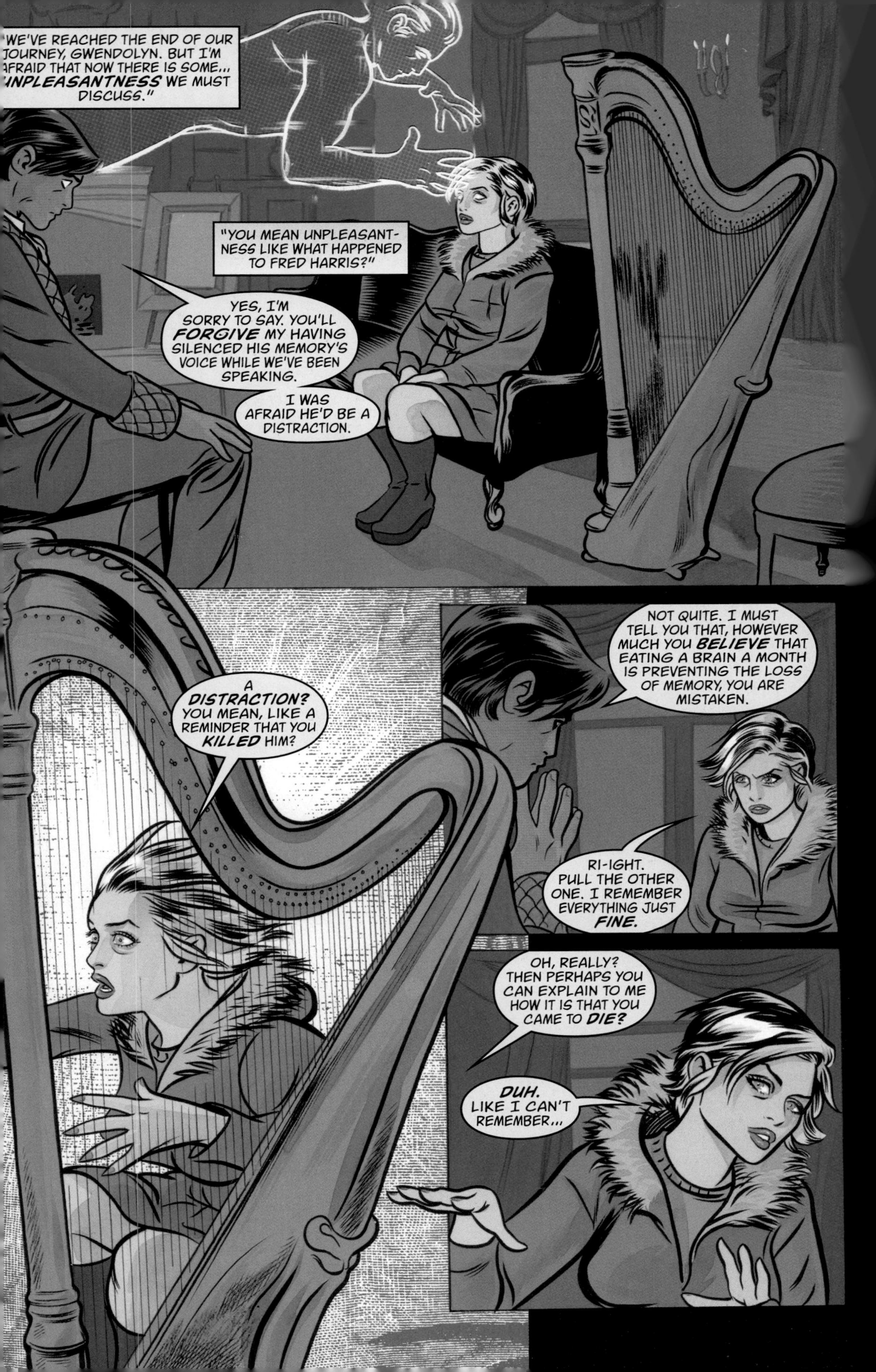
"WE'VE REACHED THE END OF OUR JOURNEY, GWENDOLYN. BUT I'M AFRAID THAT NOW THERE IS SOME... ***UNPLEASANTNESS*** WE MUST DISCUSS."
"YOU MEAN UNPLEASANTNESS LIKE WHAT HAPPENED TO FRED HARRIS?"
YES, I'M SORRY TO SAY. YOU'LL ***FORGIVE*** MY HAVING SILENCED HIS MEMORY'S VOICE WHILE WE'VE BEEN SPEAKING.
I WAS AFRAID HE'D BE A DISTRACTION.
A ***DISTRACTION?*** YOU MEAN, LIKE A REMINDER THAT YOU ***KILLED*** HIM?
NOT QUITE. I MUST TELL YOU THAT, HOWEVER MUCH YOU ***BELIEVE*** THAT EATING A BRAIN A MONTH IS PREVENTING THE LOSS OF MEMORY, YOU ARE MISTAKEN.
RI-IGHT. PULL THE OTHER ONE. I REMEMBER EVERYTHING JUST ***FINE.***
OH, REALLY? THEN PERHAPS YOU CAN EXPLAIN TO ME HOW IT IS THAT YOU CAME TO ***DIE?***
DUH. LIKE I CAN'T REMEMBER...

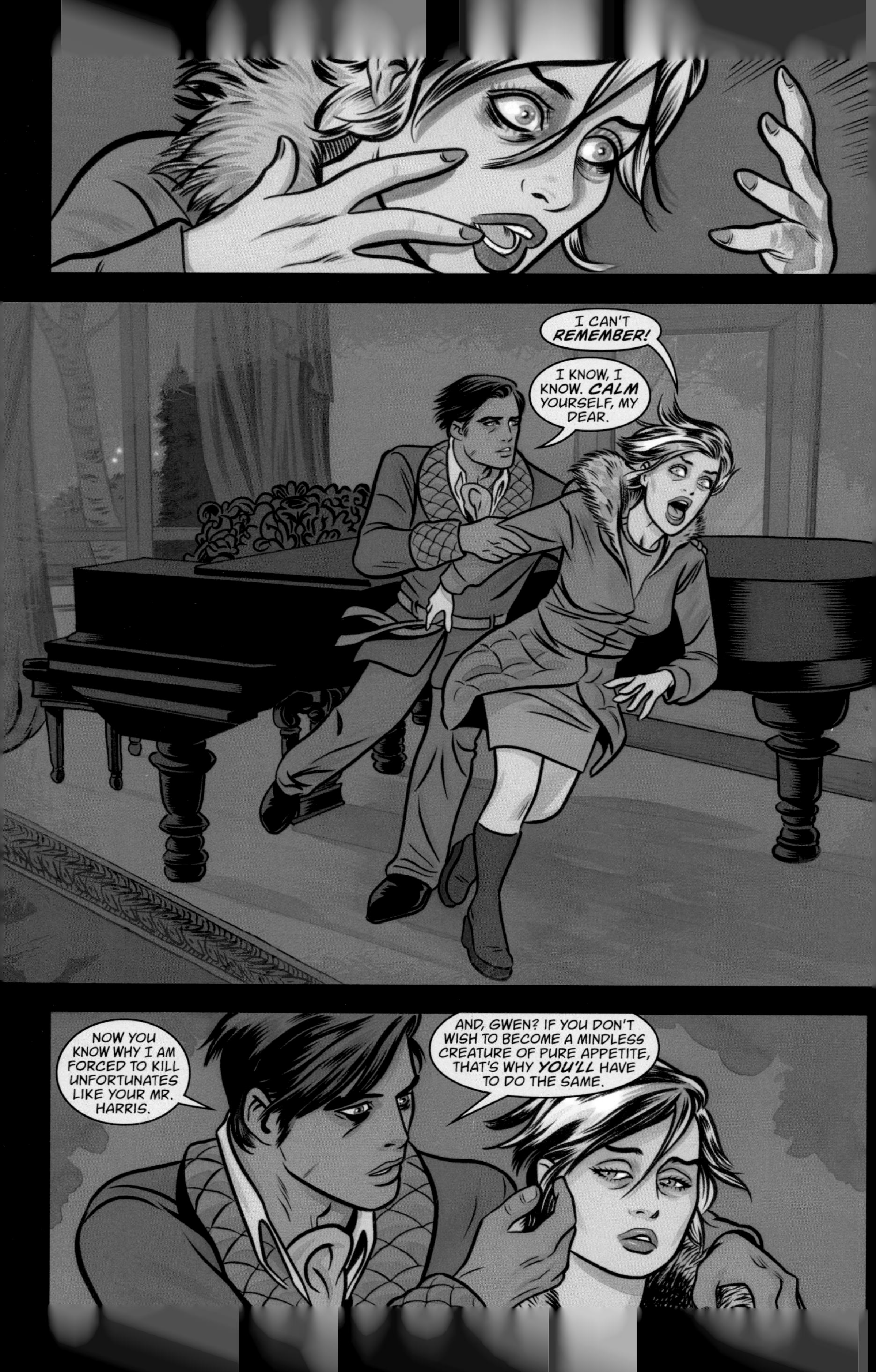
I CAN'T REMEMBER!
I KNOW, I KNOW. CALM YOURSELF, MY DEAR.
NOW YOU KNOW WHY I AM FORCED TO KILL UNFORTUNATES LIKE YOUR MR. HARRIS.
AND, GWEN? IF YOU DON'T WISH TO BECOME A MINDLESS CREATURE OF PURE APPETITE, THAT'S WHY YOU'LL HAVE TO DO THE SAME.

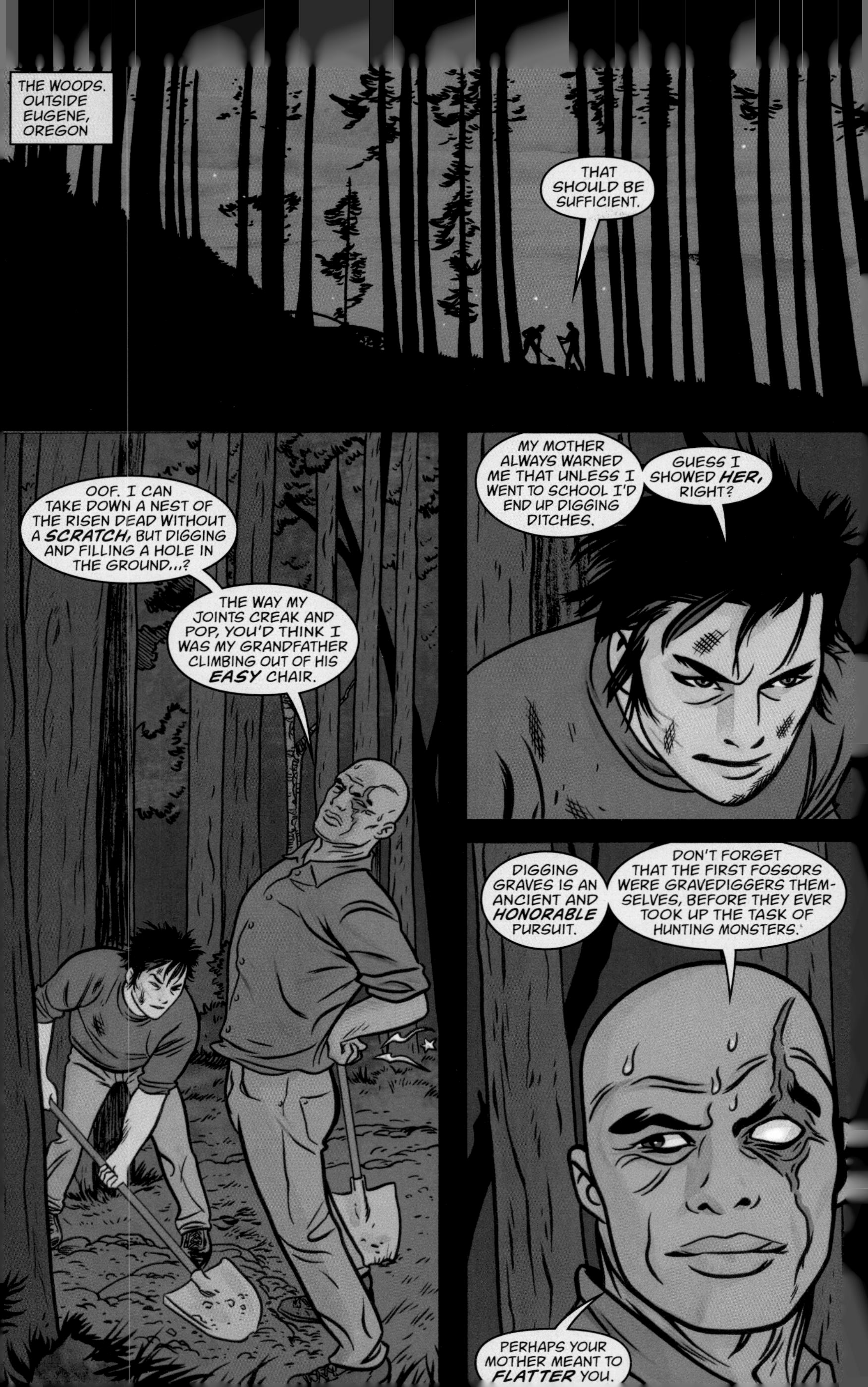
THE WOODS. OUTSIDE EUGENE, OREGON
THAT SHOULD BE SUFFICIENT.
OOF. I CAN TAKE DOWN A NEST OF THE RISEN DEAD WITHOUT A SCRATCH, BUT DIGGING AND FILLING A HOLE IN THE GROUND...?
THE WAY MY JOINTS CREAK AND POP, YOU'D THINK I WAS MY GRANDFATHER CLIMBING OUT OF HIS EASY CHAIR.
MY MOTHER ALWAYS WARNED ME THAT UNLESS I WENT TO SCHOOL I'D END UP DIGGING DITCHES.
GUESS I SHOWED HER, RIGHT?
DIGGING GRAVES IS AN ANCIENT AND HONORABLE PURSUIT.
DON'T FORGET THAT THE FIRST FOSSORS WERE GRAVEDIGGERS THEM-SELVES, BEFORE THEY EVER TOOK UP THE TASK OF HUNTING MONSTERS.
PERHAPS YOUR MOTHER MEANT TO FLATTER YOU.

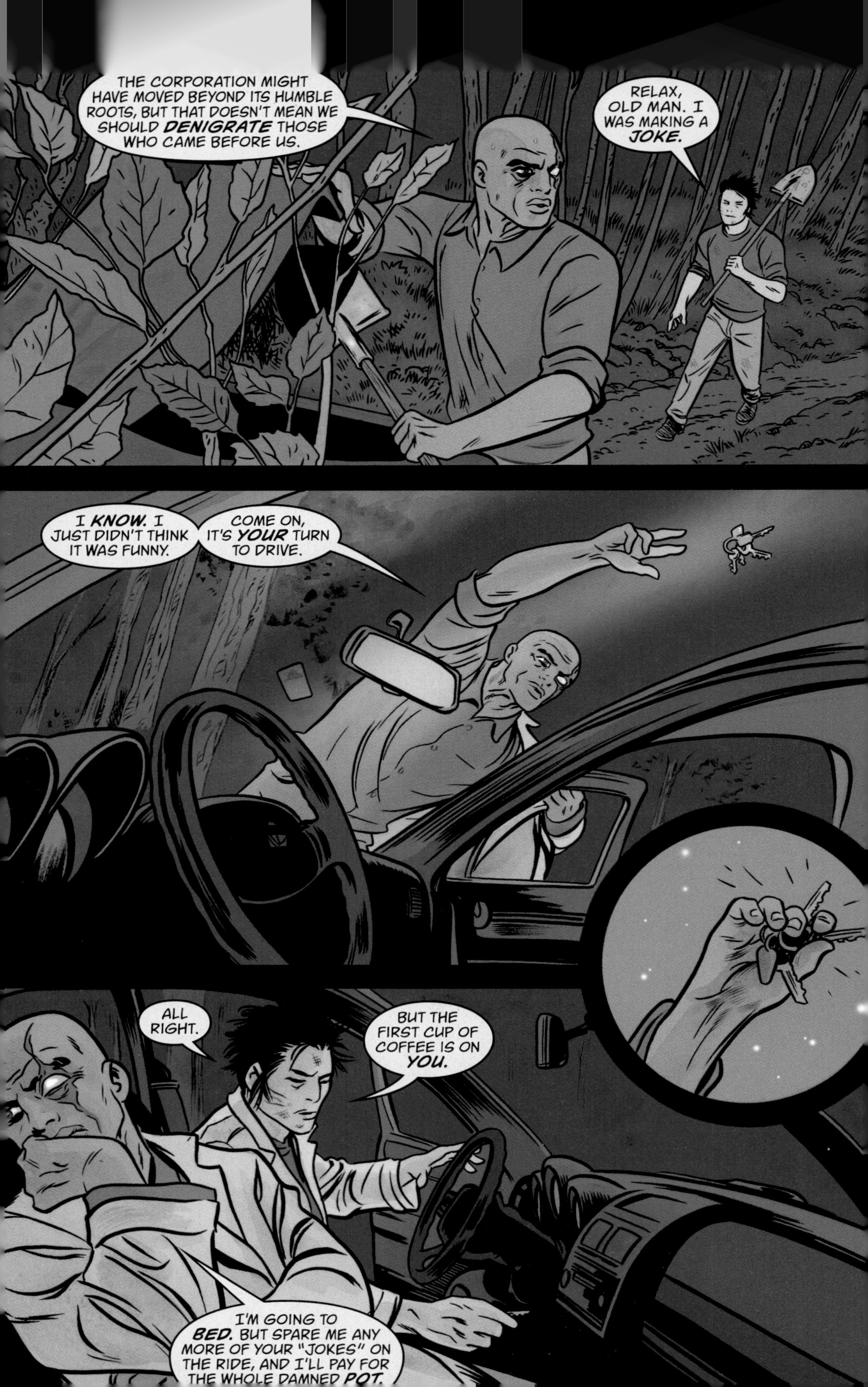
THE CORPORATION MIGHT HAVE MOVED BEYOND ITS HUMBLE ROOTS, BUT THAT DOESN'T MEAN WE SHOULD DENIGRATE THOSE WHO CAME BEFORE US.
RELAX, OLD MAN. I WAS MAKING A JOKE.
I KNOW. I JUST DIDN'T THINK IT WAS FUNNY.
COME ON, IT'S YOUR TURN TO DRIVE.
ALL RIGHT.
BUT THE FIRST CUP OF COFFEE IS ON YOU.
I'M GOING TO BED. BUT SPARE ME ANY MORE OF YOUR "JOKES" ON THE RIDE, AND I'LL PAY FOR THE WHOLE DAMNED POT.

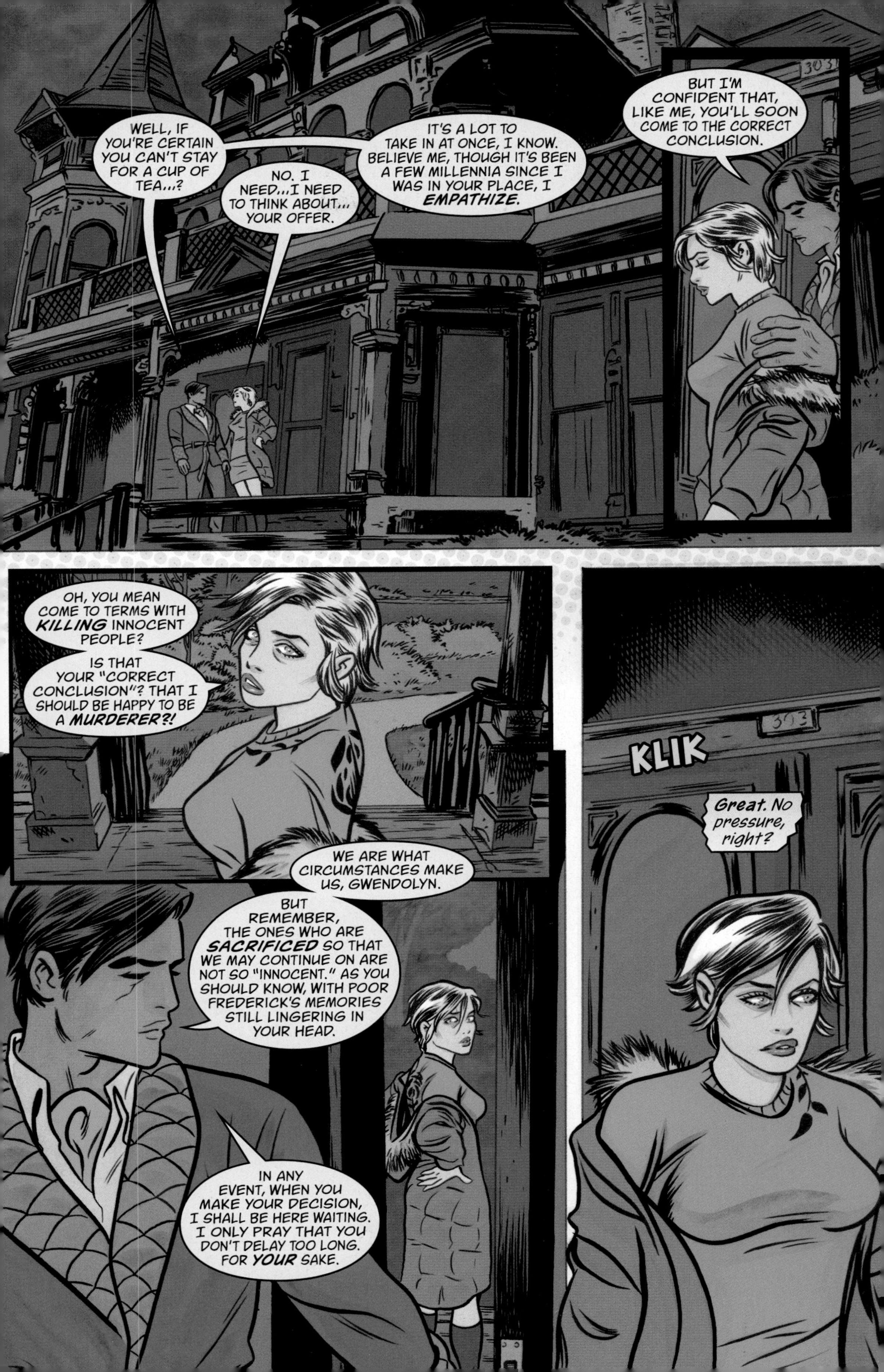
WELL, IF YOU'RE CERTAIN YOU CAN'T STAY FOR A CUP OF TEA...?
NO. I NEED...I NEED TO THINK ABOUT... YOUR OFFER.
IT'S A LOT TO TAKE IN AT ONCE, I KNOW. BELIEVE ME, THOUGH IT'S BEEN A FEW MILLENNIA SINCE I WAS IN YOUR PLACE, I EMPATHIZE.
BUT I'M CONFIDENT THAT, LIKE ME, YOU'LL SOON COME TO THE CORRECT CONCLUSION.
OH, YOU MEAN COME TO TERMS WITH KILLING INNOCENT PEOPLE?
IS THAT YOUR "CORRECT CONCLUSION"? THAT I SHOULD BE HAPPY TO BE A MURDERER?!
WE ARE WHAT CIRCUMSTANCES MAKE US, GWENDOLYN.
BUT REMEMBER, THE ONES WHO ARE SACRIFICED SO THAT WE MAY CONTINUE ON ARE NOT SO "INNOCENT." AS YOU SHOULD KNOW, WITH POOR FREDERICK'S MEMORIES STILL LINGERING IN YOUR HEAD.
IN ANY EVENT, WHEN YOU MAKE YOUR DECISION, I SHALL BE HERE WAITING. I ONLY PRAY THAT YOU DON'T DELAY TOO LONG. FOR YOUR SAKE.
KLIK
Great. No pressure, right?

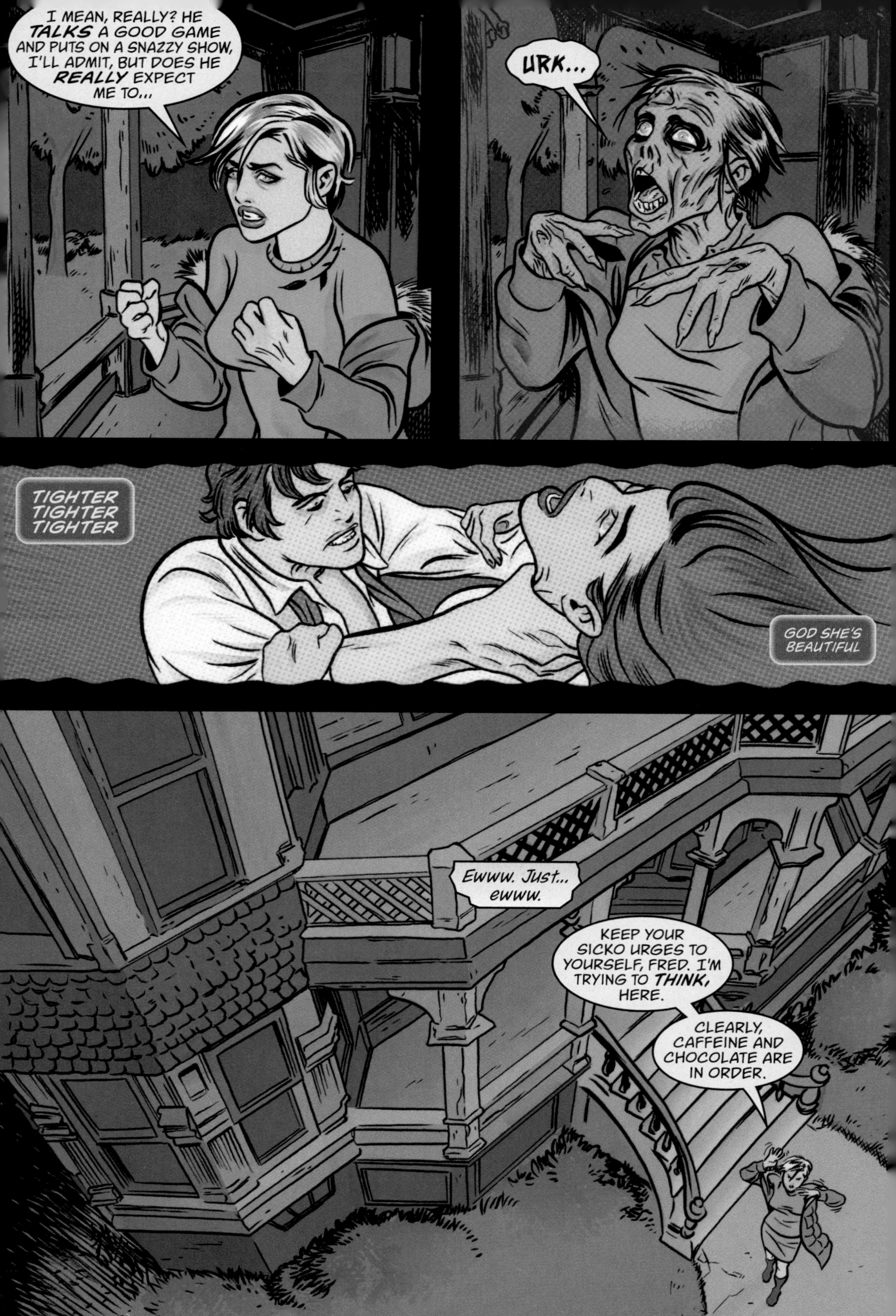
I MEAN, REALLY? HE TALKS A GOOD GAME AND PUTS ON A SNAZZY SHOW, I'LL ADMIT, BUT DOES HE REALLY EXPECT ME TO...
URK...
TIGHTER TIGHTER TIGHTER
GOD SHE'S BEAUTIFUL
Ewww. Just... ewww.
KEEP YOUR SICKO URGES TO YOURSELF, FRED. I'M TRYING TO THINK, HERE.
CLEARLY, CAFFEINE AND CHOCOLATE ARE IN ORDER.

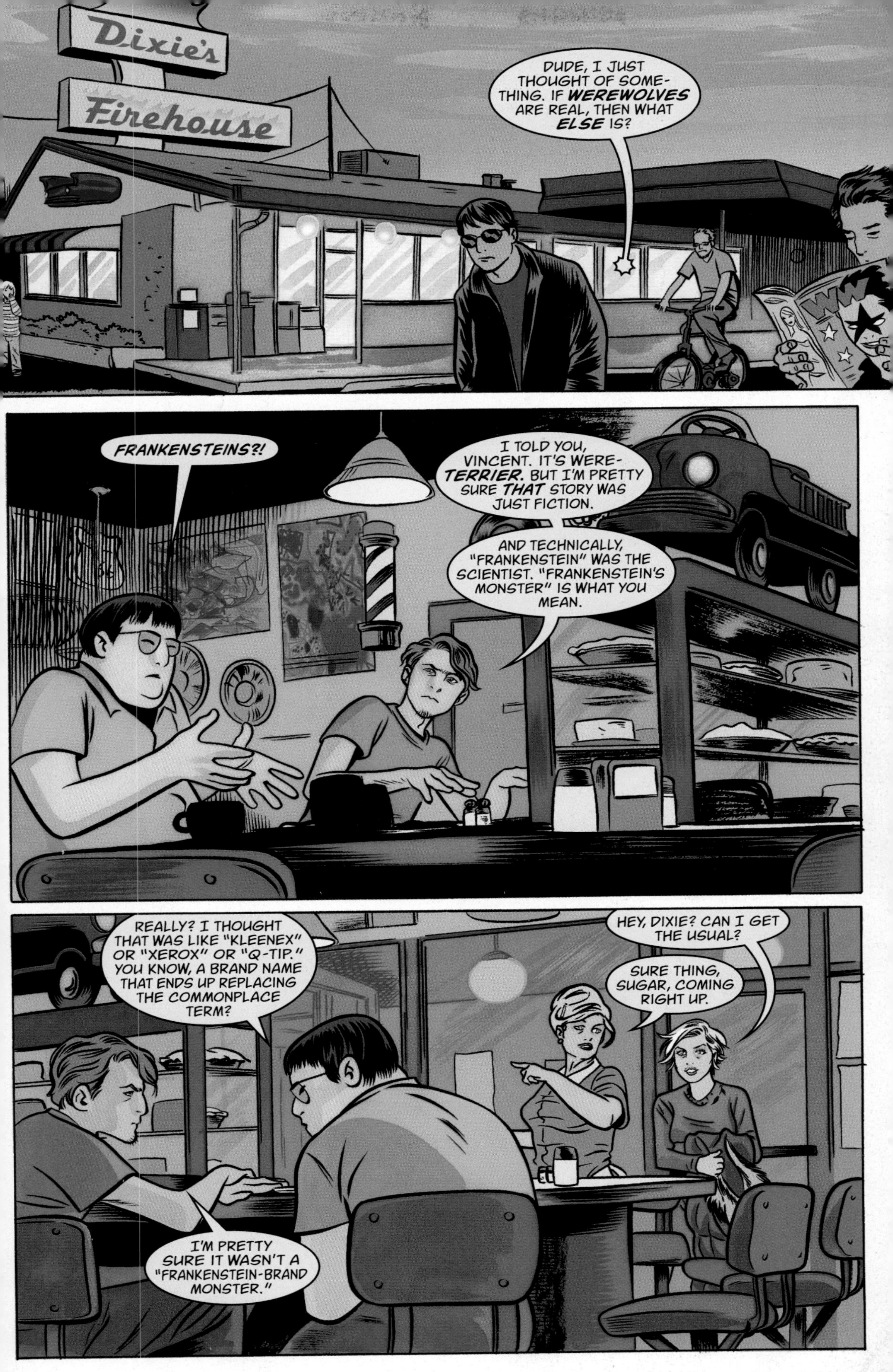
Dixie's
Firehouse
DUDE, I JUST THOUGHT OF SOMETHING. IF WEREWOLVES ARE REAL, THEN WHAT ELSE IS?
FRANKENSTEINS?!
I TOLD YOU, VINCENT. IT'S WERE-TERRIER. BUT I'M PRETTY SURE THAT STORY WAS JUST FICTION.
AND TECHNICALLY, "FRANKENSTEIN" WAS THE SCIENTIST. "FRANKENSTEIN'S MONSTER" IS WHAT YOU MEAN.
REALLY? I THOUGHT THAT WAS LIKE "KLEENEX" OR "XEROX" OR "Q-TIP." YOU KNOW, A BRAND NAME THAT ENDS UP REPLACING THE COMMONPLACE TERM?
HEY, DIXIE? CAN I GET THE USUAL?
SURE THING, SUGAR, COMING RIGHT UP.
I'M PRETTY SURE IT WASN'T A "FRANKENSTEIN-BRAND MONSTER."

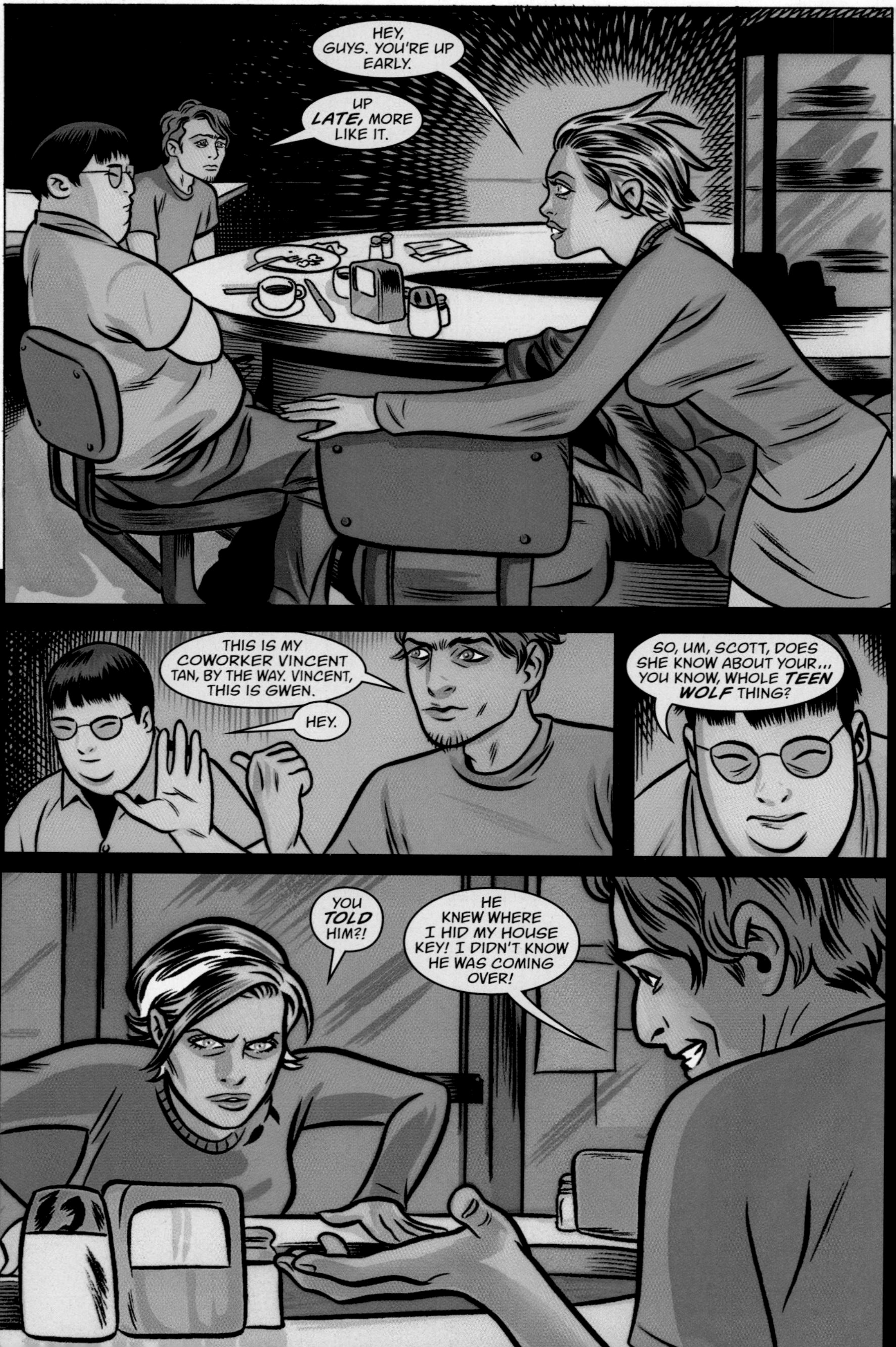

HEY, GUYS. YOU'RE UP EARLY.
UP *LATE,* MORE LIKE IT.
THIS IS MY COWORKER VINCENT TAN, BY THE WAY. VINCENT, THIS IS GWEN.
HEY.
SO, UM, SCOTT, DOES SHE KNOW ABOUT YOUR... YOU KNOW, WHOLE *TEEN WOLF* THING?
YOU *TOLD* HIM?!
HE KNEW WHERE I HID MY HOUSE KEY! I DIDN'T KNOW HE WAS COMING OVER!

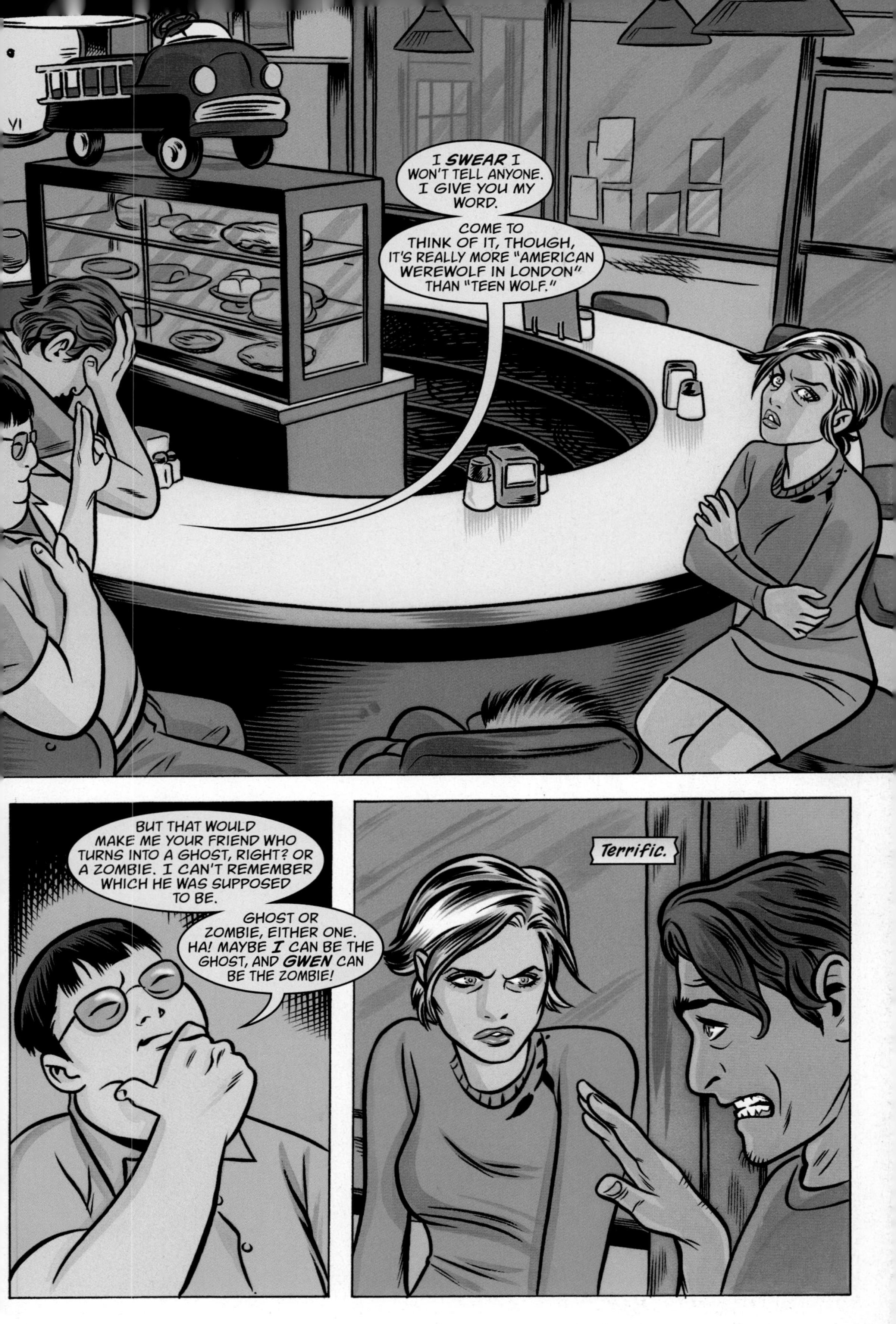
I SWEAR I WON'T TELL ANYONE. I GIVE YOU MY WORD.
COME TO THINK OF IT, THOUGH, IT'S REALLY MORE "AMERICAN WEREWOLF IN LONDON" THAN "TEEN WOLF."
BUT THAT WOULD MAKE ME YOUR FRIEND WHO TURNS INTO A GHOST, RIGHT? OR A ZOMBIE. I CAN'T REMEMBER WHICH HE WAS SUPPOSED TO BE.
GHOST OR ZOMBIE, EITHER ONE. HA! MAYBE I CAN BE THE GHOST, AND GWEN CAN BE THE ZOMBIE!
Terrific.

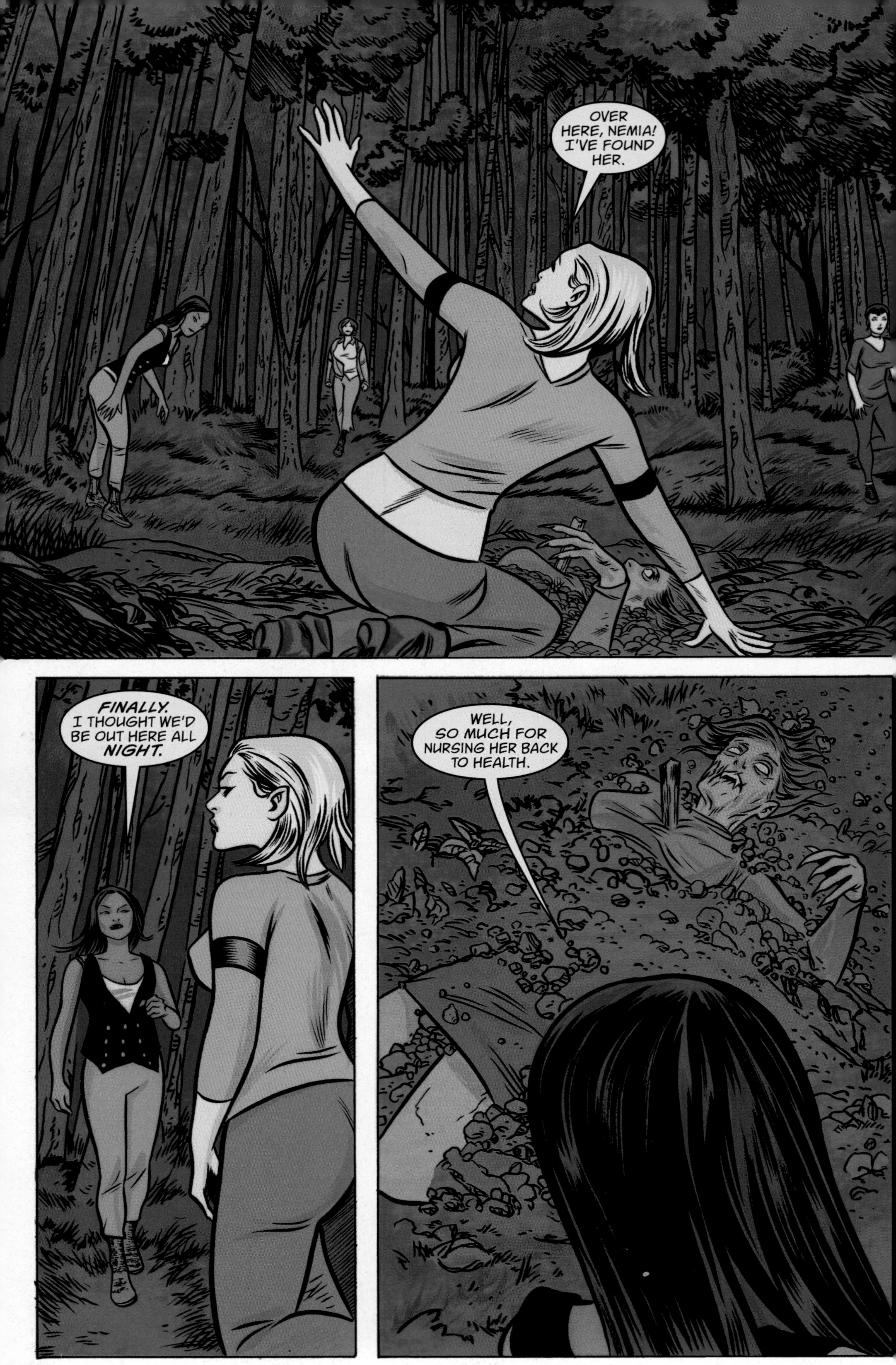
OVER HERE, NEMIA! I'VE FOUND HER.
FINALLY. I THOUGHT WE'D BE OUT HERE ALL NIGHT.
WELL, SO MUCH FOR NURSING HER BACK TO HEALTH.

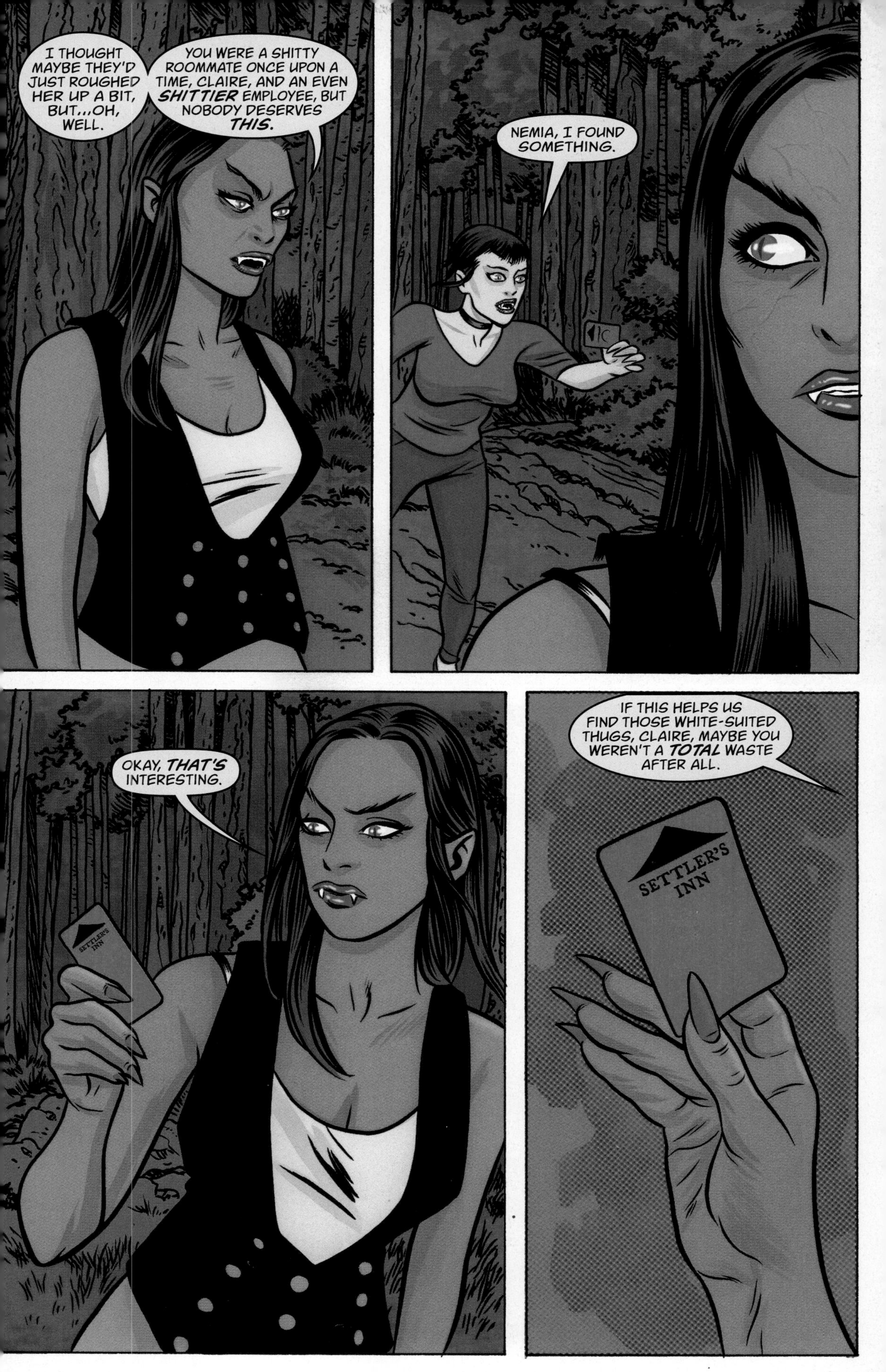
I THOUGHT MAYBE THEY'D JUST ROUGHED HER UP A BIT, BUT...OH, WELL.
YOU WERE A SHITTY ROOMMATE ONCE UPON A TIME, CLAIRE, AND AN EVEN SHITTIER EMPLOYEE, BUT NOBODY DESERVES THIS.
NEMIA, I FOUND SOMETHING.
OKAY, THAT'S INTERESTING.
SETTLER'S INN
IF THIS HELPS US FIND THOSE WHITE-SUITED THUGS, CLAIRE, MAYBE YOU WEREN'T A TOTAL WASTE AFTER ALL.
SETTLER'S INN

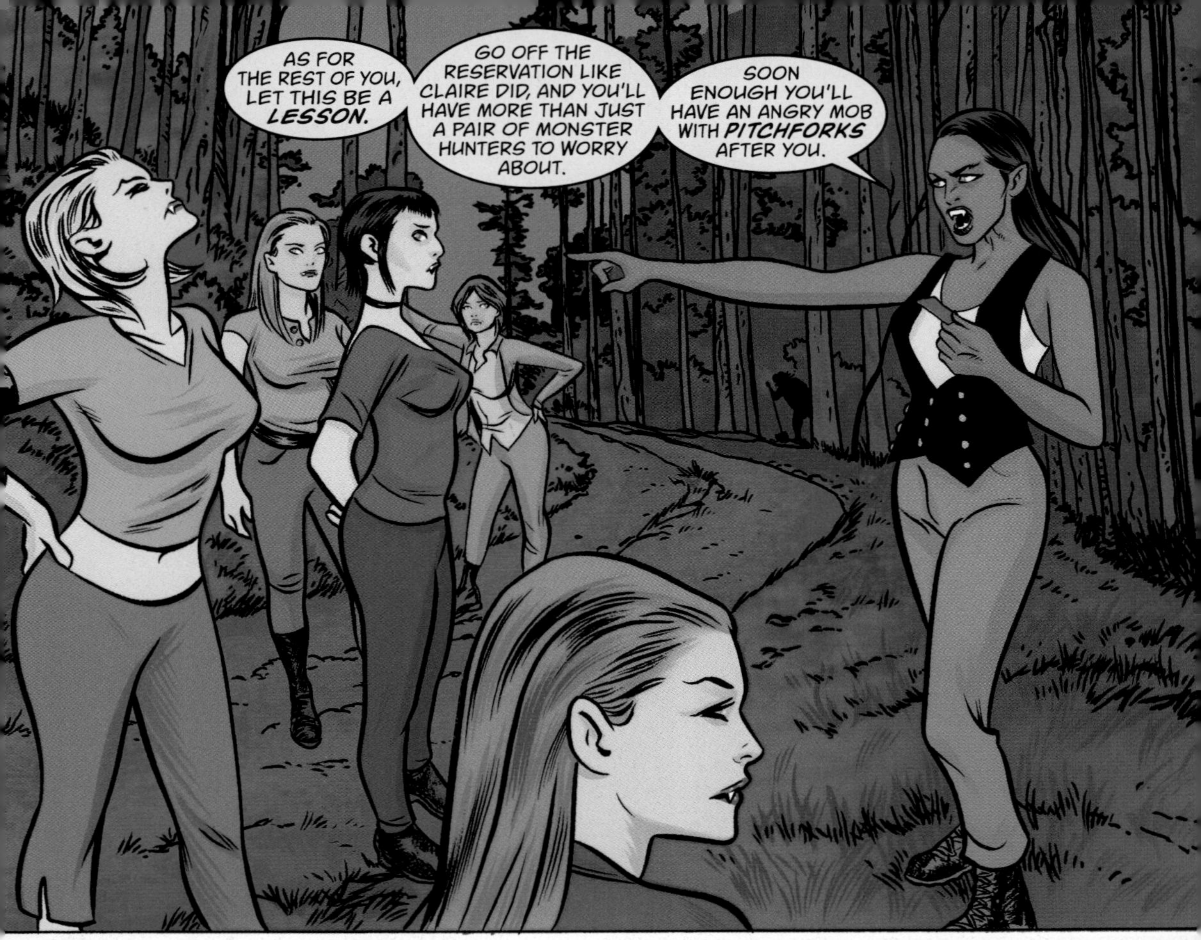
AS FOR THE REST OF YOU, LET THIS BE A LESSON.
GO OFF THE RESERVATION LIKE CLAIRE DID, AND YOU'LL HAVE MORE THAN JUST A PAIR OF MONSTER HUNTERS TO WORRY ABOUT.
SOON ENOUGH YOU'LL HAVE AN ANGRY MOB WITH PITCHFORKS AFTER YOU.

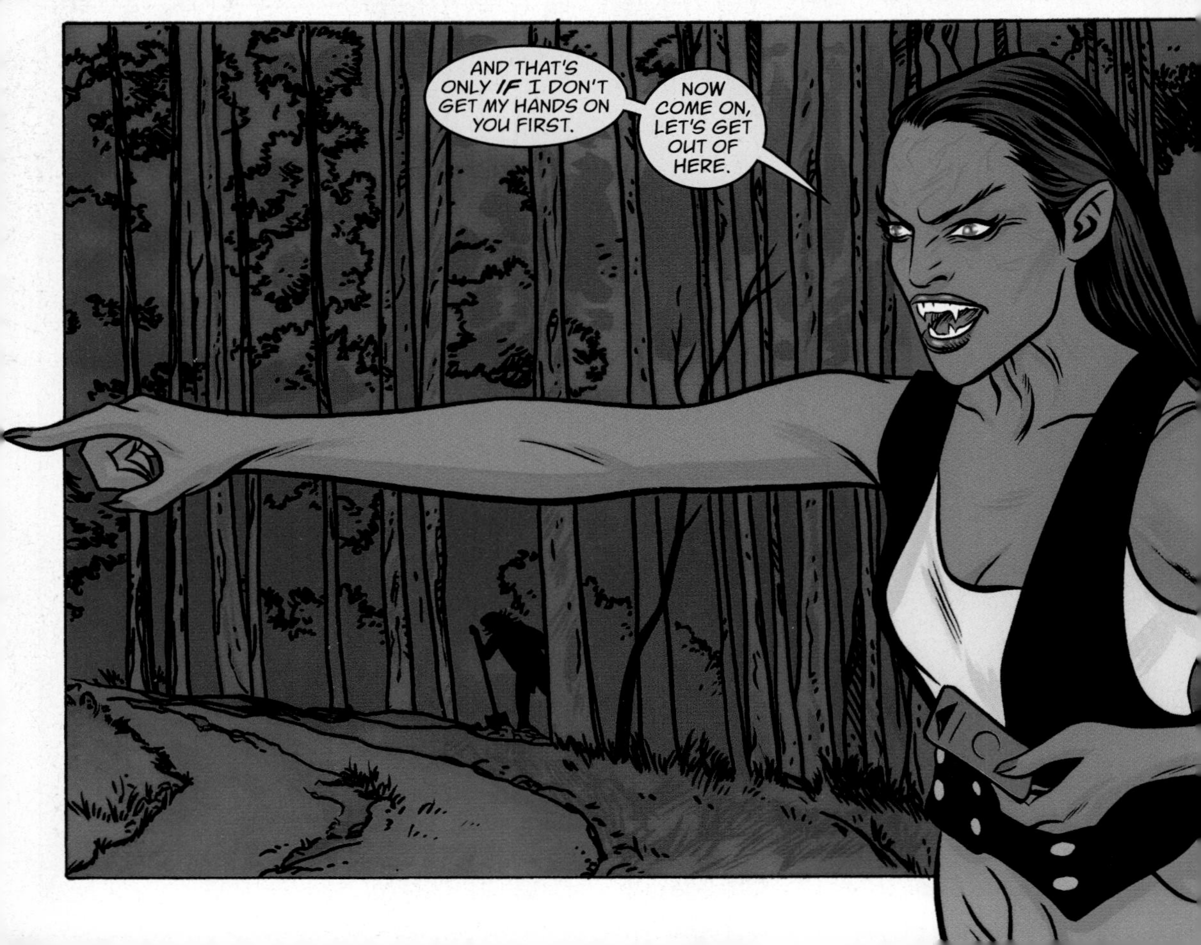
AND THAT'S ONLY IF I DON'T GET MY HANDS ON YOU FIRST.
NOW COME ON, LET'S GET OUT OF HERE.

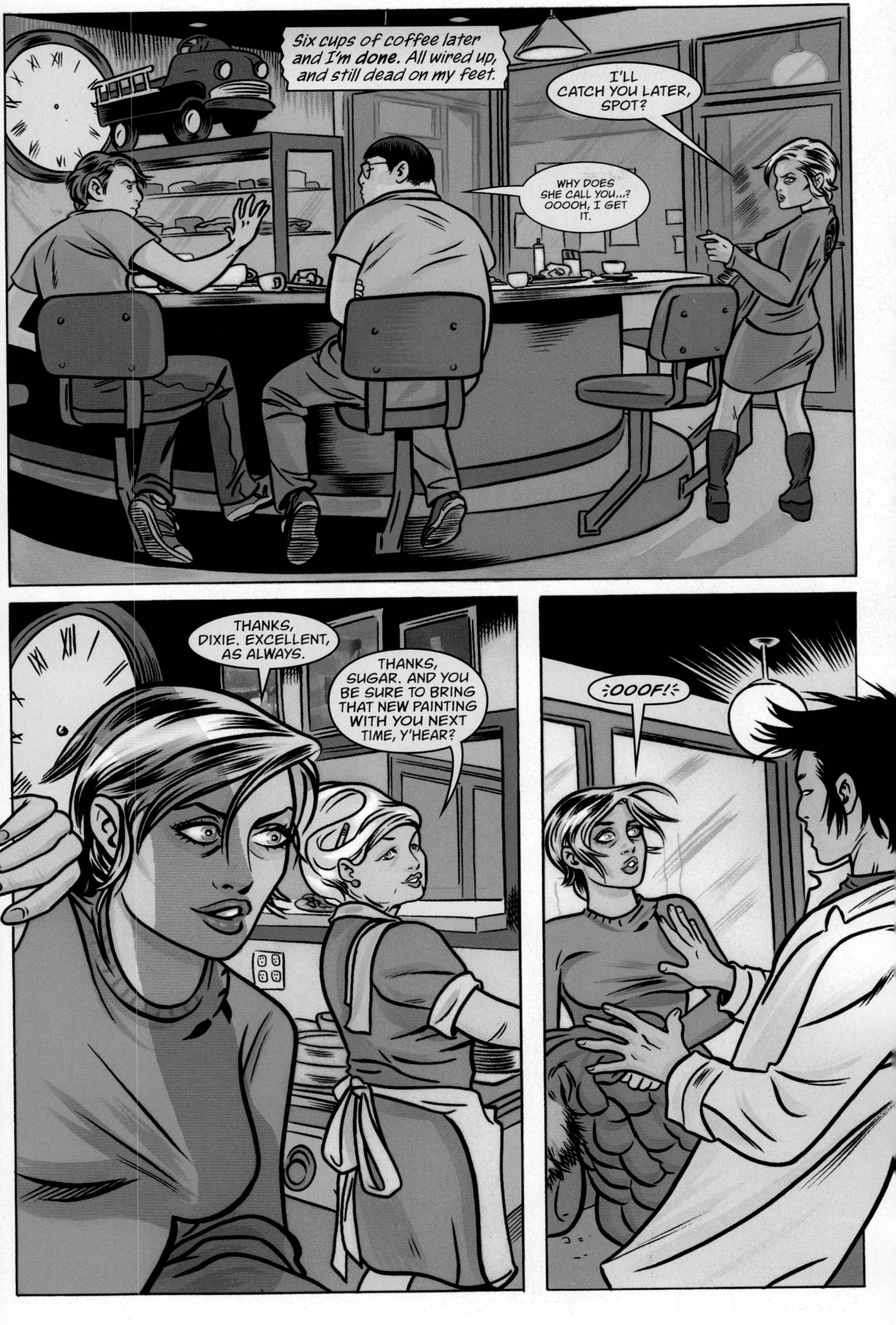
Six cups of coffee later and I'm **done.** All wired up, and still dead on my feet.
I'LL CATCH YOU LATER, SPOT?
WHY DOES SHE CALL YOU...? OOOOH, I GET IT.
THANKS, DIXIE. EXCELLENT, AS ALWAYS.
THANKS, SUGAR. AND YOU BE SURE TO BRING THAT NEW PAINTING WITH YOU NEXT TIME, Y'HEAR?
OOOF!

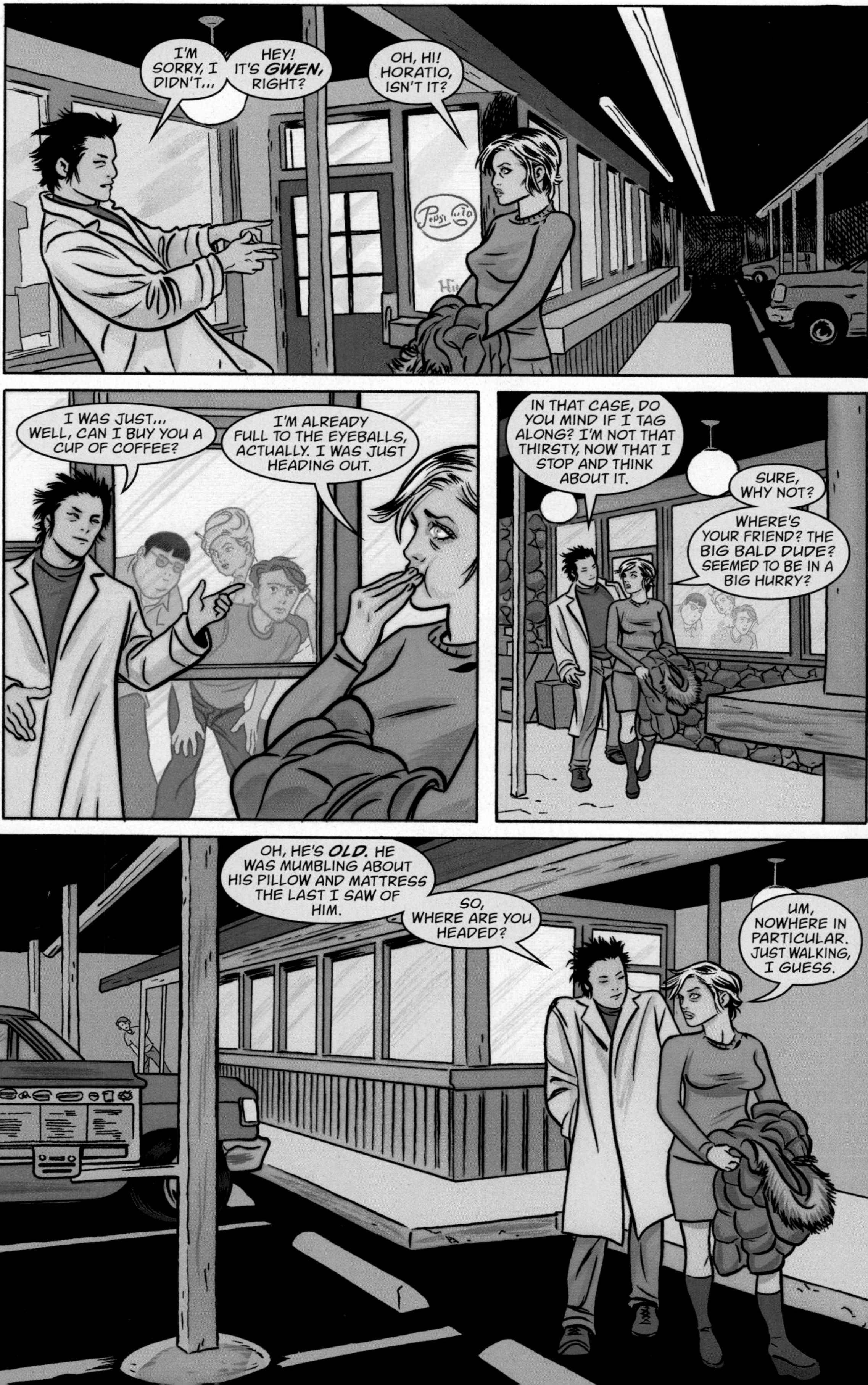
I'M SORRY, I DIDN'T...
HEY! IT'S GWEN, RIGHT?
OH, HI! HORATIO, ISN'T IT?
I WAS JUST... WELL, CAN I BUY YOU A CUP OF COFFEE?
I'M ALREADY FULL TO THE EYEBALLS, ACTUALLY. I WAS JUST HEADING OUT.
IN THAT CASE, DO YOU MIND IF I TAG ALONG? I'M NOT THAT THIRSTY, NOW THAT I STOP AND THINK ABOUT IT.
SURE, WHY NOT?
WHERE'S YOUR FRIEND? THE BIG BALD DUDE? SEEMED TO BE IN A BIG HURRY?
OH, HE'S OLD. HE WAS MUMBLING ABOUT HIS PILLOW AND MATTRESS THE LAST I SAW OF HIM.
SO, WHERE ARE YOU HEADED?
UM, NOWHERE IN PARTICULAR. JUST WALKING, I GUESS.

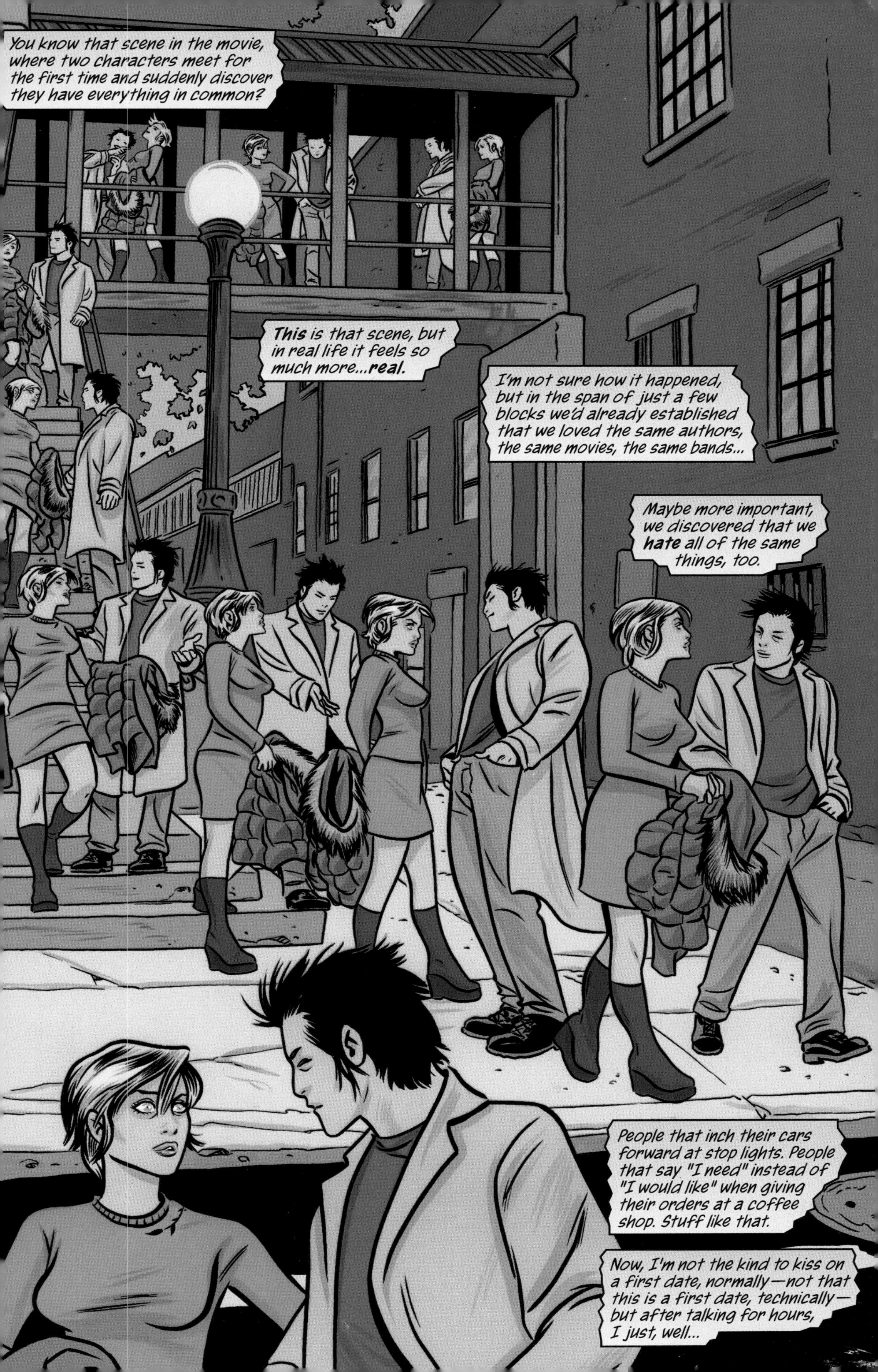
You know that scene in the movie, where two characters meet for the first time and suddenly discover they have everything in common?
This is that scene, but in real life it feels so much more...real.
I'm not sure how it happened, but in the span of just a few blocks we'd already established that we loved the same authors, the same movies, the same bands...
Maybe more important, we discovered that we hate all of the same things, too.
People that inch their cars forward at stop lights. People that say "I need" instead of "I would like" when giving their orders at a coffee shop. Stuff like that.
Now, I'm not the kind to kiss on a first date, normally—not that this is a first date, technically—but after talking for hours, I just, well...

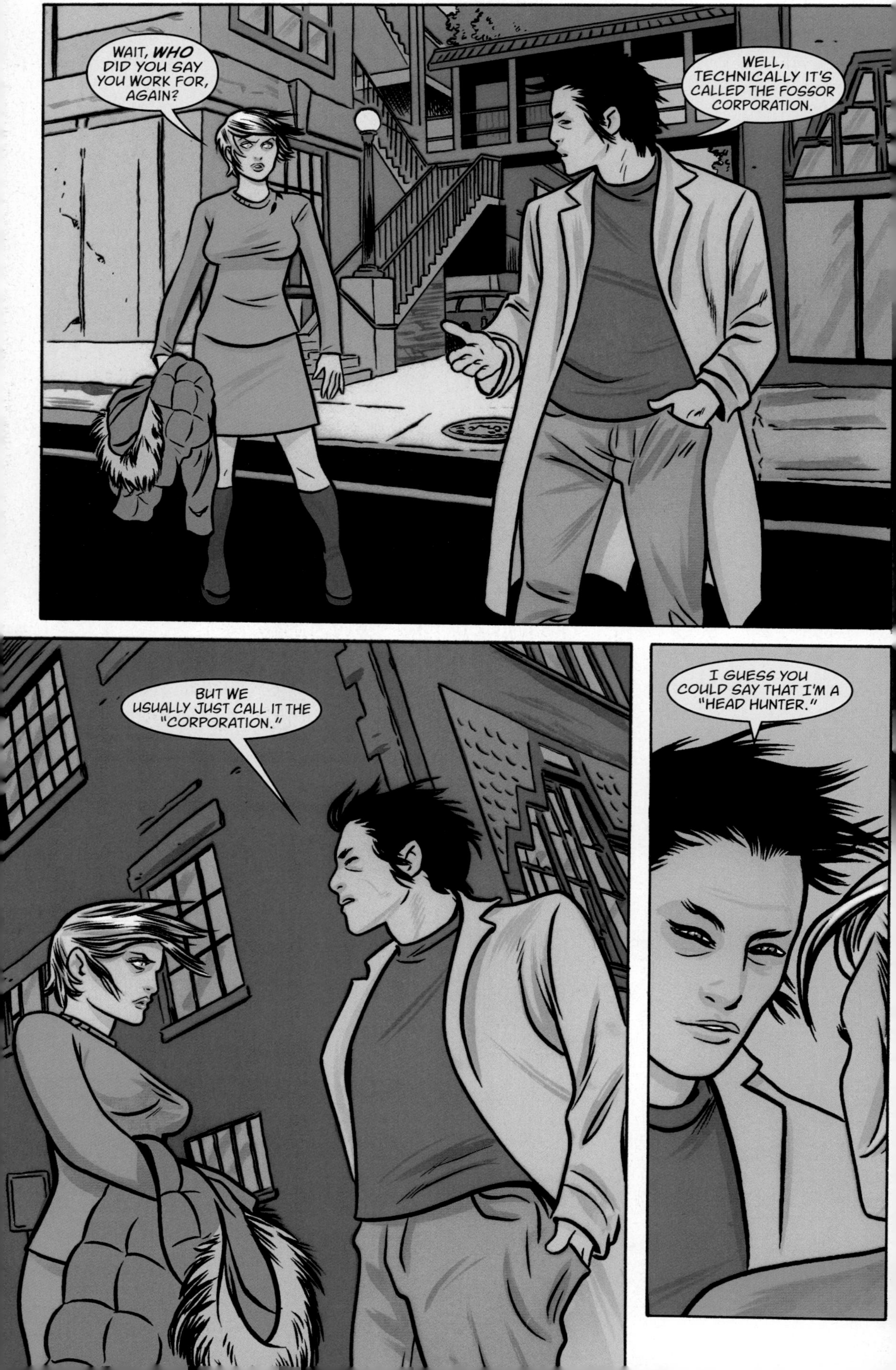
WAIT, **WHO** DID YOU SAY YOU WORK FOR, AGAIN?
WELL, TECHNICALLY IT'S CALLED THE FOSSOR CORPORATION.
BUT WE USUALLY JUST CALL IT THE "CORPORATION."
I GUESS YOU COULD SAY THAT I'M A "HEAD HUNTER."

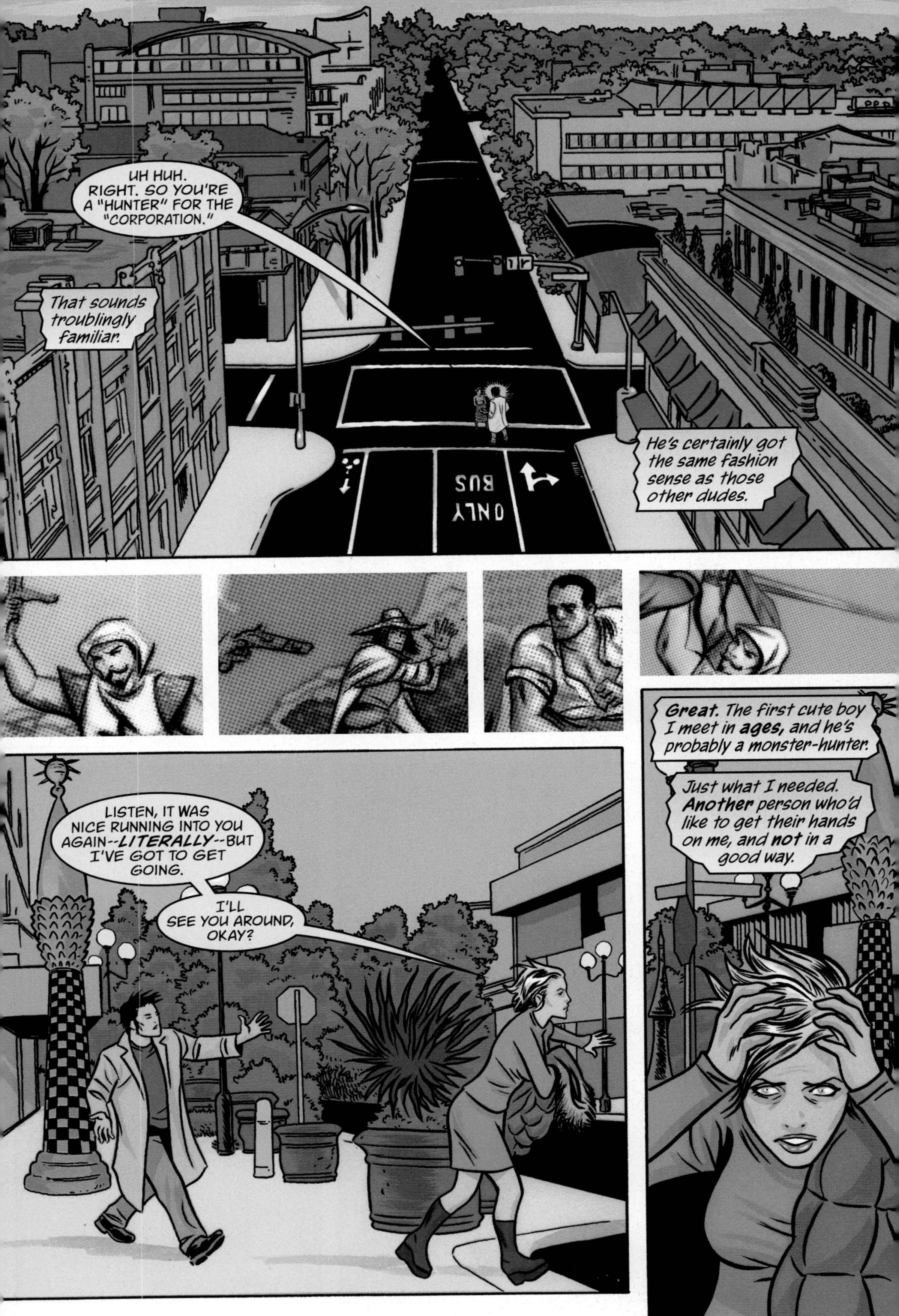
UH HUH. RIGHT. SO YOU'RE A "HUNTER" FOR THE "CORPORATION."
That sounds troublingly familiar.
He's certainly got the same fashion sense as those other dudes.
BUS
ONLY
Great. The first cute boy I meet in ages, and he's probably a monster-hunter.
Just what I needed. Another person who'd like to get their hands on me, and not in a good way.
LISTEN, IT WAS NICE RUNNING INTO YOU AGAIN--LITERALLY--BUT I'VE GOT TO GET GOING.
I'LL SEE YOU AROUND, OKAY?

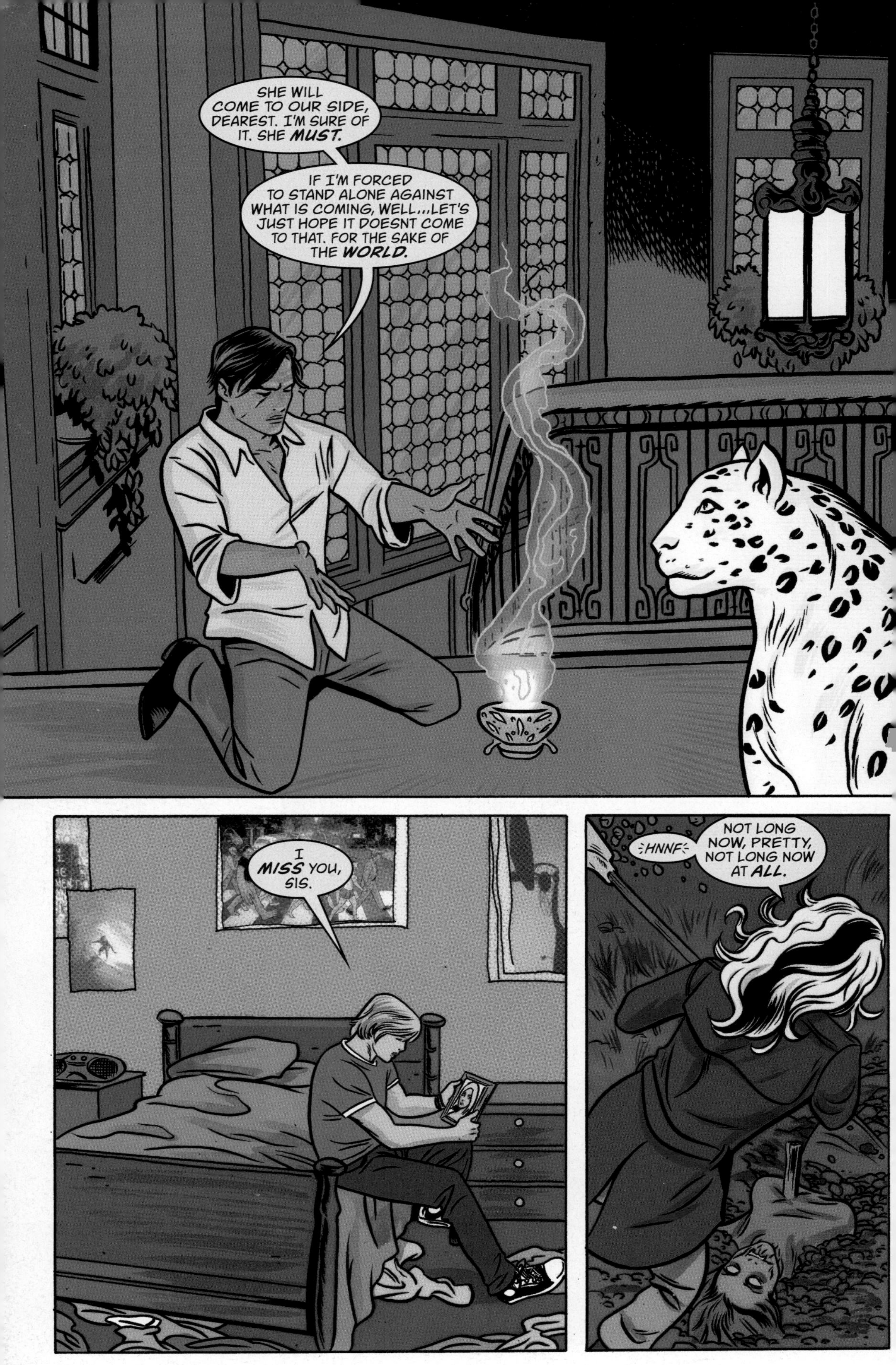
SHE WILL COME TO OUR SIDE, DEAREST. I'M SURE OF IT. SHE MUST.
IF I'M FORCED TO STAND ALONE AGAINST WHAT IS COMING, WELL...LET'S JUST HOPE IT DOESNT COME TO THAT. FOR THE SAKE OF THE WORLD.
I MISS YOU, SIS.
HNNF
NOT LONG NOW, PRETTY, NOT LONG NOW AT ALL.

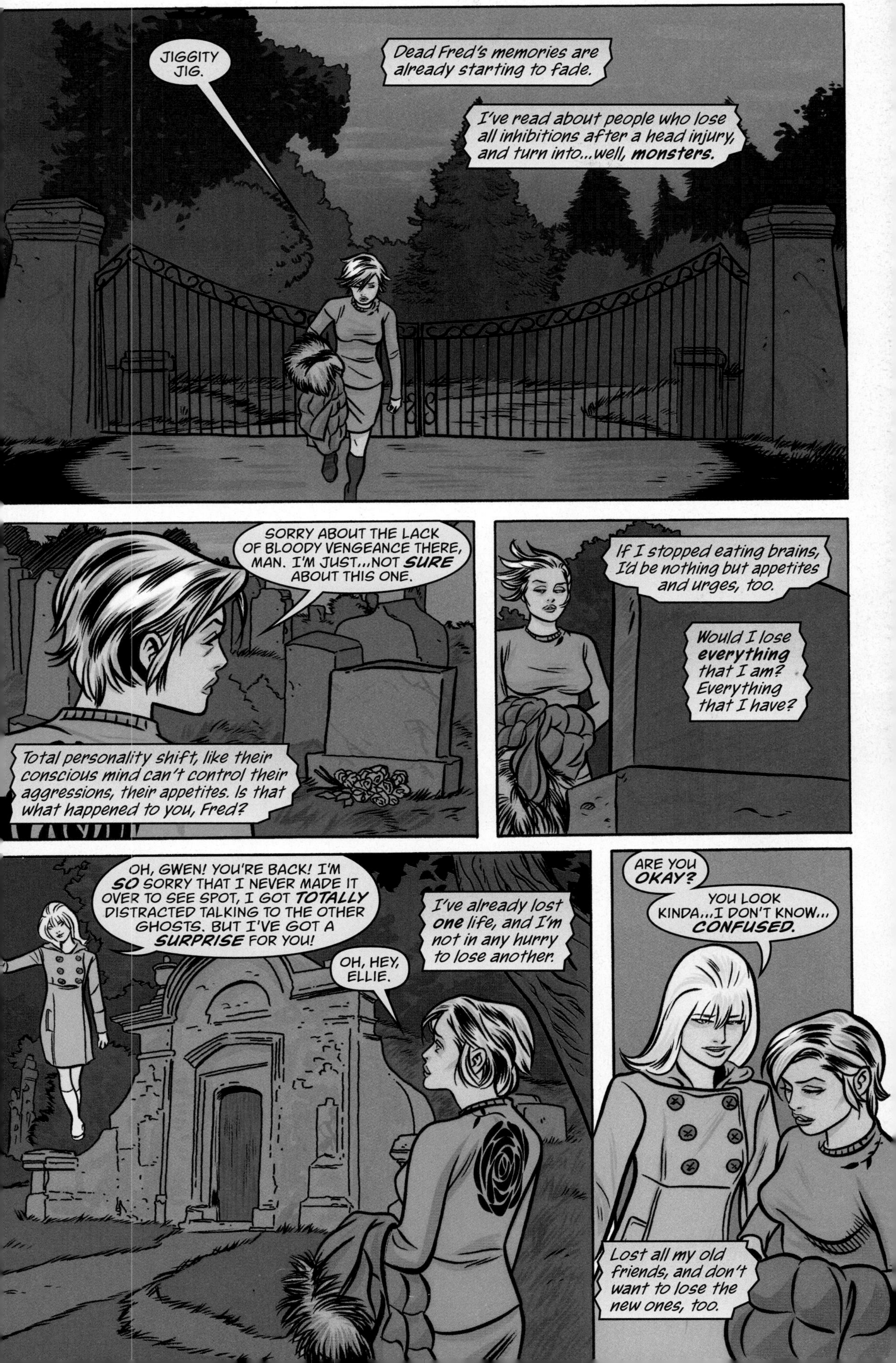
JIGGITY JIG.
Dead Fred's memories are already starting to fade.
I've read about people who lose all inhibitions after a head injury, and turn into...well, **monsters.**
SORRY ABOUT THE LACK OF BLOODY VENGEANCE THERE, MAN. I'M JUST...NOT ***SURE*** ABOUT THIS ONE.
Total personality shift, like their conscious mind can't control their aggressions, their appetites. Is that what happened to you, Fred?
If I stopped eating brains, I'd be nothing but appetites and urges, too.
Would I lose **everything** that I am? Everything that I have?
OH, GWEN! YOU'RE BACK! I'M ***SO*** SORRY THAT I NEVER MADE IT OVER TO SEE SPOT, I GOT ***TOTALLY*** DISTRACTED TALKING TO THE OTHER GHOSTS. BUT I'VE GOT A ***SURPRISE*** FOR YOU!
I've already lost **one** life, and I'm not in any hurry to lose another.
OH, HEY, ELLIE.
ARE YOU ***OKAY?***
YOU LOOK KINDA...I DON'T KNOW... ***CONFUSED.***
Lost all my old friends, and don't want to lose the new ones, too.

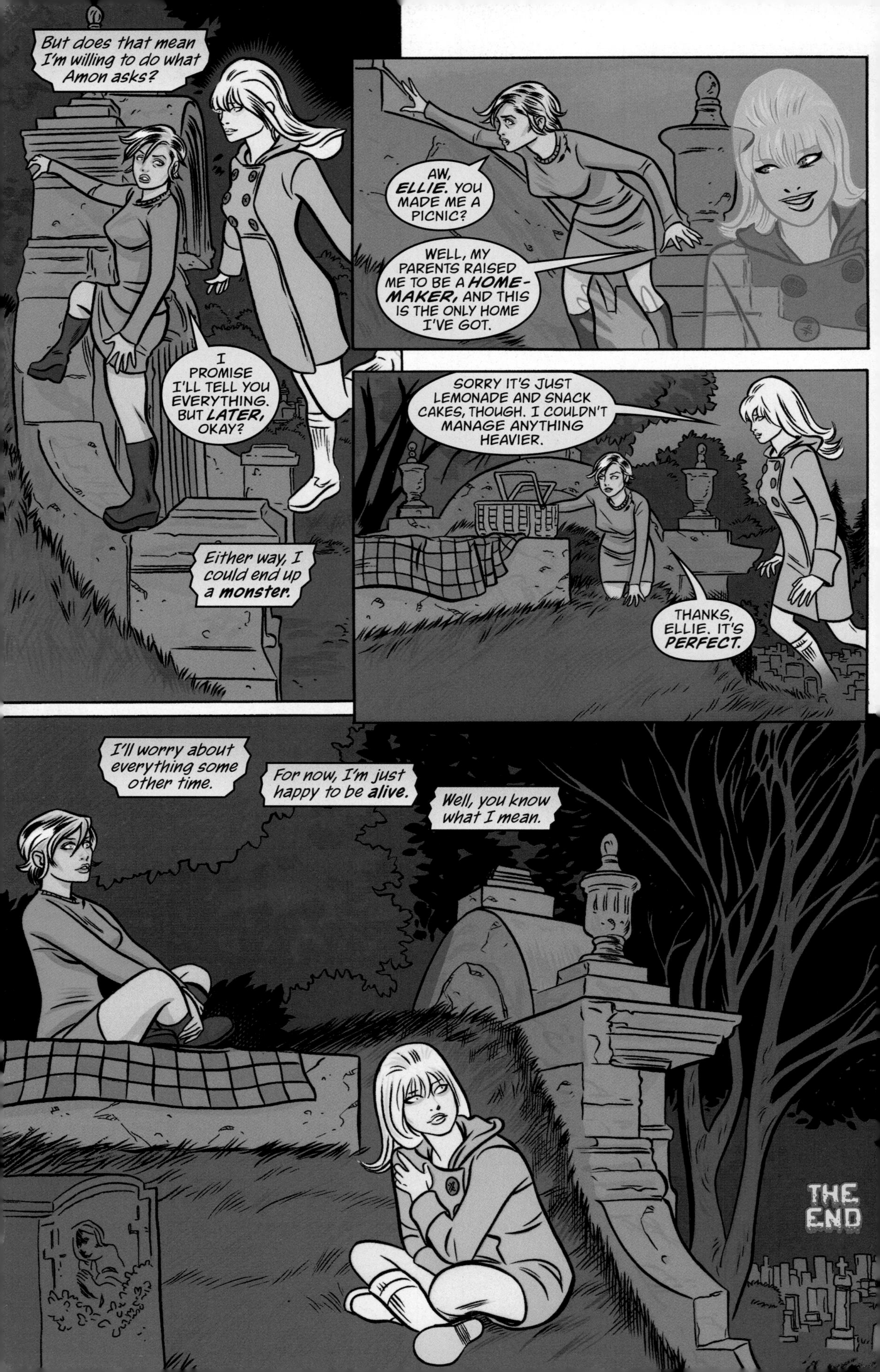
But does that mean I'm willing to do what Amon asks?
I PROMISE I'LL TELL YOU EVERYTHING. BUT LATER, OKAY?
Either way, I could end up a monster.
AW, ELLIE. YOU MADE ME A PICNIC?
WELL, MY PARENTS RAISED ME TO BE A HOME-MAKER, AND THIS IS THE ONLY HOME I'VE GOT.
SORRY IT'S JUST LEMONADE AND SNACK CAKES, THOUGH. I COULDN'T MANAGE ANYTHING HEAVIER.
THANKS, ELLIE. IT'S PERFECT.
I'll worry about everything some other time.
For now, I'm just happy to be alive.
Well, you know what I mean.
THE END

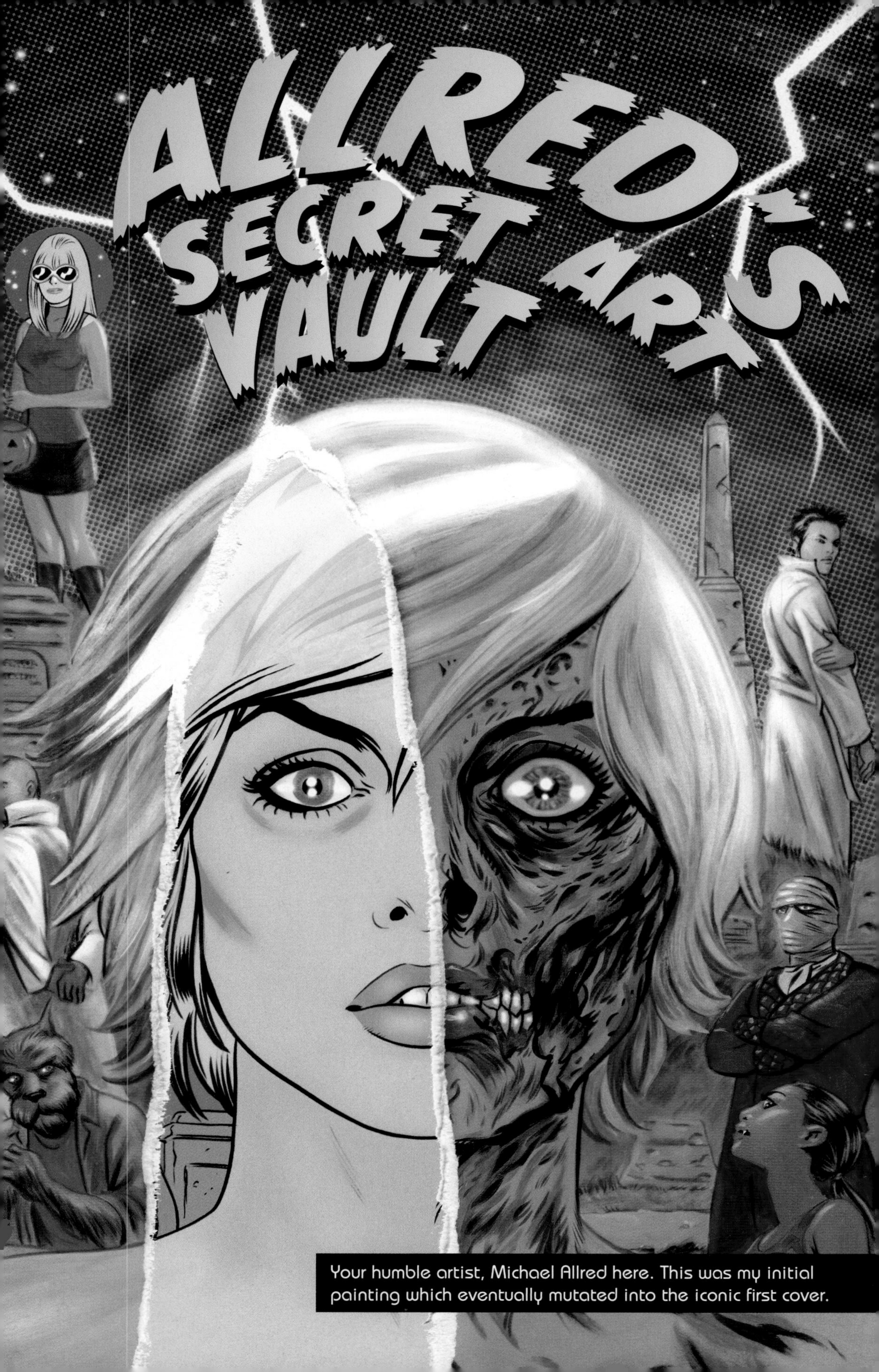
ALLRED'S SECRET ART VAULT

Your humble artist, Michael Allred here. This was my initial painting which eventually mutated into the iconic first cover.

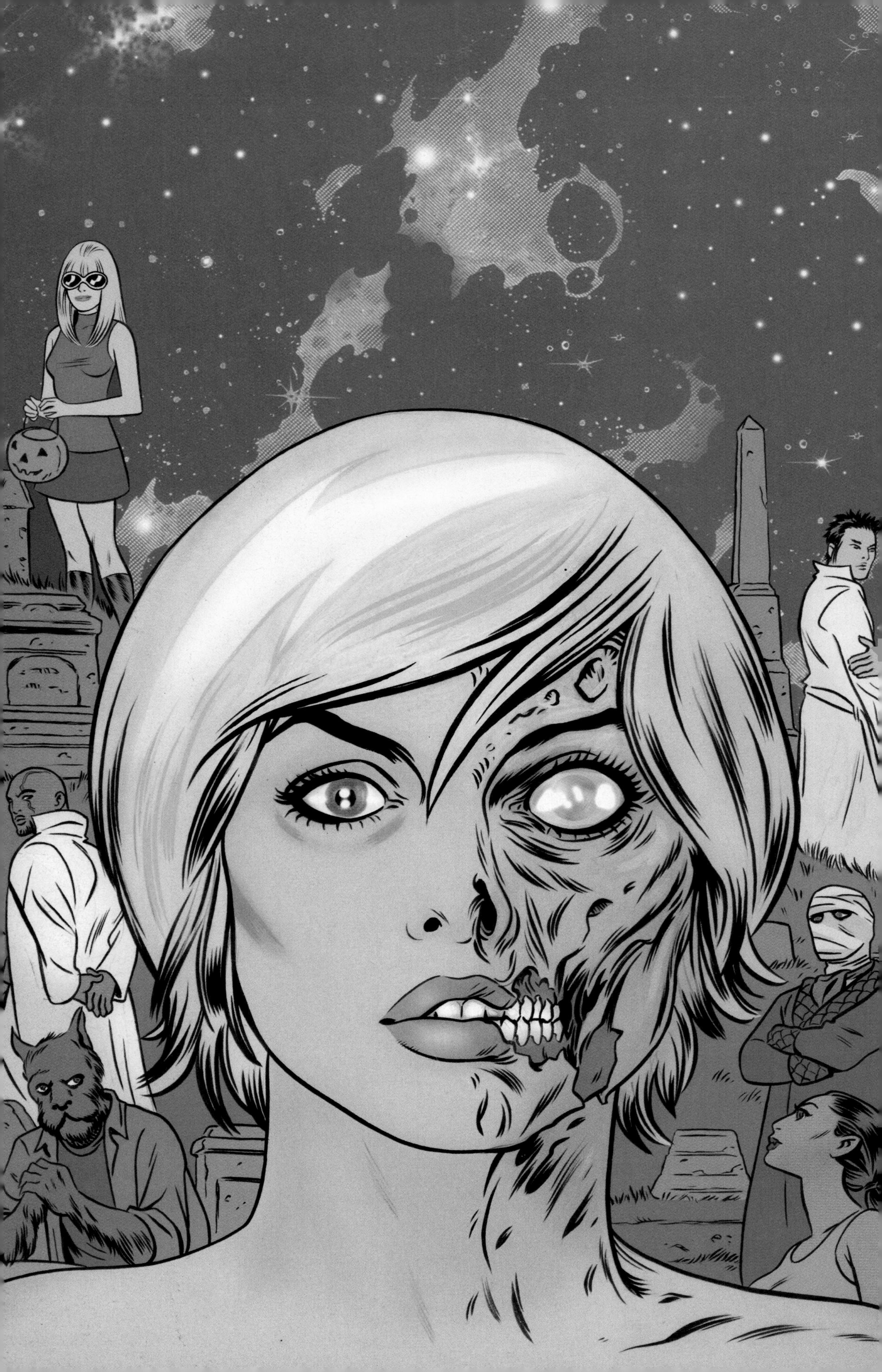

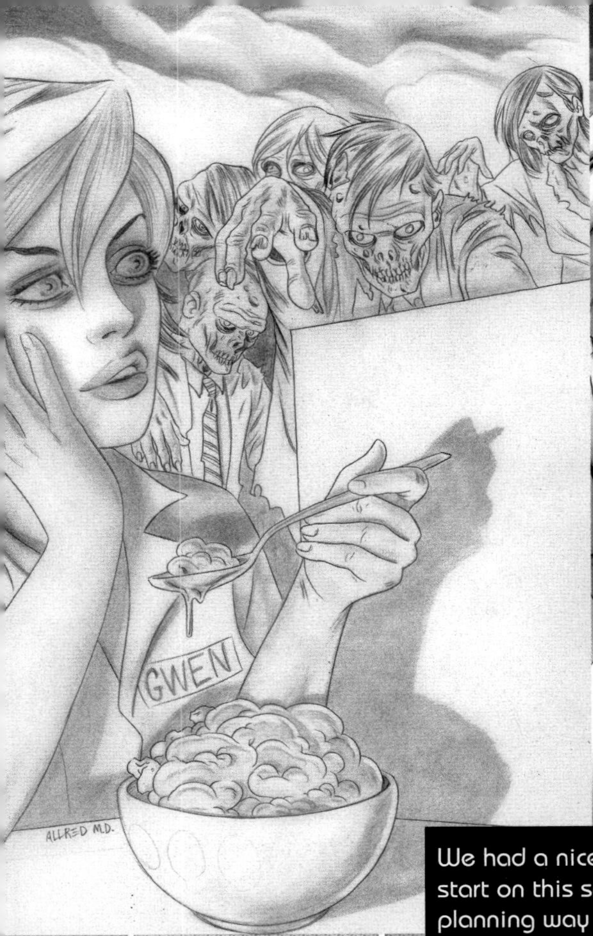
GWEN
ALLRED M.D.

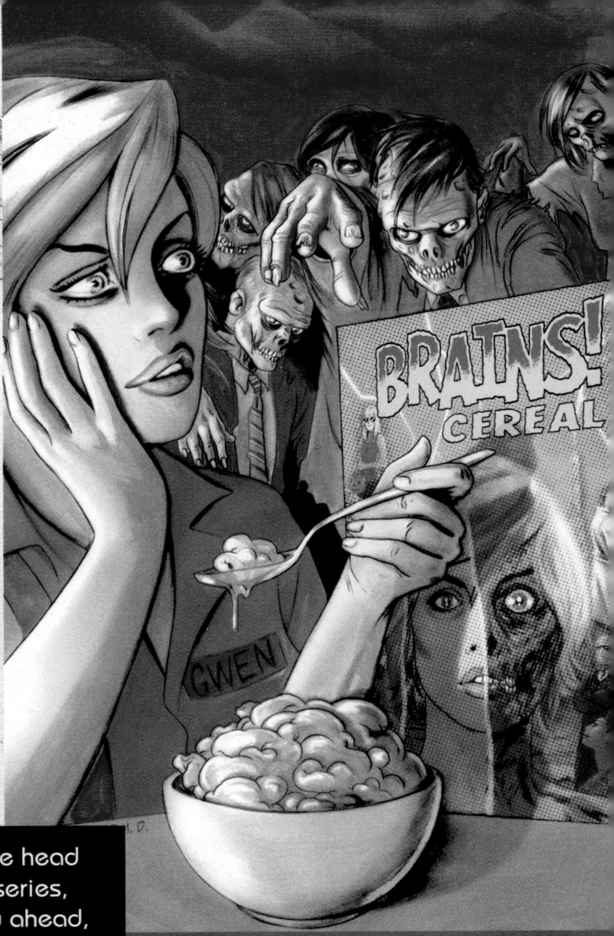
BRAINS!
CEREAL
GWEN

We had a nice head start on this series, planning way ahead, which allowed me to do several variations on the early covers.

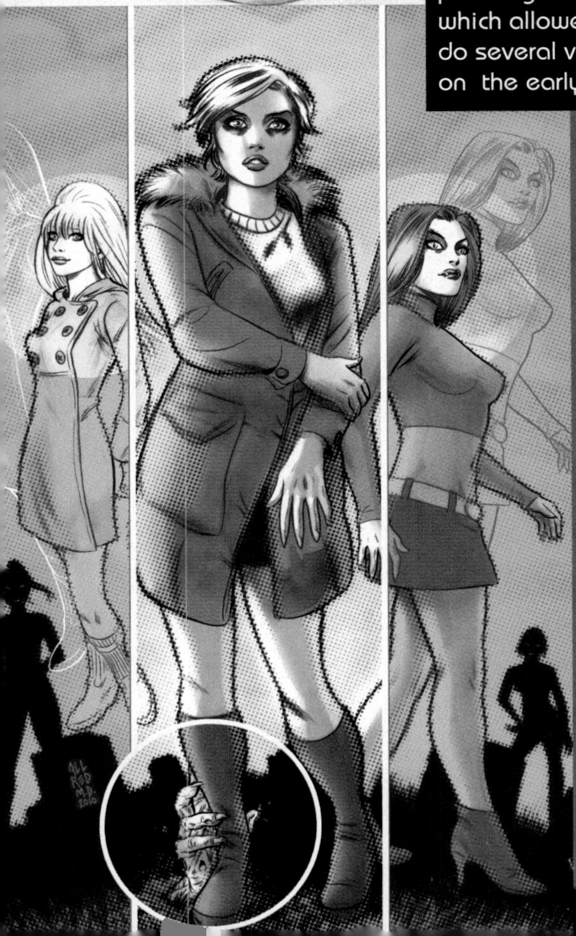
ALL RED M.D. 2010

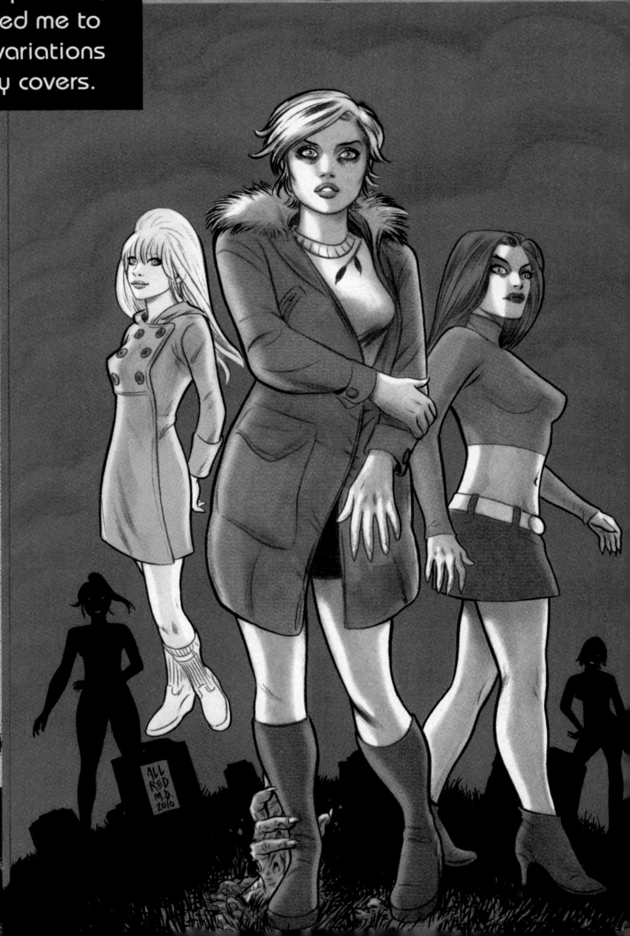
ALL RED M.D. 2010

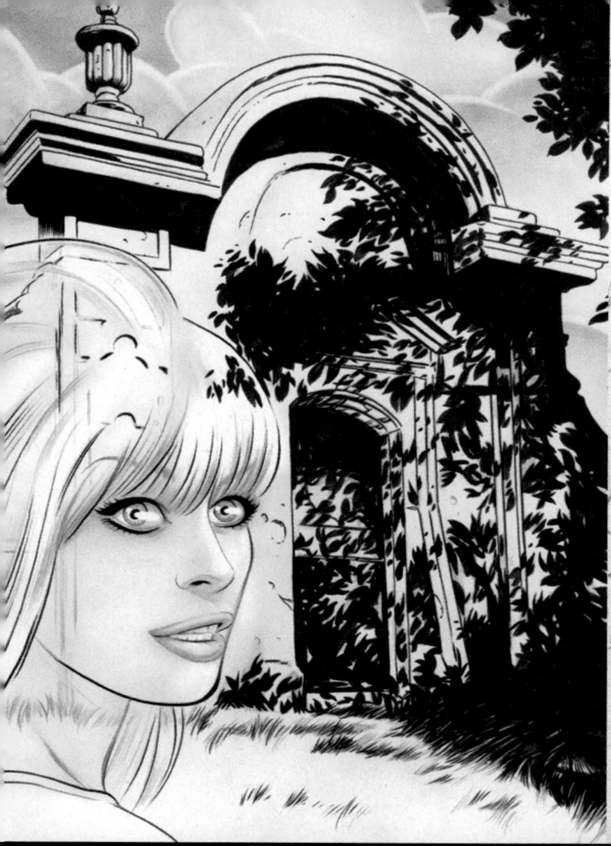

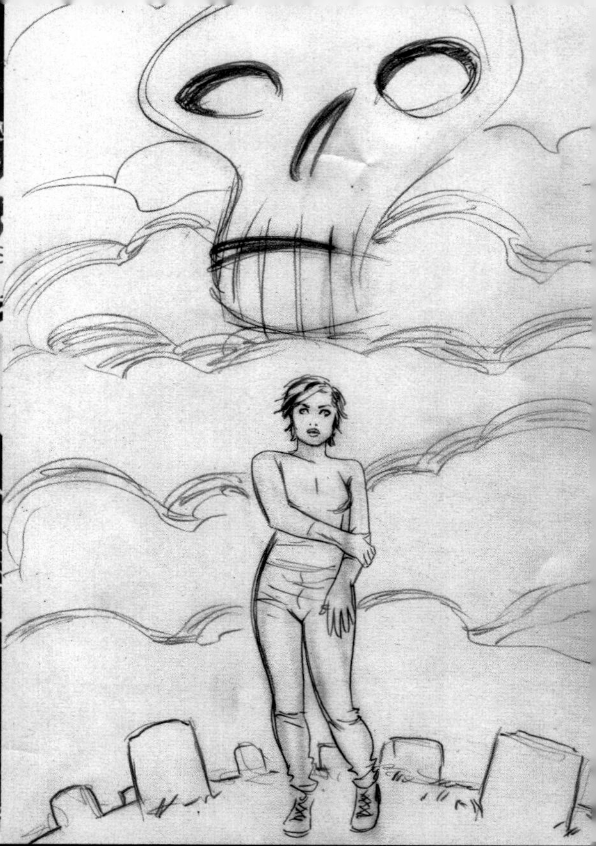

Clockwise from the upper left we have an example of the original art before Laura works her color magic; my first cover sketch for the third cover; Ellie realized, and my rough sketch for the fourth cover.

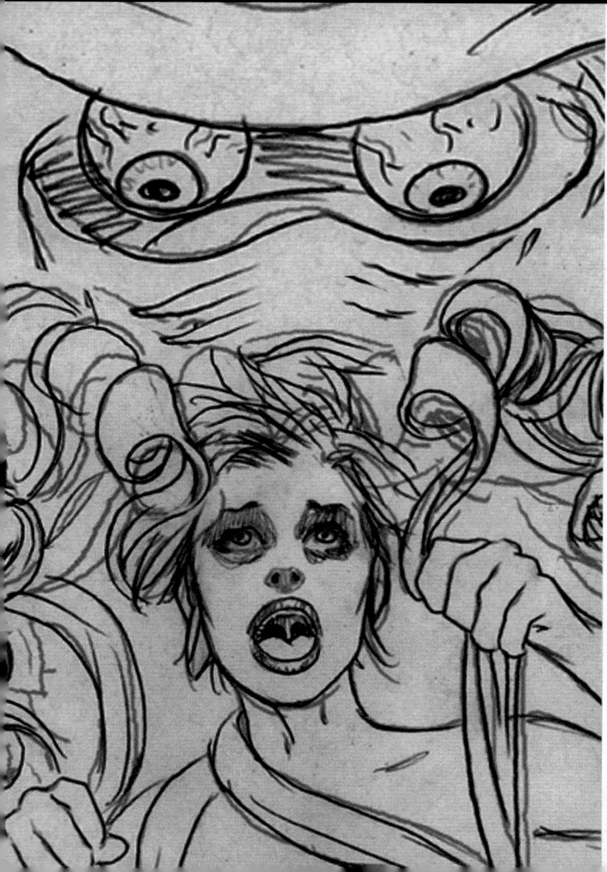

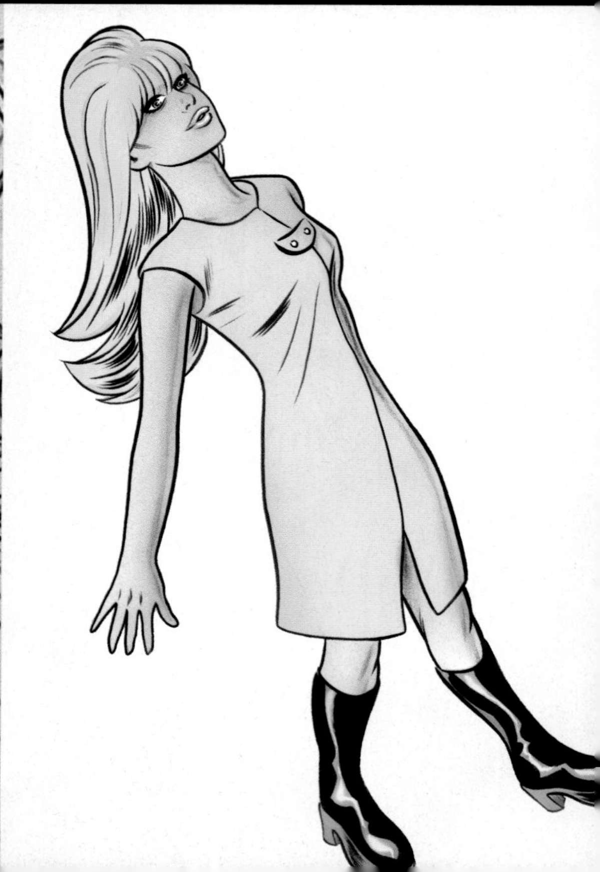

My favorite unused cover idea.
Still hope to find an excuse to
finish this up someday.

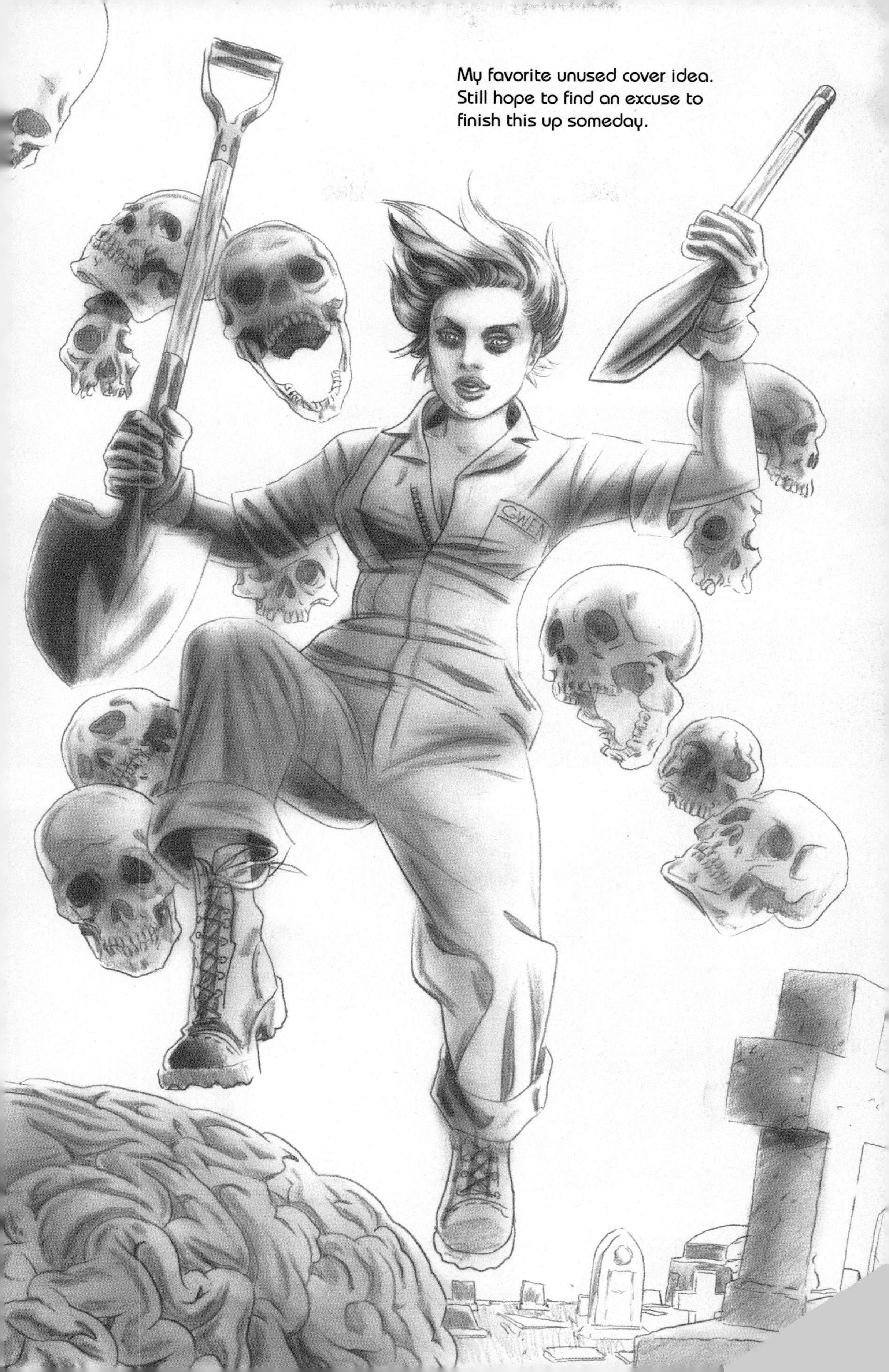
GWEN

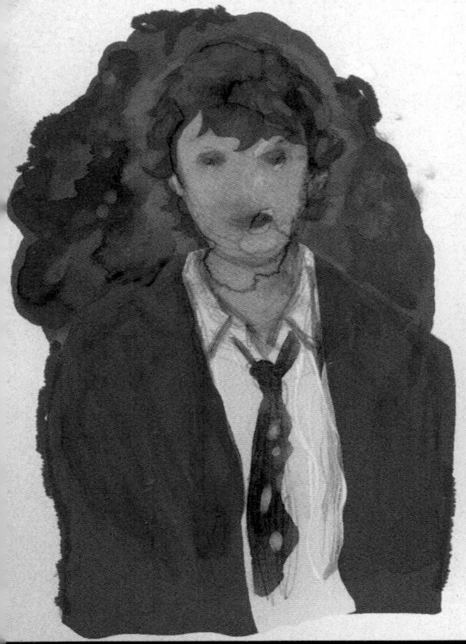
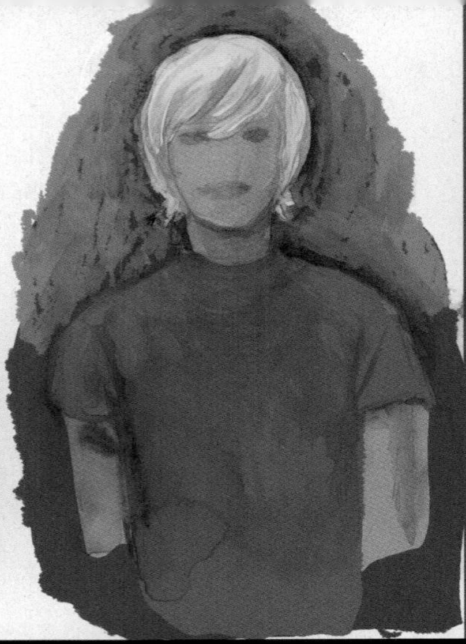
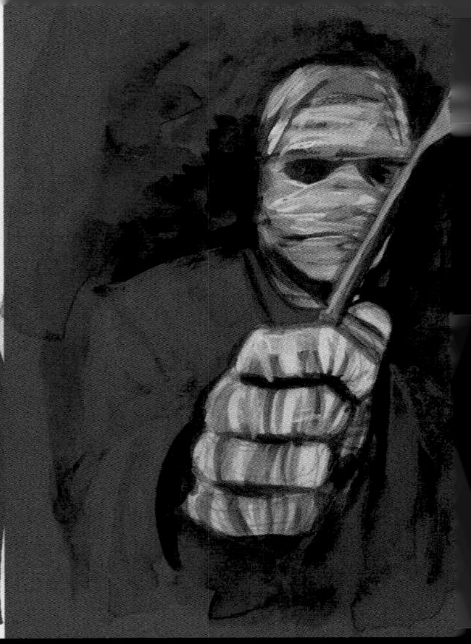

Here's a sampling of "Gwen's" paintings.

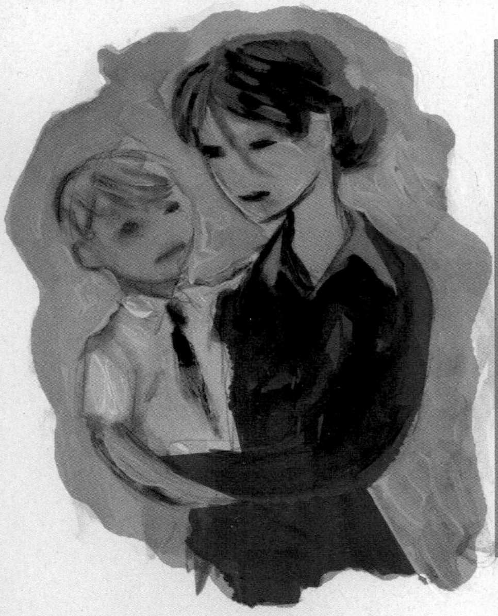
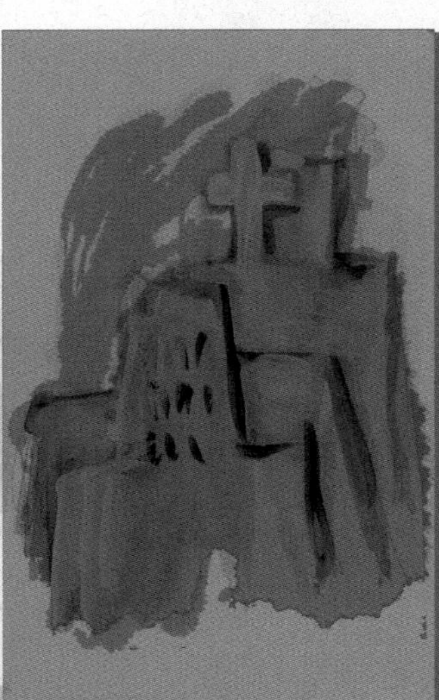
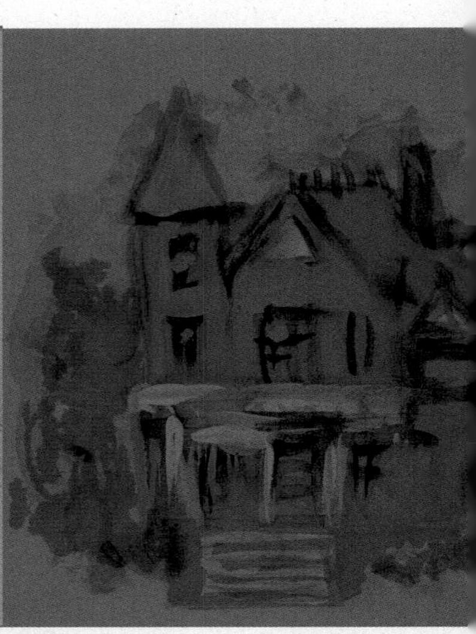
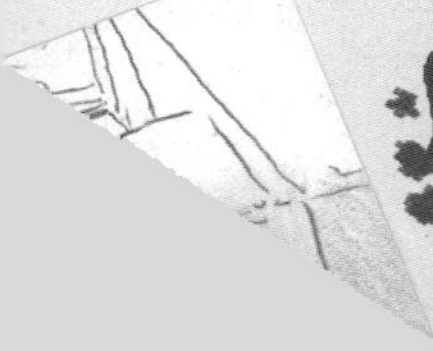
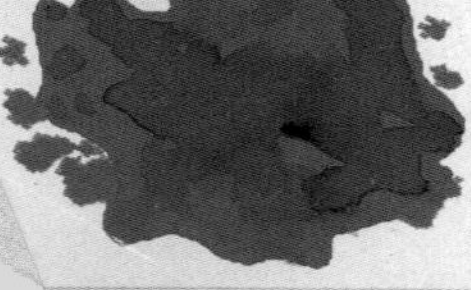
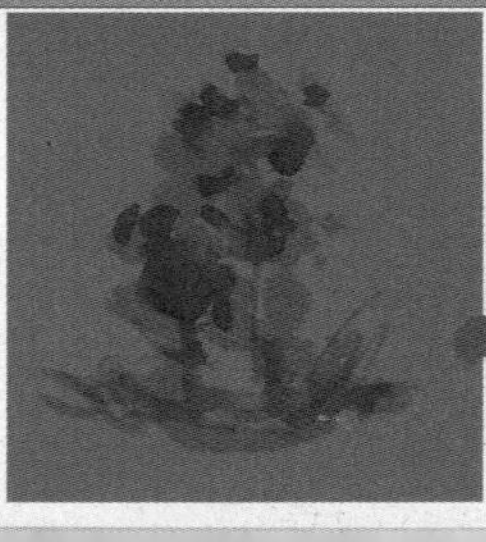
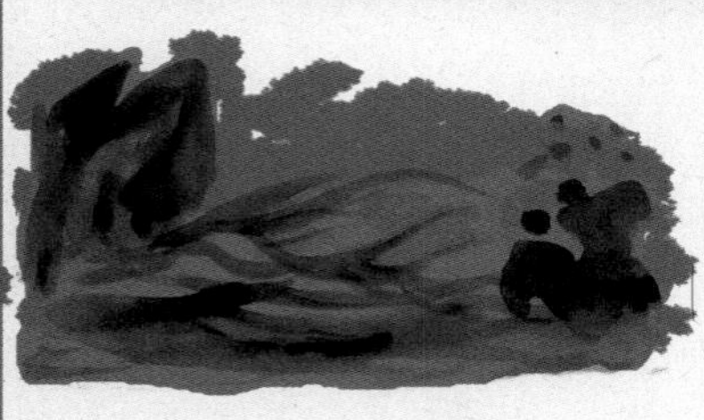

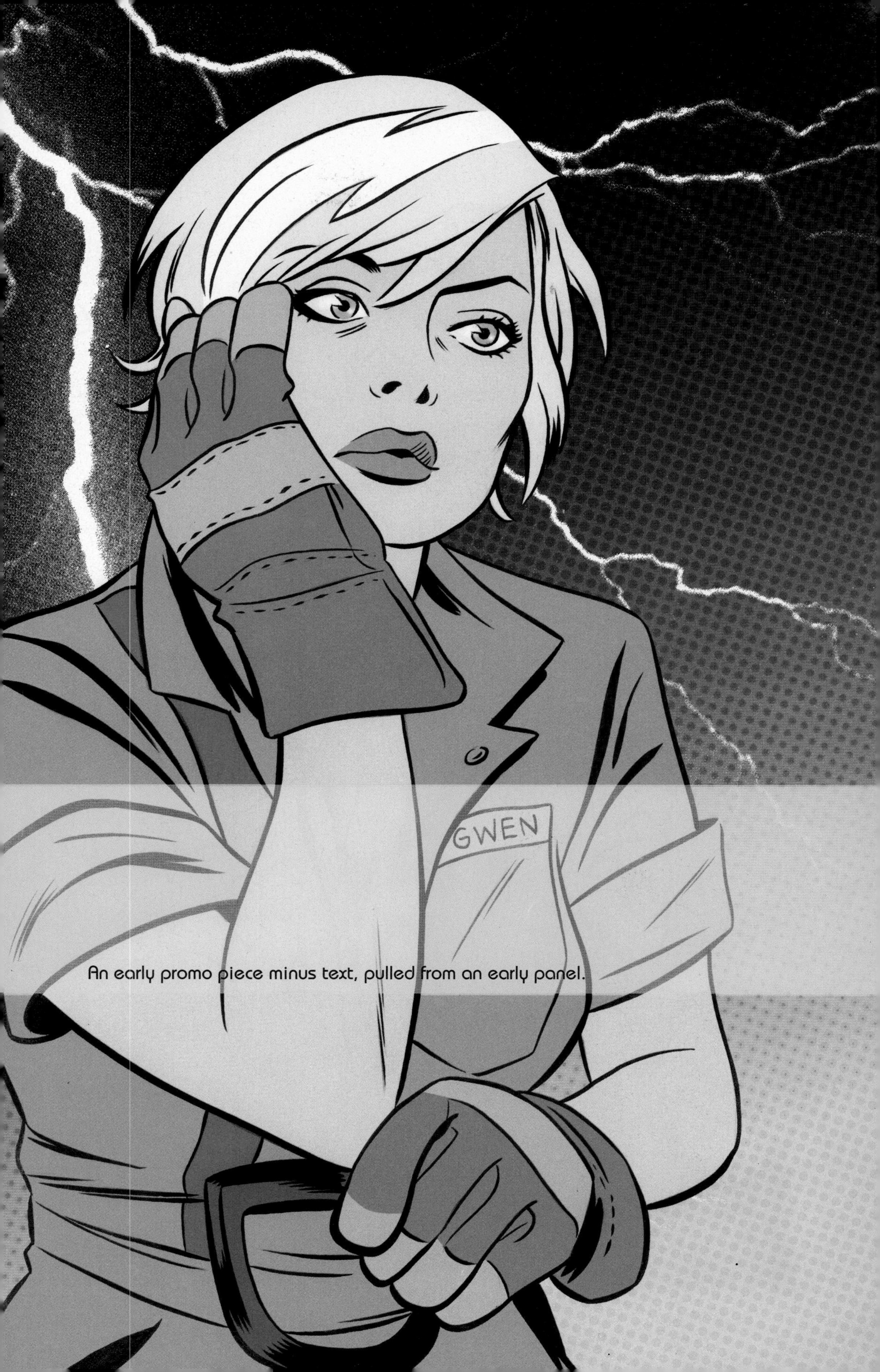
GWEN

An early promo piece minus text, pulled from an early panel.

Another favorite unused cover idea that I hope to finish someday.

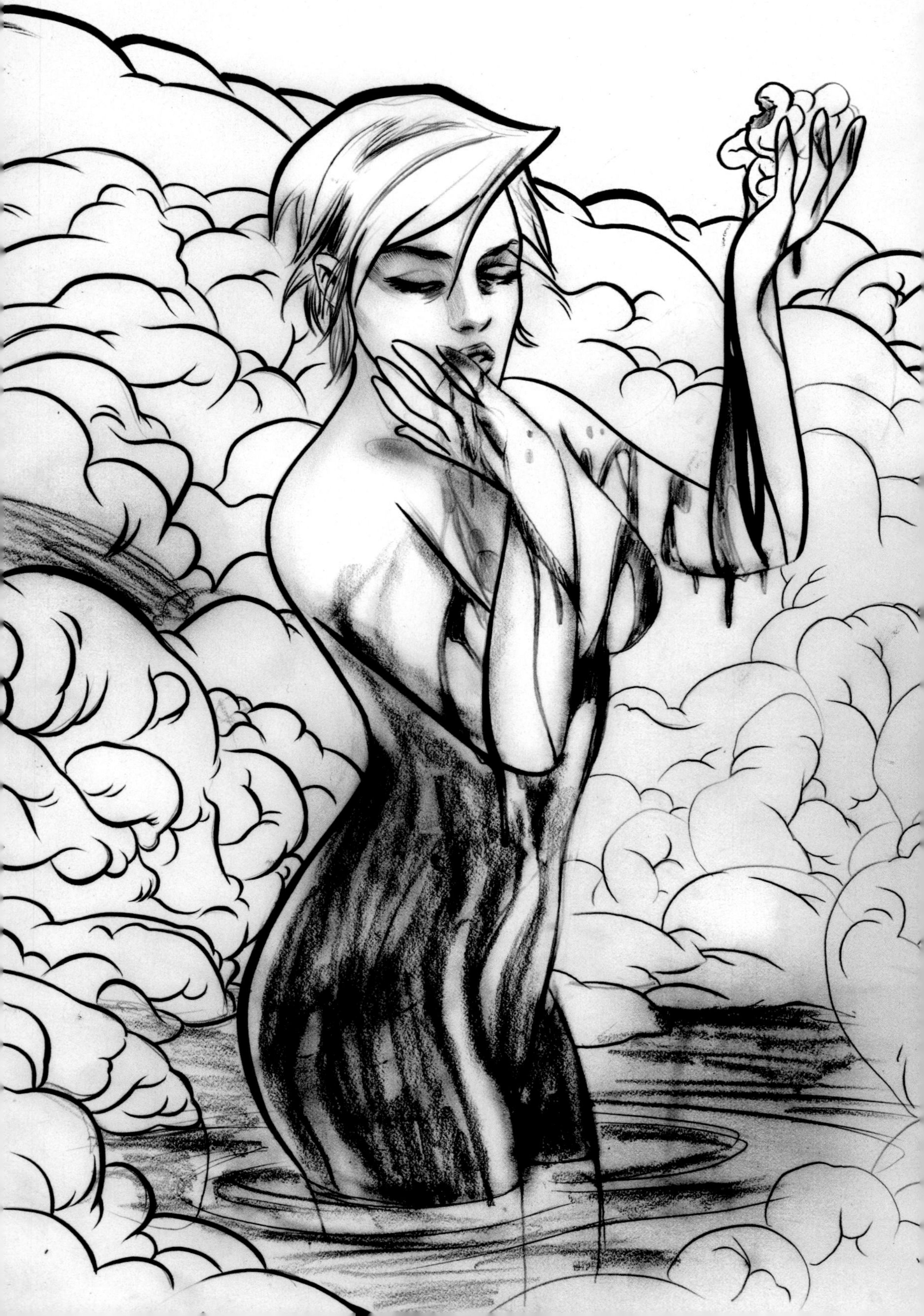

This baby will see life on the cover of *iZOMBIE* no.12.

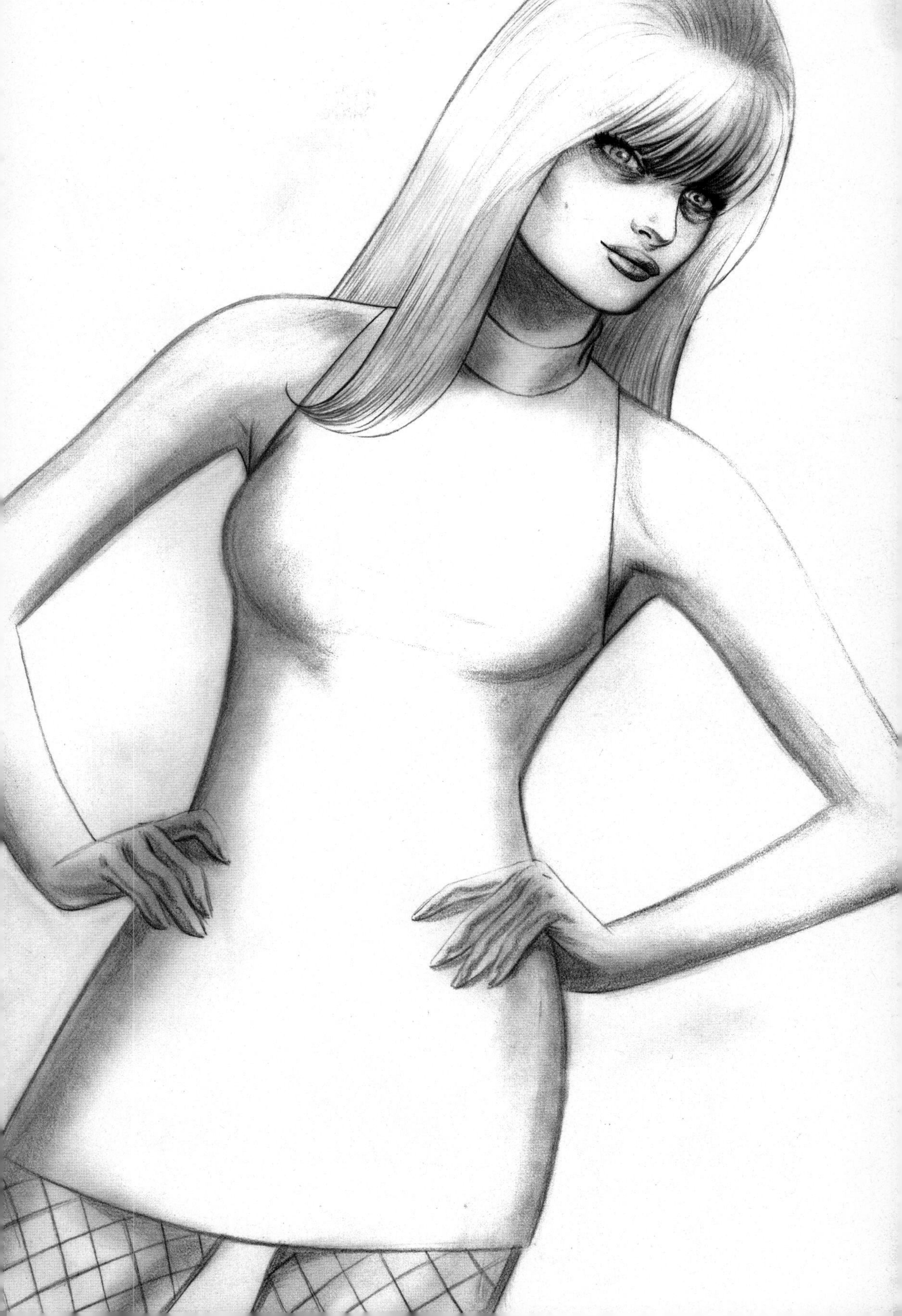

Another unused cover idea.

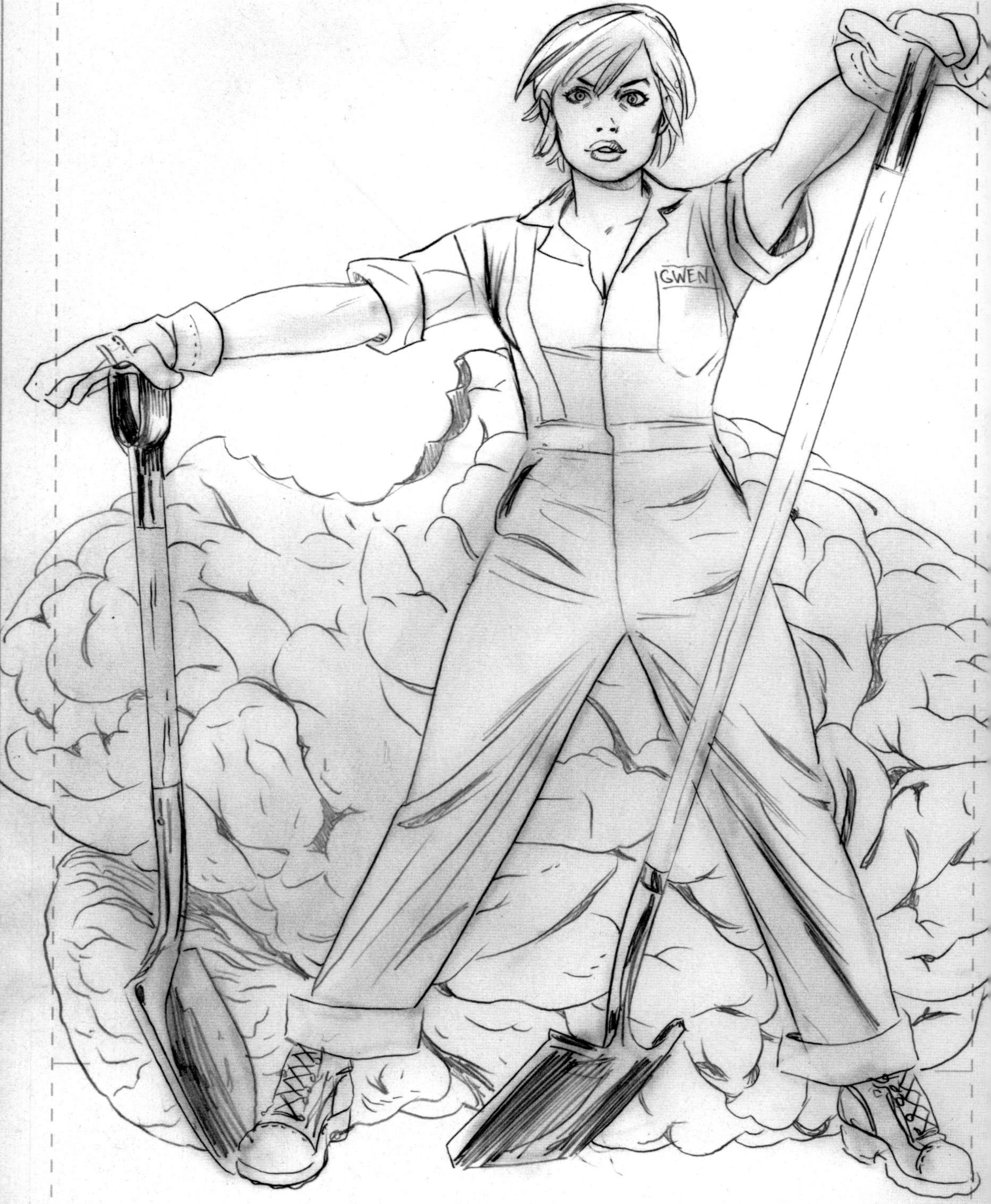
GWEN

LIVE AREA

CROP

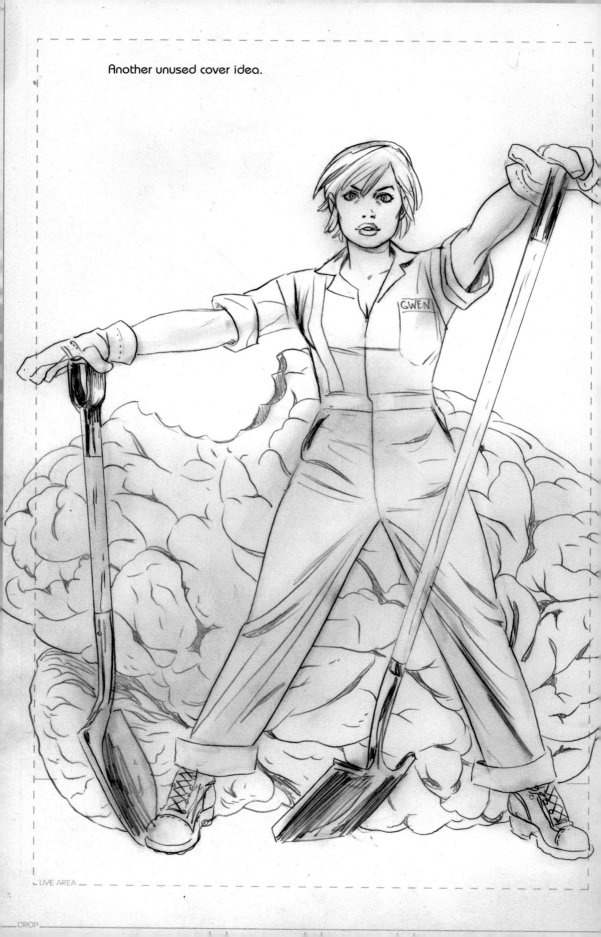

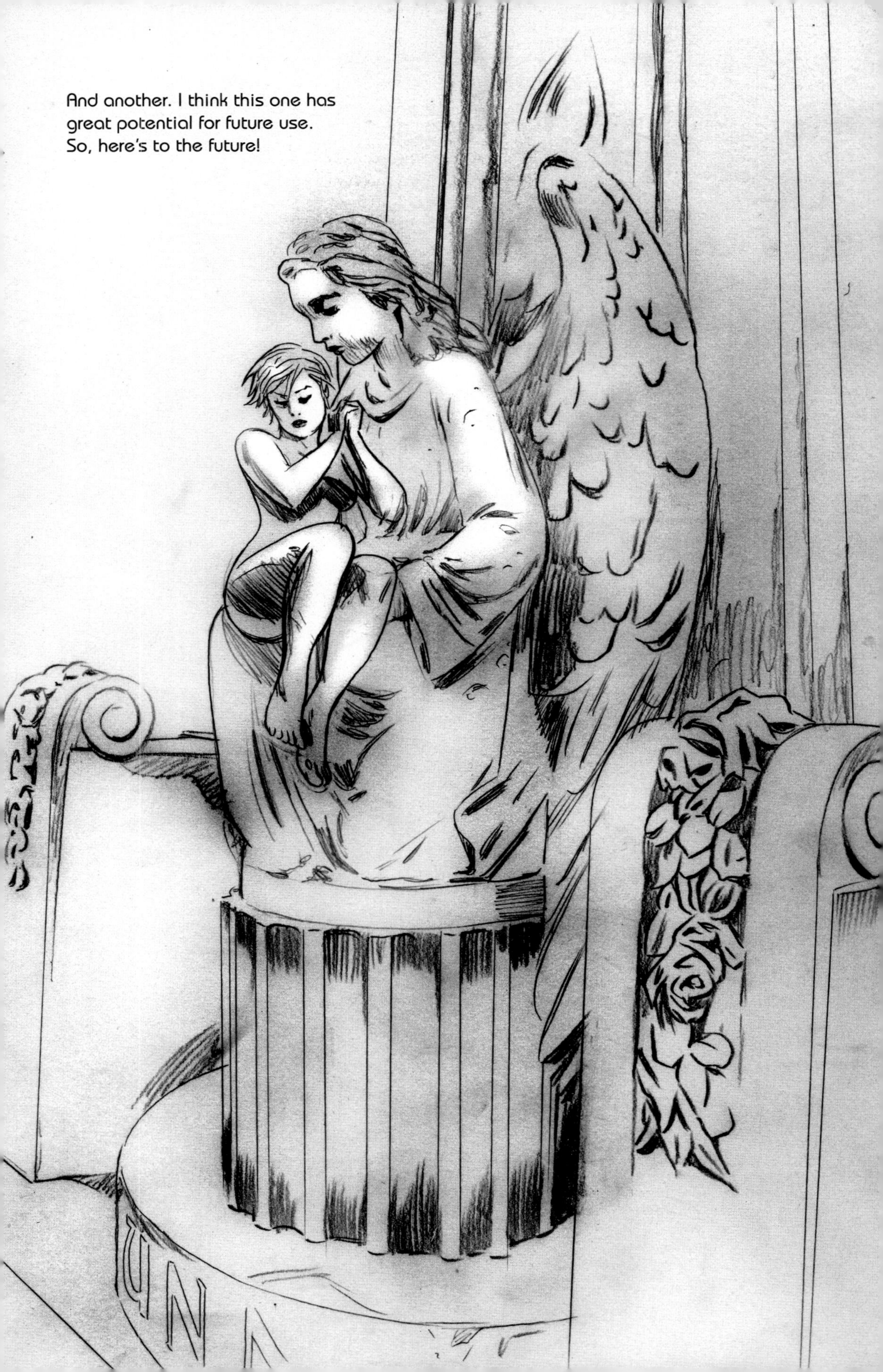
And another. I think this one has great potential for future use. So, here's to the future!